The Rule of Dons

The Rule of Dons

Rivke Jaffe

CRIMINAL LEADERS AND POLITICAL
AUTHORITY IN URBAN JAMAICA

DUKE UNIVERSITY PRESS
Durham and London 2024

© 2024 DUKE UNIVERSITY PRESS

This work is licensed under a Creative Commons Attribution-NonCommercial-NoDerivatives 4.0 International License, available at https://creativecommons.org/licenses/by-nc-nd/4.0/.
Printed in the United States of America on acid-free paper ∞
Designed by Dave Rainey
Typeset in Portrait Text, Ogg, and DIN 1451 Std Mittelschrift by Westchester Publishing Services

Library of Congress Cataloging-in-Publication Data
Names: Jaffe, Rivke, author.
Title: The rule of Dons : criminal leaders and political authority in urban Jamaica / Rivke Jaffe.
Other titles: Criminal leaders and political authority in urban Jamaica
Description: Durham : Duke University Press, 2024. | Includes bibliographical references and index.
Identifiers: LCCN 2024003706 (print)
LCCN 2024003707 (ebook)
ISBN 9781478031154 (paperback)
ISBN 9781478026907 (hardcover)
ISBN 9781478060178 (ebook)
ISBN 9781478094319 (ebook other)
Subjects: LCSH: Organized crime—Jamaica. | Organized crime—Political aspects—Jamaica. | Political corruption—Jamaica. | BISAC: SOCIAL SCIENCE / Anthropology / Cultural & Social | SOCIAL SCIENCE / Sociology / Urban
Classification: LCC HV6453.J25 J344 2024 (print) | LCC HV6453.J25 (ebook) | DDC 364.106097291—dc23/eng/20240717
LC record available at https://lccn.loc.gov/2024003706
LC ebook record available at https://lccn.loc.gov/2024003707

Cover art: Michael Elliott, *Donopoly: Episode 1*, 2010. Acrylic on canvas.

This book draws on research funded by the Dutch Research Council (NWO).

This book is dedicated
to the memory of
my mother,
Lexa Jaffe-Klusman (1941–2018), and
to the memory of
"Mama," Gwendolyn Whittaker (1932–2018)

CONTENTS

Acknowledgments ix

Introduction 1

1 Histories 22
2 Geographies 50
3 Electoral Politics 80
4 Law and Order 104
5 Taxation 133

Conclusion 161

Notes 169

Bibliography 181

Index 193

Acknowledgments

As with any research, I am indebted to the many people who helped me over the last fifteen years, during fieldwork and in the course of writing this book. The nature of this specific project, however, is such that some of the most important people must remain anonymous. I am, first and foremost, extremely grateful to the many Kingstonians who were willing to speak so frankly with me about their experiences of donmanship—in particular, the residents of "Brick Town," but also the various politicians, government officials, police officers, businesspeople, and nongovernmental organization (NGO) workers. I owe special thanks to the man I call "Roger," for introducing me to the neighborhood, and to those I call "Keith," "John," and "Lion," for their friendship throughout the years. For the many different forms of generosity they showed me in the course of conducting this research, I give thanks to Rowano Mullings, Jonathan Greenland, Oswald Kassie, Donnette Zacca, Jason Ramsay, Claudia Hucke, Allison Perkins, Silvia Kouwenberg, Pauletta Chevannes, Abena Chevannes, Amba Chevannes, Horace Levy, and Jevan Brown.

This book grew most directly out of two research projects on crime and political authority funded generously by the Dutch Research Council (NWO, grant nos. 360-45-030 and W01.70.100.001). Leading the project on the popular culture of illegality together with Martijn Oosterbaan was a great joy—I'd do it all over again in a heartbeat. My understanding of crime and the politics of aesthetics benefited immensely from our work with Tracian Meikle and Sterre Gilsing, and later on with Chelsey Kivland, Carly Barbosa Machado, and Cleaver Cunningham. I am, of course, particularly indebted to Tracian, whose in-depth ethnographic fieldwork and keen aesthetic insights on Kingston's memorial murals have closely informed my reading of the visual culture of donmanship, and who generously allowed me to reproduce some of the images of artworks she took in the context of her own research.

My understanding of donmanship was also enhanced by the ability to work as principal investigator on thematically adjacent projects on security assemblages, funded by an NWO Vidi grant and a European Research Council starting grant, and as coinvestigator with Eveline Dürr and Gareth Jones on a project on tourism in low-income, high crime urban areas funded by NWO, the German Research Foundation (DFG), and the Economic and Social Research Council (ESRC). It was a profound pleasure working across these projects with such wonderful scholars as Alana Osbourne, Carolina Frossard, Erella Grassiani, Francesca Pilo', Francesco Colona, Frank Müller, Lior Volinz, Patrick Weir, Tessa Diphoorn, Thijs Jeursen, Alessandro Angelini, and Barbara Vodopivec. I also found much inspiration in two research networks, one led with Lucy Evans on representations of crime and Jamaica, which connected us to a range of amazing colleagues including Faith Smith, Kim Robinson-Walcott, Michael Bucknor, Donette Francis, Sonjah Stanley-Niaah, and Emiel Martens and another led by Pat Noxolo on Caribbean in/securities with Anyaa Anim-Addo, Ronald Cummings, David Featherstone, Susan Mains, and Kevon Rhiney. The ideas set out in this book also developed during visits as a visiting researcher at the Institute for the Study of the Americas at the University of London, the Sir Arthur Lewis Institute of Social and Economic Studies at the University of the West Indies, and the anthropology departments of Columbia University and the University of Pennsylvania.

Over the years, I have benefited similarly from the insights, encouragement, and critical engagement of friends and colleagues in and beyond Caribbean studies, anthropology, and geography: amongst many others, David Scott, Brian Meeks, Charles Carnegie, Jovan Scott Lewis, Robert Kinlocke, Nadiya Figueroa, Yonique Campbell, Esther Figueroa, Doreen Gordon, Annie Paul, Diana Thorburn, Amanda Sives, David Howard, Imke Harbers, Julienne Weegels, Rosemarijn Hoefte, Michiel Baud, Kees Koonings, Barbara Hogenboom, Ton Salman, Jolle Demmers, Martijn Koster, Trevor Stack, Maarten Onneweer, Marianne Maeckelbergh, Sabine Luning, Annemarie Samuels, Veronica Davidov, Steffen Jensen, Dennis Rodgers, Laurens Bakker, Kedron Thomas, Cristiana Panella, Thomas Blom Hansen, Ieva Jusionyte, Lucia Michelutti, Thomas Grisaffi, Desmond Enrique Arias, Asher Ghertner, Hudson McFann, Daniel Goldstein, Rowland Atkinson, Simon Parker, Gabriel Feltran, Hebe Verrest, Fenne Pinkster, Wouter van Gent, and Willem Boterman. Barry Chevannes and Anthony Carrigan, both gone too soon, formed my thinking about Jamaica and imagination in important ways.

For their feedback on different chapters, or on earlier versions of texts that made their way into this book in a reconfigured form, I am indebted to Wayne Modest, Anouk de Koning, Petrina Dacres, Austin Zeiderman, Nikhil Anand, Dennis Rodgers, Gareth Jones, Miranda Sheild Johansson, Asher Ghertner, Emma Jackson, Hannah Jones, Shamus Khan, Madiha Tahir, Veronica Davidov, Martijn Koster, Fenne Pinkster, Mark Figueroa, Maarten Onneweer, Annemarie Samuels, and Amanda Sives. For sharing fun times, less fun times, and much chocolate, I am grateful to Richard Ronald.

Within the geography department, I feel so lucky to have been able to share my shoddy first drafts with the talented group of authors and editors who formed a writing group with me, which has included Thijs Jeursen, Tracian Meikle, Carolina Frossard, Alana Osbourne, Francesco Colona, Lior Volinz, Sterre Gilsing, Julian Isenia, Afra Foli, Solène Le Borgne, Jelke Bosma, Ceylin Idel, Dolly Loomans, Carla Huisman, Maria Hagan, Harry Pettit, Tessa Diphoorn, Erella Grassiani, Frank Müller, Francesca Pilo', Patrick Weir, Dorien Zandbergen, Tahire Erman, and Faisal Umar. And everyone should have friends like Anouk de Koning, Hebe Verrest, Eileen Moyer, and Tina Harris with whom to go on writing retreats.

I am also very grateful to Elizabeth Ault, Benjamin Kossak, and James Moore at Duke University Press for their support for this project—it has been such a pleasure working with you. And many thanks to the three anonymous reviewers for their comments and their support.

The support of three people in particular was crucial throughout the years that I have been thinking about donmanship. Anthony Harriott is the type of scholar I can only aspire to be: never less than fully rigorous in his own research and writing but animated by open-ended interdisciplinary conversations, always supportive of younger generations of academics, and with an uncommon empathy and intelligence that he ensures serve society. Deborah Thomas's work and support have been similarly formative. Like so many others, I have benefited greatly from her personal and intellectual generosity, from her many incisive and encouraging peer reviews, and more generally from her scholarship on Jamaica and on political affect—on what sovereignty feels like—which has clearly informed my understanding of dons' political authority. Petrina Dacres has had my back every step of the way. At dancehall parties and streetside pedicures, in Uptown coffee shops and art galleries, engaging in in-depth visual analysis and walking up Mountain Spring, talking, writing, and laughing together—what a privilege and a joy it has been to cross these borders and share these worlds with you in Kingston, New York, and Amsterdam.

And what a blessing to have been embraced by Gwendolyn Whittaker and her family—especially my Jamaican sister Avis and her children Dilon, Javier, Zidane, Savannah, and Skye. While she is probably still wearing green in heaven, the love that Miss Gwen had for her party was surpassed still by the love and care that she showed to her family and her community.

I don't know that this book could have been written without Anouk de Koning, my extraordinarily talented and generous friend. In cafés, on retreats, at your kitchen table, in instant messages, your editorial insight, unwavering encouragement, and overall loveliness have improved my writing and buoyed my spirits beyond compare.

Conducting this research, as always, I felt the love and support of my parents, Walter and Lexa, and my sisters, Anna and Jenny. I remember my mother's outrage when the Baltimore Police Department's "Officer Friendly" came to teach my kindergarten class that "stranger rhymes with danger." It has been a privilege to have had parents who taught me otherwise—who raised me to question authority, and who imbued me with a sense of safety and security that travels with me to Kingston and beyond.

As a parent myself, I hope to be able to do the same for Teju—who is already so skilled at observing and questioning, but also delighting in this world we live in. None of this would be possible without Wayne Modest, who is always there by my side to provide Teju with that sense of safety, reflection, and wonder. I could not have pursued this research without your critical engagement and loving support. I hope the end result honors our ongoing conversations about difference, inequality, and the extended political and personal project of *samenleven*.

Introduction

On May 24, 2010, the Jamaican military and police forced their way into Tivoli Gardens, a low-income neighborhood in the capital of Kingston, in an attempt to arrest the country's most powerful "don," Christopher Coke, more commonly known as "Dudus" or "the President." This security operation, which came to be known as the Tivoli Incursion, followed an extradition request from the United States, where Dudus was wanted on drug and arms-trafficking charges. After stalling for over nine months and with apparent reluctance, the Jamaican prime minister, Bruce Golding, had signed the warrant for Dudus's arrest in mid-May. Soon after, armed men in Tivoli Gardens began to barricade the entrances to the neighborhood with roadblocks made of abandoned cars and fridges, wooden pallets, and debris. Meanwhile, hundreds of mostly female residents, dressed in white, marched to Gordon House, the seat of the Jamaican parliament, to protest the decision to extradite their don. They held up signs that read "After God, Dudus comes next" and "Jesus die for us. We will die for Dudus!!!"

A few days later, gunmen apparently affiliated with Dudus attacked four police stations and killed two police officers in an ambush, leading Golding to declare a State of Emergency. The state security forces mounted their counterattack the following day, breaking through the barricades while snipers shot at them from the rooftops of Tivoli's high-rise apartment buildings. During the course of the operation, the security forces killed sixty-nine civilians and detained hundreds more. One soldier died. As soldiers and police combed through the neighborhood over the following days, Dudus remained elusive. A month later, he was captured and extradited to the United States. In 2012, following a guilty plea, he received a twenty-three-year prison sentence, which he is currently serving in a low-security federal correctional institution in New Jersey.

Why would hundreds of citizens march out in support of a criminal leader like Dudus, stating that they were prepared to die for him? Why would a state leader such as Prime Minister Golding jeopardize international relations to protect this don from criminal prosecution? How did Dudus manage to convince so many people to view him as a legitimate leader, rather than a criminal—how could a don like him persuade others that he had a right to rule, despite his associations with crime and violence? In this book, I argue that dons have become figures of political authority, and I explain what aesthetic, affective, and spatial strategies have enabled them to do so.

A few weeks after the Incursion, but before Dudus's arrest, I made my way down to Tivoli Gardens with two Jamaican colleagues to attend the taping of the national television program *Your Issues Live*. After entering the area through a heavily armed checkpoint, we walked in the direction of the neighborhood's community center, where the live recording was about to start. Several hundred people had gathered there, mostly women and children, many dressed up for the occasion. The police were also noticeably present, with several cars on the premises and uniformed officers visible in the audience. Less than a hundred people had managed to get seats, facing the stage. The rest of us were crowded all around, sweating in the hot lights as we pressed up against each other to catch a glimpse of the action. One woman marched off, announcing that she was going to watch it on television from her home, where she could get a better view. As things got started, Michael Sharpe, the news reader hosting the program, urged everyone to be quiet during the taping, as it was airing live.

Despite the show's title—*your* issues—the audience itself was discouraged from participating. On stage, Sharpe interviewed a series of professionals, mostly familiar talking heads who often featured on such current affairs programs: a police superintendent, the public defender, a psychiatrist, and an urban regeneration consultant. The only two "representatives of the community" were the principal of a neighborhood school and the head of a local state-sponsored youth club.

"Welcome to another edition of *Your Issues Live*," Sharpe began. "We're in Tivoli Gardens for a special program. We want to see how best we can help the people of Tivoli to heal from what took place in the community over the past few weeks, and what has been happening in the community since it was perhaps created." His tone was somber as he gazed into the camera. "It is our mission to help shape the new Tivoli and indeed the new Jamaica. Far too many have died, and it's time for us to turn a new page. We simply cannot continue like this. But before we get into the program, let's take a quick look at *how* we perhaps got into these problems to begin with."

On a large screen that had been erected near the stage, and on television screens across the nation, a prerecorded segment began to air. It provided a historical background to the Tivoli Incursion, describing the long-standing entanglement of electoral politics and organized crime known as "garrison politics." As archival footage from the 1960s onward began to screen, Damian Marley's 2005 hit "Welcome to Jamrock" played, an ironic take on tourism advertisements that welcomes listeners to a Jamaica marked by poverty and crime.

> *Welcome to Jamrock*
> *Camp where the thugs them camp at*
> *Two pounds of weed inna van back*

The crowd murmured appreciatively at the soundtrack, as the narrator intoned: "Tivoli Gardens has notoriety for being Jamaica's most feared garrison . . ."

"Lie!!" the woman next to me shouted.

"This image is often scattered across the local and international media as a prototype for Jamaican gangsters and gun-slinging and assault," the recording continued, "but for some residents there's no place like home." Featuring scenes of armed clashes and the sound of gunshots, the segment continued: "It is a situation which reveals the two Jamaicas and the clash of identity that is often debilitating towards fostering unity and progress. When manifested physically the clash has proven deadly, as born out of the confrontations between the security forces and armed thugs in 1997, 2001, and now in 2010. But to understand Tivoli one has to go back to its roots."

Moving back in time, the narrator located these roots in the years following Jamaica's independence in 1962: "Tivoli emerged through the vision of Edward Seaga. Seaga, who was a Member of Parliament and Minister of Development in the 1960s, sought to create a new community out of the decadence that postcolonial neglect and urbanization had thrust on Western Kingston. In the 1960s, the squatter settlement Back-o-Wall was bulldozed and up went Tivoli Gardens. It was a bold and ambitious move, which perhaps would have been successful were it not for political tribalism, which manifested in the 1970s."

The soundtrack shifted to "Political Fiction," a 1970s reggae classic by Half Pint. Its lyrics critiqued the political antagonism that accompanied garrison politics:

> *Due to political fiction*
> *Man and man gone in a different segregation*
> *We living so near and yet so far*
> *All because of political war*

The historical footage moved from images of Seaga in the 1960s to scenes of electoral violence in the 1970s and 1980s while the narrator explained how different low-income communities became embroiled in what was in essence a geopolitical conflict. "It was a war much bigger than the communities, in fact, it was bigger than Jamaica. At the heart of it were two clashing political ideologies, a breed of socialism backed by the USSR and democracy-slash-capitalism backed by the United States. This was the Cold War, the so-called war between the AK and M-16 and it was being played out in little Jamaica in communities such as Tivoli."

On the screen, the images of politicians were replaced by a number of well-known dons, from communities across Jamaica. "Today, the Cold War has ended, at least in terms of the physical clashes," the narrator continued, "but communities such as Tivoli never quite recovered, they were taken over by the area leaders. These so-called dons converted the poor, often-neglected communities into enclaves for drug and gun running. Whereas in the past they got their guns and money from unscrupulous politicians, today these dons get their money from wealthy drug cartels, who solicit their help to move drugs, guns, and other illegal merchandises through our ports and territorial waters. Many provide security for their communities and are quick to provide other services which the state fails to provide. Christopher 'Dudus' Coke . . ."—the crowd began to cheer "Bap! Bap! Bap!" (mimicking celebratory gunfire), making it hard to hear the rest of the sentence—"is one such don."

Dudus's photograph appeared on screen, and a loud roar of approval went up. Amidst the hubbub, the segment concluded, "It is believed that in order for Jamaica to progress, the state would have to get rid of area leaders such as Dudus and start playing its rightful role as the protector of communities." Hearing these last lines, the audience's response turned to displeasure. "No sir, this is serious!" a woman close to me called out angrily, evidently upset at the suggestion that the road to progress required getting rid of Dudus. Following so closely after a dramatic instance of state violence, the crowd as a whole seemed unconvinced of the Jamaican state's "rightful role" in protecting them.

As the television program returned to its live format, the host, Michael Sharpe, seemed rather taken aback by these reactions. His face, projected onto the screen, was sweaty and he looked nervous. "Thank you. Welcome back!" he said as he tried to resume control of the narrative, sketching a nation that had experienced a shared trauma. "It's interesting you know, twenty-three days ago there was a lot of stuff happening here in Tivoli Gardens, there were barricades that were set up and there were some of us who were inside the barricade and many of us who were outside the barricade, all of us were traumatized." Sharpe returned to the leader at the heart of the crisis: "Tonight, I note with interest that there is a US$20,000 man on the run." Mentioning a recent public opinion poll, he highlighted the support Dudus enjoyed both within and outside Tivoli Gardens: "Two things happened tonight. When the poll came out, and they say, the people in Tivoli Gardens said 'Yay.' A while ago they saw his picture on television and some of them said 'Legend . . .'"

The crowd applauded and shouted in agreement. "Legend! Legend! Yeah!" the woman behind me cried approvingly.

"Legend . . ." Sharpe went on, "or runner. Legend or runner?" "*Legend!*" the crowd answered as one. "Legendary runner! No runner nuh deh yah," no runners here, my neighbor corrected Sharpe. "Presi live!" a man next to her called out, using the don's other popular title. "President to the world!" another man chimed in.

How does a don like Dudus become a legend?

Outsiders frequently use labels such as "drug kingpin" or "vicious predator" to describe these men. Yet locally they do not only or primarily inspire fear, but also respect, trust, and even love. The most powerful ones are known as "heroes," or indeed "legends," to the Jamaican poor. In many of Jamaica's underprivileged urban neighborhoods, residents see dons as legitimate rulers.

Dons are often important actors in the transnational drugs and arms trade. And they do play a major role in perpetuating Jamaica's high rates of violent crime. In fact, their reputation for violence and business savvy contributes to the mystique that surrounds the persona of many dons. Yet they are also key governance actors within marginalized urban areas: they provide impoverished residents with access to security, conflict resolution, and various forms of welfare. This governance role is facilitated in part through their own resources, and in part through their long-standing connections to Jamaica's two main political parties, the Jamaica Labour Party (JLP) and the People's National Party (PNP). While dons' authority derives to some extent from their reputation as outlaws, their strategic engagement with state institutions, from electoral politics to the police, is equally important.

How can we understand the political authority that these neighborhood leaders, most of whom are linked to criminal organizations, enjoy?[1] How do they achieve and consolidate a position of power not only or primarily through violent means, but through aesthetic, affective, and spatial forms of persuasion?

In this book, drawing on over a decade of ethnographic research in Kingston, I explain how dons' power—that is, their ability to get others to obey them—comes to be viewed as legitimate not only by many low-income residents, but also by other political and economic leaders. Once political power is perceived as legitimate, it becomes political *authority*. Where media reports often assume that donmanship involves a reign of terror, my research suggests that their rule relies much more on consensus and consent than on coercion. This book analyzes the various ways that dons actively seek to claim authority and the conditions under which their claims are recognized, both by those who live in the territories over which they rule and by other rulers.

In so doing, I develop a conceptualization of political authority as shaped both in and beyond the state. The authority of men such as dons, I suggest, lies precisely in their ability to combine an embodied, personified form of leadership with a close yet ambivalent relationship to state institutions. Their form of authority operates through a complex choreography with state institutions and ideals that involves balancing an autocratic form of rule with an established democratic order. In so doing, dons draw on deeply felt experiences of social and political exclusion—many residents feel that they live in a nation controlled by elites, who regard the urban poor with a mix of contempt and fear. Dons' physical and social proximity to these residents allows them to assume a type of political leadership that may feel more "representative" than the formal electoral system.

With the analysis of donmanship I set out in this book, I seek to develop an understanding of how autocratic, violent rulers may be entangled with democratic systems. This manifestation of political authority extends beyond the specific Jamaican phenomenon of donmanship. It displays similarities with forms of extralegal rule in cities across the world, from Brazilian *comandos* and the Haitian *baz* to Italian *capos* and South Asia's Mafia Raj.[2] These examples might seem to suggest that these political formations are restricted to postcolonial states such as Jamaica, or as indicative of "failed states" or "disjunctive democracies." Yet this type of authority can be recognized in a broad range of political contexts, including "established" or "well-functioning" democracies. I draw on the case of Jamaica's dons to highlight how such leaders convince citizens to embrace them, both through their ability to embody the figure of the antiestablishment outlaw *and* through their engagement with established state institutions. The "strongman" character who utilizes state institutions even as he destabilizes them is found not only in notionally informal, or local, power struggles. The appeal of this style of leadership is also evident within representative politics at the national level, as the popularity of elected leaders from Trump and Bolsonaro to Putin and Orbán has attested.

BEYOND "TWO JAMAICAS"

In seeking to identify the factors that had led to the Tivoli Incursion, Michael Sharpe's *Your Issues Live* drew on a familiar narrative, sketching a "clash of identity" between "two Jamaicas" that hampered the nation's progress and that manifested itself in armed violence between criminals and the security forces. This idea of a clash—in which two distinct cultural fragments or parallel orders are pitted against each other—has been dominant in attempts to explain donmanship and comparable political formations. The "two Jamaicas" framework is useful in that it highlights entrenched social inequalities and spatial segregation; these types of divisions do feed the distrust and disappointment expressed by marginalized "Downtown" residents toward "Uptown" politicians. However, in suggesting that dons derive their authority primarily from a *cultural* division, and that they represent a *parallel* order to that of the state, this analytical lens may end up obscuring as much as it reveals.

The frequent emphasis on cultural difference risks presenting support for donmanship as a form of cultural deviance, shaped by clashing norms and values.[3] Such culturalist explanations ignore the fact that many of the social and political values attributed to "ghetto" residents are shared much more broadly. By emphasizing cultural values, it may also play down the classed and raced structures of exclusion within which dons may appear to represent "rightful rule" and protection as much as the state. Meanwhile, the trope of the parallel order or the "state within a state" implies a much stricter separation of donmanship and the Jamaican state than is actually warranted. It ignores the many ways in which dons are entangled with various forms of bureaucracy, with electoral politics, with the justice system, and indeed with the police force. Dons' political authority derives from *both* their larger-than-life outlaw persona and their consistent engagement with these state institutions.

Understanding donmanship requires moving beyond "the clash between two Jamaicas" that was mobilized in *Your Issues Live*. This narrative of a postcolonial nation split in two along lines of identity, and hampered in its progress by a lack of social integration, is a dominant one. Why does this narrative of a cultural clash have such appeal? Importantly, this explanation of donmanship is rooted in long-standing academic and political debates on Jamaica's purported cultural fragmentation, first formulated in the pre-independence period.[4]

The most influential iteration of the cultural fragmentation thesis was the mid-twentieth century "plural society" theory first developed by J. S. Furnivall in Southeast Asia and elaborated for the Caribbean by Jamaican anthropologist M. G. Smith. In an era of decolonization, Smith's theory posited a profound disunity wrought by colonialism, characterized by culturally distinct groups. The lack of a normative consensus based on shared national values, he suggested, posed specific problems for postcolonial nations, as social dissolution was likely to take place in the absence of colonial political coercion.[5] While acknowledging the raced and classed nature of Jamaica's divisions, he stressed that the "plural society" should be understood as a *cultural* phenomenon rather than as a form of social stratification. In privileging a framework of cultural opposition over one of social inequality and exclusion, Smith established an approach that continues to inform contemporary analyses.

In the early twenty-first century, analyses of donmanship frequently draw on this conception of Jamaica's cultural fragmentation. Increasingly, these discussions are concentrated on *urban* conflicts and segregation as a way to understand

Jamaica as a whole. The reverberations of the plural society thesis are evident, for instance, in two prominent readings of the dons' popularity, by social and political theorist Brian Meeks and anthropologist David Scott. Both scholars read the support for dons as expressions of profound cultural difference, although they diverge in their views on the necessity—and indeed the possibility—of generating a cultural consensus.

Brian Meeks reads the support that dons enjoy as part of a "popular, subaltern insurgency" and "a widening fissure, from below, from the ways and means of official Jamaican society."[6] In contrast with M. G. Smith, he suggests that Jamaica's early post-independence years *were* characterized by a normative consensus. However, following the political violence of the 1970s and 1980s, Meeks identifies a process of what he calls hegemonic dissolution. Many Jamaicans no longer believe in the divisive "political fiction" that reggae artist Half Pint identified in the song broadcast during *Your Issues Live*, lamenting the segregation that had emerged "because of political war." In light of this normative dissensus, Meeks understands mobilizations in defense of dons as forms of subaltern politics. Discussing the 1998 protests following the arrest of Donald "Zeeks" Phipps, a prominent West Kingston don, Meeks suggests that these events—known as the Zeeks riots or the Zeeks uprising—"demonstrate the re-emergence of the Jamaican poor and working people on the political stage after almost two decades of quiescence."[7]

More than a decade later, in the wake of the Tivoli Incursion, Meeks identifies a phase of cultural separation in the widespread support for Dudus. He identifies "substantially new cultural and philosophical spaces" that go beyond "the rebellious distancing of subaltern classes from the Anglophilic, Christian and creole notions of the traditional Jamaican middle classes." These new worldviews, Meeks suggests, include elements of "moral relativism, neo-fascist authoritarianism and the glorification of violence."[8] As a political formation, the Dudus "movement," as he describes it, represents "a turn toward a ruthless, monopolistic, and hierarchical approach to governing and a slide toward barbarism," even if Dudus's supporters included "plaintive and powerful advocates of equality arguing for an end to discrimination based on color, class, or geographical location."[9]

David Scott offers a related reading of the support for dons as an expression of cultural difference. Yet where Meeks echoes M. G. Smith's concern in identifying the lack of a national cultural consensus as a key postcolonial challenge, Scott contests this reading of difference-as-a-problem. In an influential essay on "the permanence of pluralism," he draws on the Zeeks riots to rethink the political meaning of difference. While concurring with Smith's view of Jamaica as constituted by relatively autonomous social and cultural sections, Scott argues against understanding this difference as a political *problem* that needs to be overcome through cultural integration. Jamaica's historically constituted difference should be viewed as "ineradicable and indeed central to human flourishing," not as a hindrance to national progress.[10] Like Meeks, Scott's assessment of the Zeeks riots recognizes the dissolution of the political project of acculturation and assimilation that was intrinsic to postcolonial nation-building. Yet, he insists, it is precisely this project that has lost its credibility: we must reject the "moral-politics of improvement in which the unassimilable and indigestible identities Zeeks and his supporters embody are to be re-educated for middle-class civility."[11] The promise of national progress-through-acculturation that Scott skewers is still recognizable in Michael Sharpe's depiction of Jamaica as hampered by "a clash of identity that is often debilitating towards fostering unity and progress."

Similar narratives of violently clashing segments, and related frameworks of pluralism and parallelism, have been mobilized to explain the power of criminal leaders in contexts beyond Jamaica. Where authors such as Meeks and Scott were primarily interested in understanding donmanship as expressing *cultural* difference, other scholars have framed criminal organizations such as those led by Dudus or Zeeks as parallel *political* orders, rather than as cultural fragments. Drawing on Weberian definitions of the state as an entity that can claim a monopoly of the legitimate use of violence within its territory, they describe these organizations and their leaders as "parallel states" or "shadow states."[12] Such terms suggest that these criminal organizations are both separate from, and competitive with, the nation-state. The idea of pluralism also features in influential work on "violent pluralism," a concept mobilized to understand how multiple subnational armed groups that operate with impunity may coexist within formally democratic states.[13]

In Jamaica, the garrisons over which dons rule have frequently been described, both by academics and by the general public, as "states within a state."[14] This common conception of donmanship as competitive, and ultimately incompatible, with the democratic state came out clearly in two cartoons by the popular artist Clovis, published in the *Jamaica Observer* immediately before and after the Tivoli Incursion. In the first cartoon, two gunmen stand guard at the entrance to Tivoli Gardens, which has been barricaded with debris. The informal border that they are securing is marked by a makeshift flag proclaiming the territory to be "the Republic of Tivoli." As a Jamaica Constabulary Force vehicle drives up to the barricades, the gunmen demand to know "Where unoo going, unoo have unoo visa?" asking where the police officers think they are going and whether they have a visa. Here, Tivoli under Dudus—marking its own territory, policing its own borders—is understood as a parallel polity at war with the nation-state. A second cartoon, published a few days later, after the security operation had begun, depicts a scene of burning debris. The barricades have been torn down and the nation-state has proven victorious.

In the foreground, a tough-looking Jamaica Defense Force soldier, his smoking weapon strapped to his back, plants the official Jamaican flag, reclaiming the territory. Tivoli's flag, previously flown so defiantly, slumps next to it, the branch to which it was tied broken, its claim to sovereignty defeated.

My own research in Kingston—and specifically in a garrison community that I refer to as "Brick Town"—suggests that such portrayals of donmanship as separate and antagonistic obscure much of the workings of this political formation. To frame donmanship primarily in terms of parallelism or pluralism misrecognizes its enduring entanglement with not only political parties but the entire state bureaucracy and even the police. Given the various state-like functions dons fulfill, from welfare provision and security to taxation, I was initially also inclined to understand donmanship as "alternative governance systems" that mirrored and supplanted the state. Increasingly though, I came to appreciate the difficulty of drawing any clear boundaries between "the state" and "organized crime."[15] To give just a brief example, the local youth leader who was interviewed during *Your Issues Live* in Tivoli Gardens was on stage representing the Presidential Click Police Youth Club. Police youth clubs have been a long-standing component of the Jamaica Constabulary Force's community policing efforts aimed at improving relations between young people and the police in low-income urban neighborhoods. The Tivoli branch was named after Dudus's entertainment company Presidential Click—apparently, the authority of "the President" and that of the "Police" were not experienced as incompatible.[16]

This lack of a clear distinction lies not so much in any particularly Jamaican tendency toward corruption. Designations of "narco-states" or "failed states" generally serve to reproduce simplistic understandings of governance "elsewhere," celebrating Western Europe and North America as the democratic ideal. Yet the intermingling of business and political interests, and of legal and illegal economic activities, is similarly entrenched in these countries. As political anthropologists have long recognized, the boundary between "state" and "society" is always an unstable effect.[17] Acknowledging the blurred and performative character of this boundary is all the more important in the context of neoliberal models of governance, where public service provision is established through networks of state, commercial, and voluntary actors. This is certainly the case in Jamaica: in addition to state agencies, dons take on a range of governance roles. But so do local and international corporations, NGOs, and churches, often in provisional, fragile coalitions.

My interest in this book is not just to emphasize the hybridity of states or the networked nature of governance. More specifically, I seek to understand how dons both produce and straddle this line between "state" and "nonstate," and how this strategic engagement is central to their political authority. Credible performances of authority will at times involve dons positioning themselves as outsiders or outlaws, working against the oppressive agents of the state to the benefit of "the people." Indeed, such performances may implicitly or explicitly speak to long-standing experiences of cultural difference and antagonism. They draw on shared experiences of "sufferation"—on feelings of cultural intimacy that pit an impoverished black Jamaican "Us," represented by the don, against an elite outsider "Them."[18] This type of claim to authority enacts a clear and antagonistic boundary between state and nonstate rule. Yet simultaneously, dons' authority relies on their ability to cross this same boundary that they help to produce. The feeling that they have a right to rule is enhanced precisely through their close connections to political parties, their success in attracting government investment to their neighborhoods, and their ability to credibly appeal to democratic aspirations such as "freedom" or "equal rights and justice."

AUTHORITY AS CONSENT AND CONSENSUS

By approaching donmanship through the lens of authority, I also aim to shift our analyses of don-like rulers beyond a dominant focus on violence. This emphasis on violence has frequently led scholars researching "nonstate armed actors" to frame the political formations that emerge around them in terms of sovereignty, understanding them as "informal," "social," or "street" sovereigns.[19] Such analyses resonate with anthropological understandings of sovereignty, which center violence. In an influential article, Thomas Blom Hansen and Finn Stepputat argue that all sovereign power is, at its basis, "premised on the capacity and the will to decide on life and death, the capacity to visit excessive violence on those declared enemies or on undesirables."[20] They distinguish between informal and formal sovereignty, defining informal or de facto sovereignty as "the right over life" or "the ability to kill, punish and discipline with impunity," in contrast with formal sovereignty, which is "grounded in formal ideologies of rule and legality."[21] The scholarship associated with this approach has been important in challenging the idea of sovereignty as located only in the nation-state. Yet in privileging violence, and in contrasting it with legality, this framing in terms of sovereignty may obscure the salience of other sources of power on which dons draw.

While dons' ability to use violence with a level of impunity is certainly an important element of their power, in practice they do not rule solely or even primarily through coercion, conflict, and fear, but also through consent and consensus. How does a don's ability to force people to do things come to feel normal, natural, and right? Why do many people accept their rules and obey their commands relatively willingly? In short, how does power become authority?

Authority is generally understood as the ability to rule *without* resorting to violence. As Hannah Arendt notes in her classic text on the concept, "Since authority always demands obedience, it is commonly mistaken for some form of power or violence. Yet, authority precludes the use of external means of coercion; where force is used, authority itself has failed."[22] However, she also warns against equating authority with persuasion through argumentation, suggesting that this presupposes an egalitarian order, where subjects consciously decide to follow a course of action: "If authority is to be defined at all, then, it must be in contradistinction to both coercion by force and persuasion through arguments."[23] Authority, she argues, involves both ruler and ruled recognizing the rightness of the hierarchical relation between them. This commonsense recognition of a leader's rightness—the *consent* of the governed—is where authority can be located.

What, then, is the source of this recognition? On what basis is this right to rule conferred? Following Weber, classic sociological theory distinguishes three ideal-types of authority: traditional, rational-legal, and charismatic authority. In contexts of traditional authority, the right to rule is based on custom and on hereditary or ascribed status; rational-legal authority is based on modern state institutions and achieved status; and charismatic authority on the exceptional supernatural qualities of an individual leader.[24] While Weber recognized that these types were often blurred, much subsequent scholarship has been marked by a rough division of interest in either individual leaders and their specific, charismatic qualities *or* in political institutions, from monarchies to the state. In this book, I am interested in locating political authority at the intersection of individual leaders and state institutions. In understanding why people come to accept, and even embrace, dons and the often violent systems of rule these leaders develop, it is this intersection that is important.

In focusing on this intersection, my interest is in the relational dimension of political authority: in how authority is claimed by rulers, but also in how it is recognized by the ruled, *and* by other rulers. Understanding how authority is claimed means studying carefully how dons, consciously or unconsciously, rely on embodied performances of authority while also making use of established institutional mechanisms. Understanding, in turn, how authority is recognized means concentrating on how residents of marginalized urban areas, as well as other political figures across the city, assess these claims, and on what basis they recognize them as legitimate. Certainly, not everyone supports donmanship. Yet within Downtown Kingston, and equally importantly, in more privileged spaces, there is a level of *consensus* that dons have a leadership role to play.

Authority is a relationship, if always a hierarchical one. Here, I am interested in exploring it as a three-way relationship between individual leaders, state institutions, and political communities. These political communities, however, are not necessarily preestablished. Rather, they emerge—and political subjects are formed—precisely through the acceptance of specific forms of authority. When residents of a marginalized neighborhood come to accept a leader's right to rule as a commonsense "fact," this also shapes their sense of themselves as a community, a body politic. Across such neighborhoods, I frequently heard residents distinguish between good dons and bad dons. This distinction reflects the extent to which donmanship as a system is no longer in question—it has become a social fact. Within this system, however, individual dons can be good or bad, effective or greedy, a blessing or a curse. The shared recognition, or conversely the rejection, of a don's claim to authority is an important element in becoming a political "Us." When a crowd shouts "*Legend!*" in unison, they not only confirm the authority of their don, they also establish their belonging to the same political community.

AFFECTIVE ATMOSPHERES OF AUTHORITY

I approach this dynamic, relational formation of authority by considering factors that go beyond violence. An interview with "Derek," second-in-command to a powerful Central Kingston don, brought this point home to me forcefully. He explained to me how leadership worked: "If they fear you, they will do what you say. But if they love you, they will jump in front of a bullet to save your life." Effective donmanship is built on this dimension of love. Criminal power does not rely solely or primarily on coercion. But mindful of Arendt's caution, authority cannot be understood as a conscious decision either; it does not result from careful argumentation and deliberation.

In approaching authority as a matter of both consent and consensus, I am particularly interested in the shared linguistic roots of these two concepts in *consentire*, literally, "feeling together."[25] The relational recognition of the dons' right to rule takes shape in a sensorial fashion—their power comes to *feel* normal and natural. Their power becomes authority not so much through the rhetorical, rational forms of argumentation that Arendt references, but through the senses and through emotions. Grasping this dimension involves a conceptual and methodological emphasis on the embodied, often precognitive modes through which authority is claimed and recognized. As I show throughout this book, dons' authority works through the bodies of their constituents. I focus in particular on the role of popular culture—reggae music, street dances, and mural art—in this process. While dons themselves strategically create or encourage some of these art forms as legitimizing practices, other forms develop more spontaneously, at the initiative of residents, artists, or other supporters. In the music, dance, and visual art that celebrate dons, we can identify aesthetic-affective practices that enact forms of sensorial persuasion through residents' listening, seeing, and dancing bodies.

In Jamaica, music has always been political, as the lyrics of "Welcome to Jamrock" and "Political Fiction," played during the Tivoli edition of *Your Issues Live*, attest. But the political power of art goes beyond lyrics and textual forms of persuasion. At street dances held to celebrate dons, from "birthday bashments" to memorial dances, residents move together to the same bass-line, but also in honor of the same leadership. Being moved in this way by sonic immersion in reggae and dancehall music, revelers experience a powerful physical sensation of both community and political order.[26] Such street dances involve a manifestation of power through pleasure rather than through force.[27]

The aesthetic forms through which donmanship works also include visual culture: the walls of Kingston's low-income neighborhoods are decorated with memorial murals, including images of deceased dons. These artworks are public reminders of local histories of political leadership, normalizing dons' authority visually. They make dons visible as individual icons—indeed, as "legends." At the same time, by inserting their portraits into a Jamaican tradition of mural art that celebrates elected politicians and other national heroes visually, these artworks also depict dons' leadership as compatible with the nation-state and its institutions.

In emphasizing the aesthetic and affective dimension of authority, I also highlight how donmanship feels normal, natural, and right *within specific urban spaces*. Emotions and affects are not static—they circulate between bodies within specific sites and through specific objects. Authority, then, is also produced in an emplaced fashion, reflecting and reproducing specific political geographies.[28] The political effects of aesthetic forms such as music, street dances, and visual art are embodied, but they are also embedded in neighborhood histories. In addition, the aesthetic-affective practices that generate authority work through the built environment of these same neighborhoods—their streets, walls, and zinc fences—to generate affective atmospheres that envelop residents visually and sonically. This enveloping spatiality can produce an immersive experience of intimacy and comfort, of being watched over and protected within a don's territory, although this atmosphere may also include more ambiguous affective impacts, such as wariness and tension.[29] In explicitly approaching political feelings as spatial, I draw attention to the crafting and experience of such affective atmospheres, to the "currents and transmissions that pass between bodies and which congeal around particular objects, materials and bodies in specific times and spaces."[30]

My argument in this book, then, is that dons' political authority is fashioned relationally and sensorially. In understanding authority as established not through coercion, but through consent and consensus, I argue for particular attention to the various aesthetic, affective, and spatial practices that constitute claims to authority and their reception. Dons' power becomes legitimate only when their role as leaders is recognized both by those who live in the neighborhood territories over which they rule and by political figures who operate from within more formal spaces of state power. Being recognized as legitimate leaders involves a balancing act, in which dons claim a position both as charismatic individuals who are a law unto themselves and as part of established state institutions. But this recognition is also achieved sensorially. In addition to positioning themselves both in and beyond the state, successful dons generate connections between people, spaces, and objects in a way that *feels* right.

RESEARCHING DONMANSHIP

In analyzing donmanship through this lens, this book draws on extensive ethnographic fieldwork in Kingston. Roughly speaking, it follows two interrelated extended case studies. The first is the "Dudus affair," which started with the United States' extradition request in 2009. The impact of the Tivoli Incursion, with its spectacular display of state violence, reverberated in the decade that followed. The handling of the extradition request and the security operation itself were the focus of two Commissions of Enquiry, and these events became the main point of reference for shifts in urban and security policy, from frequent calls to "revitalize Downtown Kingston" to a marked militarization of urban policing. My second extended case is of one low-income Kingston neighborhood. From 2010, I conducted research in "Brick Town," an area formerly ruled by an influential don, "the General." (I use pseudonyms for the neighborhood and its former leader—and for all individual interlocutors mentioned throughout this book.) Brick Town and the General were associated with a criminal organization I call the "West Side Posse," which had long-standing connections with the PNP, one of Jamaica's two main political parties. Working in one "garrison community" helped me to understand how Jamaica's urban and national transformations—including the Tivoli Incursion and its aftermath—intersect with neighborhood-level histories and power struggles, and how these are also entangled with residents' transnational mobilities and connections.

This research involved long-term participant observation in Brick Town, which mainly entailed a lot of "deep hanging out": eating and drinking at neighborhood cook shops, watching television and DVDs with residents, sitting on street corners chatting and watching passersby, shopping at the local market, and occasionally attending festive events such as street dances, or going on outings with friends to other parts of the city. In addition to this neighborhood-level fieldwork, I did research throughout Uptown and Downtown Kingston, organizing a survey in multiple low-income areas and spending time with politicians, policymakers, bureaucrats, businessmen, NGO workers, police officers, and a number of smaller dons and their seconds-in-command, some of them retired. By using pseudonyms and omitting or changing identifying details such as gender or political affiliation, I have sought to anonymize my interlocutors and fieldsites; I do refer to public figures and places where specific political events occurred by their real names.

More broadly, this book draws on my long-term engagement with Kingston, which started with research on urban pollution in 2000, a project that first alerted me to the importance of dons in urban governance. From 2006–2007, I lived and worked in Kingston as a university lecturer and began to learn more about dons' connections to economic and political elites. Focusing specifically on donmanship, I conducted a total of twelve months of fieldwork in Downtown Kingston during the period 2008–2012, followed by shorter return visits to Brick Town over the decade that followed, along with phone calls and WhatsApp conversations in between. My analysis of donmanship set out here also draws on a larger research project on plural policing that I developed from 2013 onward, which included work with police, military, and private security companies, and which helped me understand better how dons are inserted in Kingston's broader geographies of protection.

Conducting research on criminal leadership, and concentrating on a neighborhood known for its high rates of violent crime, raises a number of methodological and ethical issues. Hearing about my research, common responses amongst friends and colleagues, both Jamaican and international, were "Isn't that dangerous?" and "Aren't you scared?" Often, these questions were explicitly raced and gendered: people wanted to know how a *white woman* was able to do such research.[31] Kingston's segregation along lines of race and class, combined with its high rates of crime, produce invisible boundaries that many are loath to cross. White women, in particular, are rarely seen outside the gated enclaves of Uptown Kingston.

In general, I did not experience this research as risky, certainly not while I was doing fieldwork. In the months that followed the United States' request for Dudus's extradition, dons became *the* national topic, dominating newspaper headlines, talk shows, and everyday conversations across the country. Nearly everyone I spoke to, from Brick Town residents to police officers and politicians, was surprisingly open in speaking—anonymously, but on tape—about dons. Moreover, being a foreign white woman largely seemed to make neighborhood-level research easier rather than harder, as Chelsey Kivland also found during her fieldwork with young male *baz* leaders in an impoverished Port-au-Prince neighborhood. She explains how her status as a *blan* woman generally worked to her advantage, allowing these leaders to approach her "with a degree of neutered professionalism," where their encounters with Haitian women might have been read in a more sexualized fashion. At the same time, Kivland's gender often worked to temper her racial and foreign privilege.[32]

My experience in Downtown Kingston was roughly similar. As I had also found during my earlier fieldwork, which concentrated on urban pollution in low-income neighborhoods, the appearance of a white-looking female researcher often elicited surprise, but only very rarely generated any hostile or otherwise overtly negative responses. My foreignness generally appeared to facilitate rather than limit access, and few residents seemed to experience my presence as threatening or otherwise unwelcome. Rather, they seemed invested in keeping me safe, and also in ensuring that I *felt* safe. As in other neighborhoods where I had worked, many people went out of their way to make me feel comfortable. Friends would block off a parking spot for me when they knew I was coming to Brick Town, walking me back to my car to see me drive off safely, or escorting me to the border of the community if I was leaving on foot, especially at times when things were "running hot." They would intervene if they felt vendors or passersby were too assertive or nosy in their interactions with me, but would also warn me if I engaged in behavior that might be read as suspicious, such as taking photographs of street scenes. Being married to a Jamaican and becoming a mother during the course of my fieldwork—and being accompanied by my husband and son on various occasions—perhaps also helped frame my presence as a friendly one.

During the first few years of my research, Brick Town was relatively calm. I was first introduced to the neighborhood by one of the General's relatives, and following some initial awkwardness I struck up a number of fieldwork friendships and felt increasingly comfortable showing up unannounced. The fact that Brick Town was not involved in any active gang feuds, and remained calm in the run-up to the 2011 national elections, contributed to my feelings of safety. Even when, starting in 2012, an escalating conflict between two factions competing over leadership within Brick Town led to multiple murders, I still felt relatively comfortable visiting. The murders generally took place at night; I experienced the daytime "vibes" around the market area of the neighborhood where I spent most of my time as more or less unchanged and I did not feel that I would be a target. The fact that residents seemed to carry on with their everyday activities, seemingly without feeling too much fear, also helped.

In short, my research rarely felt actively risky to me. Of course, the risk involved in a certain research project may be borne less by the researcher than by her interlocutors. In Jamaica, where the don's rule is *informer fi dead*, snitches must be killed, this is an evident concern. The frankness of my interviewees in discussing dons as rulers—as opposed to discussing their role in drugs and arms trafficking—suggested that donmanship was not a taboo topic in itself. Indeed, Jamaican newspapers also publish regularly on the issues discussed in this book. Nonetheless, my research obviously involved potential risks for my interlocutors, both for those who were (or had been) involved in criminal activities and for those who were not. In writing up my ethnography, in addition to creating pseudonyms for interviewees, I have often limited or altered my descriptions of persons or places, sacrificing context and ambience for anonymity. As I began working to publish my research, I asked two Brick Town friends, whom I call "Keith" and "Mikey" here, to read a manuscript I had submitted for review. I was relieved to find that they did not recognize themselves where I quoted from my conversations with them. In discussing the text with Keith, I asked him explicitly whether he thought my research was risky, for the people interviewed or for me, and whether it would be safe to publish the article. Fortunately, he said he did not see any risk, not as long as I used pseudonyms, adding: "One thing me have to rate [commend] you for. Me rate that you never get into the drugs thing and the guns thing." Those things, he advised me, were kept very secret and if I started asking about those things people would get upset.

On the whole, these discussions and experiences gave me a sense of relative openness, but this had its limits. During an early visit, one of the General's relatives, "Lorraine," made a quasi-casual remark aimed at me, warning that "We don't want no *Born fi' Dead*, it mash up the thing." This was a reference to *Born fi' Dead* (literally, "born to die"), a popular, semi-ethnographic book by Laurie Gunst, a white American historian.[33] Recounting the violence perpetrated by transnational criminal "posses" as they moved from dealing with Jamaican politicians to assuming a central position in the US drugs trade, Gunst had apparently failed to properly anonymize the individuals and events she had observed, and allegedly this resulted in at least one revenge killing. Given my outward similarity to Gunst, and my intention to publish my ethnographic research in written form, I was quite shaken by what I interpreted as Lorraine's implicit threat. I was not sure how to react and in the end, I more or less avoided her section of the neighborhood until I left to go home to the Netherlands, three weeks later. However, on my next return visit, almost a year later, she greeted me warmly with a hug and never made mention of Gunst's book or my writing project again. Perhaps, as a Jamaican colleague suggested, she was just "testing" me to see how I would respond. Nonetheless, the incident, even if it consisted of no more than a nonchalant remark, made me consider even more carefully what I was writing, how it might be perceived by those associated with organized crime, and what the consequences might be for my interlocutors or for me if they took offense.

Such warnings have no doubt resulted in some level of conscious or unconscious self-censorship on my part, especially with regard to drugs and arms trafficking.

These illegal activities are an important source of income and weapons, and in so doing shape dons' ability to rule. Yet knowing or discussing the details of such activities is not necessary to understand their authority.

Violence in itself, whether legal or illegal, seemed much less taboo as a topic. However, and perhaps surprisingly, violence did not necessarily present itself as a dominant theme within my fieldwork. In academic circles, my analytical and ethnographic decentering of violence often elicited surprise and sometimes disbelief or even disapproval. In addition to asking about the dangers of fieldwork, audience members at conferences and seminars where I presented my research, and peer reviewers assessing manuscripts, would frequently ask, "Aren't you *romanticizing* the dons?" This charge referred specifically to my lack of emphasis on the violent activities associated with organized crime and "inner-city life." Such questions resonate with responses to Austin Zeiderman's research on insecurity in Bogotá, which also lacked a direct focus on violence. "Where's the blood?" his audiences would ask, literally or in so many words.[34]

In truth, violence and crime were significant background features of life in Brick Town, but they were not the only or the dominant theme, and residents did not appear to go about their daily lives in a state of fear. Throughout the years that I visited, residents would sometimes discuss historical or recent incidents of gang-related violence or police brutality amongst each other, and in interviews with me, but it was not a constant preoccupation. In their discussions of donmanship, they did not restrict their discussions to dons' nonviolent activities, which included providing local access to a range of public goods and services, from welfare and employment to solid waste management and the construction of public parks. They also confirmed the dons' use of violence although they tended to justify its use as necessary to maintain local peace and order, as I discuss in chapter 4. (A "good don" uses violence proportionately and in service of the community, a "bad" one is excessively violent or uses force primarily to further his own interests.) Dons and seconds-in-command I interviewed did not deny the need to use violence in maintaining their rule, although they were quick to emphasize that the threat of violence, or a reputation of historical involvement in violence, could in itself be sufficient. With respect to crime more broadly, quite a few of my interlocutors turned out to have been deported from foreign countries after having been involved in "a little drugs business," or had spent time in prisons in Jamaica, but they were generally not treated as scary, violent individuals.

The lack of "blood" in this book, then, reflects the fact that I did not observe many violent incidents during fieldwork, nor did stories of violence dominate in the interviews and informal conservations I held with residents. Beyond this relatively low exposure to violence—which may, of course, have been shaped by my reluctance to look for it, or ask after it explicitly—I realize that my tendency to write "around" the violence associated with dons might in part be a form of self-censorship. My emphasis on nonviolent practices is also informed by an interest in countering more sensationalist, culturally essentialist accounts of sadistic Jamaican criminals and morally deviant inner-city residents. There is a persistent popular and scholarly imagery of urban Jamaica that centers on violence, and this tradition of representation sometimes also evidences an undercurrent of racialized essentialism.[35] While I recognize the dons' agentive role in perpetuating Jamaica's high rates of violent crime, to give it narrative centrality would be to misrecognize the extent to which their rule relies on consent and consensus. It is this fashioning of authority that is my central concern in this book.

THE BOOK

Based on this research in Jamaica, this book develops an analysis of political authority. I theorize authority as shaped both in and beyond the state: successful claims to authority involve credibly embodying an outlaw persona that stands outside of the political establishment while also connecting strategically to state institutions and mobilizing democratic ideals such as freedom and equality. Political authority is the outcome of mutual recognition by rulers and ruled—it requires the consent of the governed. In addition, a leader's authority within a specific sphere or territory must be recognized by *others* who hold positions of power—for dons, this means politicians, state bureaucrats, the police, and influential businesspeople. Showing how dons' power relies on a widespread belief in their right to rule rather than on a reign of terror, I explain how the urban poor come to experience donmanship as legitimate. Consent and consensus are produced and reproduced, and occasionally contested, in everyday urban life, as dons activate the space of the neighborhood and a range of aesthetic forms to foster deeply felt experiences of political belonging. I am particularly interested in highlighting how affective atmospheres of authority—those immersive, material-affective relations that lie in between bodies, objects, and material spaces—generate shared political sensations, making donmanship feel normal, natural, and right.

In chapters 1 and 2, I highlight, respectively, the histories and geographies of donmanship. Chapter 1 traces histories of political leadership, exploring how these have been narrated and contested in official historiography, popular culture, and everyday discussions. In so doing, it describes how donmanship developed from Jamaica's colonial past into its postcolonial present. Chapter 2 concentrates on the spatial dimension of dons' authority, demonstrating how their power is always rooted in those marginalized urban areas associated most closely with Kingston's impoverished black population. It highlights the significance of Kingston's geographies of inequality, showing how conflations of race, class, and urban space allow dons to appear more proximate and more representative than elected politicians.

Chapters 3, 4, and 5 examine how dons' authority takes shape at the intersection of individual, embodied forms of leadership and strategic relationships with state institutions. Each of these chapters focuses on one such institution, emphasizing how dons rely on personified leadership and sensorial strategies to craft a relationship to electoral politics, law, and taxation, respectively. In chapter 3, I discuss how dons' authority connects to electoral politics, building on their historical role as brokers within the clientelist system of "garrison politics." Dons' claims to authority are strengthened when elected politicians actively recognize dons' right to rule, framing their leadership in terms of participatory democracy. In addition, dons' party-political allegiance can strengthen their bonds with residents by allowing them to draw on the aesthetic, affective dimensions of partisan identities in ways that go beyond the transactional benefits of clientelist relations. Chapter 4 focuses on how dons derive authority from their ambiguous relationship to the law, showing how the violently enforced "community justice" system centered on dons can be perceived as more legitimate than Jamaica's formal legal system. Community justice connects to dons' role as security providers: despite their central role in Kingston's high homicide rates, within their own neighborhoods, the most powerful dons are credited with ensuring peace and safety. Chapter 5 analyzes dons' ability to extract money or goods from a broad range of people who conduct business within their territory. By taking seriously the widespread framing of such payments in terms of "taxation" rather than extortion, I consider how such a performance of consent reflects and reinforces dons' political authority. In the conclusion, I extend the general analysis outlined throughout this book, arguing that while donmanship represents a historically and culturally specific type of political authority, my analysis of this phenomenon can offer insights into the entanglement of violent autocratic rule and democratic institutions with implications extending far beyond Jamaica.

1
Histories

In their song "Flames" (2016), reggae artists Protoje and Chronixx engage in the Rastafari practice of "burning" injustice, targeting social wrongs with lyrical fire.[1] Here, they critique the popular practice of blaming dancehall artists, such as Vybz Kartel and Alkaline, for Jamaica's high rates of violent crime:

> *When the government cyaan fight crime*
> *Dem blame Kartel or blame Alkaline*
> *Wha'ppen to the parents dem*
> *Weh not tryin' fi tell di youth dem*
> *Make up dem own mind*
> *Haffi think deeper, overstand me*

> When the government can't fight crime
> They blame Kartel or blame Alkaline
> What's happened to the parents
> Who aren't trying to tell young people
> To make up their own mind?
> You have to think deeper, do you understand me

While pointing to the responsibility of parents to raise young people capable of independent decision-making, Protoje and Chronixx encourage their listeners to "think deeper," to connect Jamaica's violent conflict to political history, and to reflect on the role of its earliest political leaders. Specifically, the song moves on to call out two politicians and trade union leaders, Alexander Bustamante and Hugh Shearer. Bustamante, Jamaica's first prime minister after independence in 1962 and one of Jamaica's seven official National Heroes, was the leader of both the JLP and the Bustamante Industrial Trade Union (BITU), the union out of which the political party grew. Shearer, who succeeded Bustamante as BITU leader, assumed Bustamante's JLP constituency seat after the latter retired from politics and served as prime minister from 1967 to 1972.

> *All of this start so underhanded*
> *Like all a man like Bustamante*
> *How you get me trust that man deh?*
> *National Hero, who? You tan deh*
> *Hugh Shearer ban Walter Rodney*
> *None a dem ting nuh teach inna di school*
> *Dem take man fi fool*

> All of this started so underhanded
> Even a man like Bustamante
> How did you get me to trust that man?
> National Hero, who? You must be crazy
> Hugh Shearer banned Walter Rodney
> None of those things are taught in school
> They take us for fools

"Flames" pushes back against Jamaica's official history, taught in schools, which celebrates the heroic acts of a small set of political leaders as central events in the birthing of the independent nation. Proposing an alternative understanding of how "all of this" started, the song critiques the idea of National Heroes, painting Bustamante as a devious, "underhanded" figure to be distrusted rather than venerated. Bustamante's successor, Shearer, fares no better, featuring here not as Jamaica's "first black prime minister" (as he is often described), but as the man who expelled the Guyanese historian and activist Walter Rodney from Jamaica in 1968. Alarmed by Rodney's ties to Rastafari leaders and by the potential of his Pan-Africanist, Marxist scholarship to foster a revolutionary coalition of Black Power supporters, Shearer declared him a *persona non grata* in Jamaica. Indeed, his deportation led to heated protests and riots that united university students and the urban poor.[2]

It is precisely Rodney's black radical critique of established historical narrative that Protoje and Chronixx revive. Their lyrical reassessment of official historiography continues toward the end of the song, as they vow to continue commemorating an infamous episode of state persecution and violence, the 1963 Coral Gardens "incident" during which the Jamaican government detained and tortured hundreds of Rastafari.[3]

> *And we nah stop talk 'bout Coral Gardens*
> *Until we dead*
> *And we nah stop burn dem*
> *False leaders and presidents*

> And we won't stop talking about Coral Gardens
> Until we're dead
> And we won't stop condemning those
> False leaders and presidents

Summarizing their position, Protoje and Chronixx assert that they will not stop "burning" those they call "false leaders": they will continue to reject the authority of those political leaders who foment violence and division, and of the official histories that rewrite those leaders' actions as heroism.

How might we understand donmanship as a political formation that is situated in longer histories?

Any attempt to historicize dons' authority involves looking past the borders of the urban neighborhoods where their rule is most visible to consider their relationships with national political leaders, trade union activism, and electoral politics. It also requires a recognition of how international political and economic interests have informed "local" conflicts, from centuries of colonial slavery to the geopolitical machinations of the Cold War era. As evidenced by anticolonial uprisings and other overt forms of contestation, and by less spectacular forms of everyday politics, such histories of domination were always also characterized by ongoing efforts "from below" to transform the established order and to redefine the parameters of political personhood.[4]

In this chapter, I trace a number of the historical relationships and conflicts that have informed donmanship. My interest here is not so much in sketching linear trajectories that suggest a direct or inevitable pathway from specific pasts to a present of donmanship, but rather in providing a context for the connections that many Jamaicans make between political past and present. While drawing on academic texts, I also look to popular Jamaican music and oral history interviews to understand how mainstream political histories are contested, rewritten, and mobilized to explain present-day conditions. In engaging with such lyrical and everyday historiography, I am particularly interested in the alternative canons of political leaders we might encounter through this lens, and in the distinctions made between political legitimacy and legality in such processes of memory-making. What if a closer scrutiny of elected political leaders and certain National Heroes revealed them to be "underhanded" crooks, whose divide-and-rule strategies incited enduring urban warfare? And under what circumstances might men involved in formally illegal activities actually be better models of authority, heroes even? Such questions are constantly posed, and answered in various ways, in reggae and dancehall songs, but also in everyday discussions.

HISTORY AND THE POLITICAL IMAGINATION

In approaching political history with attention to such cultural narratives, I seek to draw attention to the centrality of the political imagination as it unfolds in everyday talk and in creative expressions, popular music in particular. I use the term political imagination here to refer to the imagination of political order, of how power works and how it should work.[5] These forms of political imagination that I am interested in work as analytical, normative, and affective frames. Analytically, they guide us in our understandings of how power works, and where and in whose hands it is concentrated—our attention is drawn to specific locations of power and responsibility, and not others. Normatively, the political imagination shapes our perceptions of the workings of power as just or unjust, and affectively, it imbues our responses to these workings with anger or pride, with sadness or excitement. Beyond delineating the sites and mechanisms of power, the political imagination is central in how we come to see ourselves in relation to others: with whom we feel affinity or community, what forms of authority and hierarchy we find acceptable.

We can also understand the political imagination as frameworks that suggest specific attributions of causality and blame, and delineate the conditions of citizenship and other forms of political community. For instance, it involves specific understandings of the causes of urban poverty and violence—whose fault is it that some neighborhoods suffer from high levels of conflict and deprivation, and who might be able to remedy this? Who should and can protect vulnerable citizens—the state, or other powerholders such as dons? To what established or yet to be realized political community does one belong? What normative sense of rights and responsibilities accompanies this belonging, and what emotions does it elicit? These analytical, normative, and affective frames can legitimize or delegitimize specific structures of decision-making, shifting our sense of how political decisions should be taken, implemented, and enforced, from a preference for top-down, violent authoritarianism toward a preference for electoral democracy or horizontal collective action, or vice versa.[6]

Engaging with such forms of political imagination in relation to Jamaica's histories, we see specific moments in time and specific political leaders emerging as key concerns: labor protests, election years, and other periods of violent transformation and the role of unionists, politicians, and dons in these episodes. As later chapters in this book also show, these historical figures and these episodes continue to resonate in contemporary experiences of political authority. Attending to such central conjunctures and figures, the rest of this chapter concentrates on Jamaica's political history and its narrative negotiations. In the next section, I start by discussing how both dons and politicians have often been understood as conforming to a specific historical model of leadership, with roots in colonial rule, glossed as "the hero and the crowd." The most powerful dons may have displaced politicians as political "heroes," but this process has not been a linear one.

This historical reconfiguration of political leadership is the focus of the sections that follow, as the chapter moves roughly from the late colonial past into the postcolonial present: from the anticolonial nationalist movement that emerged in the 1930s, through the consolidation of "garrison politics" in the 1960s and 1970s, and the broader governance role that dons took on in the late twentieth and early twenty-first century, to the aftermath of the Tivoli Incursion.[7] While the chapter is organized in a roughly chronological fashion, it takes a less-than-linear approach to history that resonates with anthropologist Deborah Thomas's interest in assembling "archives of affect." Such archives include a range of texts, sounds, and images in order to understand "how the sphere of the political has been imagined and felt at various junctures and . . . the kind of politics that are possible at these junctures."[8] Here, I am interested specifically in assembling an archive that helps understand how political *leadership* has been imagined, felt, and made possible at different conjunctures over the past century.

THE HERO AND THE CROWD

"Runner or legend?" Journalist Michael Sharpe posed the question to the crowd that had assembled in Tivoli Gardens shortly after the 2010 security operation, at a point in time when Dudus was still on the run from the police. The response was immediate and unanimous. "Legend!!" The crowd's support echoed that of the hundreds of mostly female residents who had marched out directly before the incursion, just a week earlier, waving signs asserting "Taking the boss is like taking Jesus."

But Dudus is not the first legendary don whose heroic status is evidenced by his crowds of followers. Tivoli Gardens has been associated with Jamaica's most famous criminal leaders: before Dudus, his father, Lester "Jim Brown" Coke, ruled over the area, gaining the title "don of dons." And before Jim Brown there was Claudius Massop, Tivoli's original godfather. In Matthews Lane, the PNP garrison that borders Tivoli to the east, a series of leaders achieved a similarly iconic status—from Aston "Bucky Marshall" Thompson in the 1970s to Glenford "Early Bird" Phipps in the 1980s, who was succeeded by his brother Donald "Zeeks" Phipps.

Zeeks in particular assumed a quasi-mythical status, cemented through the so-called Zeeks riots, mentioned briefly in the introduction.[9] In September 1998, the Jamaica Constabulary Force (JCF) arrested Zeeks and took him to the local police station. Enraged Matthews Lane residents blocked off the roads with barricades, set old tires and other debris on fire, and marched to the Kingston Central police station. At this time, a peace treaty between Zeeks and Dudus had ended the historical rivalry between their two garrisons and allegedly even JLP-affiliated gunmen came out to support Zeeks. Like Dudus's supporters in 2010, the 1998 protestors held up placards with slogans such as "Justice for Zeeks" and chanted "No Zeeks, no peace!" The march itself was not peaceful, and the protestors threatened to storm the police station if their leader was not released. The crowd only calmed down after Zeeks was led out onto the building's balcony. He assured his followers that he was unharmed and would soon return, telling them: "Mi soon come. Mi have a little business to take care of."

The event inspired Louie Culture and Cocoa Tea's "Zeeks," a reggae song that includes the following lyrics:

> From Downtown to Uptown, inna every shopper's fair
> All of the people from down in the ghetto was there
> And them a set roadblock, burning fire, 'cause them just don't care
> Revolutionary soldiers, them take over, 'cause them just nah fear
> Well, them bawl out Zeeks, them bawl out Zeeks
> The man who set the history in the streets
> Yeah them bawl out Zeeks, well them a bawl out Zeeks
> The man who cause the history in the streets
>
> Well, mi nah look nuh sorry, nah beg nuh pity
> But if them diss the program, man will lock the city
> Well, equal rights and justice haffi win, we got the key
> If them diss it, we will lock the city . . .
>
> When you right, him say you right, when you wrong, him say you wrong
> Help the poor to get some more and help the weak to get so strong

The song sketches a clear dynamic between a hero and his followers. It depicts Zeeks as a don who could summon scores of people from across the city, from Downtown to Uptown, a man who could rally fearless "revolutionary soldiers" to block the roads, to set the city on fire, to take over. The singers are uninterested in eliciting apologies or pity, they assert: "nah look no sorry, nah beg no pity." Rather, channeling the crowd, they demand "equal rights and justice," drawing a moral distinction between an "us" and a "them." If *they*, the police, "diss the program"— that is, disrespect the order that the don has arranged—then *we*, "all the people from down in the ghetto," can and will lock down the city, in the name of democratic values of equality and justice. Zeeks, they make clear, is an honorable leader, punishing wrongdoers and supporting the poor and the weak. With the people "bawling out" for their leader in anger, as the song's chorus proclaims repeatedly, Zeeks ended up writing history in the streets.

Indeed, this account of a legendary leader persecuted by the police and defended by his revolutionary soldiers echoes historical accounts of Jamaica's National Heroes. Specifically, the song "Zeeks" resembles narratives of iconic events associated with Alexander Bustamante. During the labor riots that spread across the island in the 1930s, Bustamante led large crowds of angry protestors through Downtown Kingston. As a hostile colonial police force threatened to open fire at the marchers, Bustamante confronted them with a keen sense of political drama. As he later recollected: "I turned to the policemen, bared my chest, and said 'Shoot me, but leave those unfortunate hungry people alone.' I dispersed the crowd and told them to be calm."[10]

Such iconic scenes, of Zeeks and Bustamante alike, evoke the idea of "the hero and crowd," an influential analytical frame developed by political scientist A. W. Singham in the 1960s.[11] Singham argued that Caribbean electoral politics should be understood as rooted in the colonial polity. Focusing on the final days of colonial rule and the political leaders who led the fight for independence, he identified two types of "heroes": the trade union leader who leads his working-class peers to power and the middle-class leader who sacrifices his career (often in law or academia) to help "the people" achieve self-sovereignty. In their anticolonial struggle for independence, both types of heroes were able to mobilize large and loyal "crowds" of followers, sometimes resembling millenarian movements. Yet as these heroes become professional politicians, Singham suggests they cleaved to a model of political leadership rooted directly in the region's plantation history: a personalistic, authoritarian type of leadership that demanded submissiveness from followers. He saw these "native politicians" as proto-dictators who had no interest in "a genuine political socialization of the mass of people" that might meaningfully challenge colonial patterns of authoritarianism.[12] Their tendency was to regard the political party as a vehicle for personal advancement and to actively discourage its development as an institution of mass political emancipation.[13]

The most successful dons slot easily into this model. In addition to being able to summon large crowds of fervent supporters, they draw on some of the tropes Singham associated with politician-heroes. They are able to present themselves as working-class protagonists whose endeavors to improve the lot of their peers can be framed in terms of sacrifice: taking Dudus is "like taking Jesus." The heroism of the don lies in his ability not only to present himself as the embattled but generally victorious protagonist of various political dramas. He must also take care of his adherents, "to help the poor to get some more and help the weak to get so strong," as Louie Culture and Cocoa Tea sang of Zeeks.

As discussed below, this persona, which combines charisma, care, and authoritarianism, can be recognized in the stories told about Jamaican politicians *and* dons. In many cases, such stories show how these different types of political leaders have been able to assume the role of the strong, personalist hero, or heroine, who can take care of their crowd of loyal followers. Yet there are always other accounts—some of them written, others sung, or muttered in private—that show how heroes can tumble from grace, their political leadership proving to be an unstable, temporary achievement.

EARLY POLITICAL HEROES

As a British colony in which the majority of the population of African descent had been enslaved until full Emancipation in 1838, Jamaica had a very restricted franchise until the mid-twentieth century, with the right to vote and the right to stand for election largely restricted to light-skinned, land-holding elites. Universal suffrage was only granted in 1944, nearly twenty years before independence in 1962. This extension of voting rights to all Jamaicans followed the emergence of the nationalist movement and severe labor unrest throughout the British West Indies in the 1930s. These labor rebellions were at the basis of the joint formation of Jamaica's first political parties and trade unions in the 1940s. The BITU, led by Alexander Bustamante, formed the basis of the JLP. The founder of the PNP, Norman Washington Manley, was involved in the development of the rival Trades Union Council (TUC), later superseded by the National Workers Union (NWU).

Both Bustamante and Manley became larger-than-life figures during this period. The government conferred the title of National Hero on the two men in 1969, following Manley's death, but they had achieved heroic status much earlier. From the start, music played an important role in this process of iconization. In mobilizing their supporters, the unions and the associated political parties drew on existing musical traditions. Campaign rallies regularly sought to raise participants' spirits by singing battle-themed religious songs, such as "Onward Christian Soldiers." The lyrics of familiar religious music—Christian hymns and gospel songs, but also African-Christian "sankeys" and Revival songs—were often adapted in support of the union or the party, with politicians' names replacing those of biblical figures. "Go before us, Lord, go before us," for instance, would become "Go before us, Manley" or "Go before us, Busta."[14] During the strikes Bustamante led in Downtown Kingston, his followers would sing:

I will follow Bustamante till I die
Busta power is moving just like a magnet
It moves in me and it moves in you
Jus' like the day of the Pentecost[15]

Such songs not only portray these political leaders as commanding, magnetic men endowed with spiritual powers and able to generate an affective atmosphere that literally moved their followers. Their lyrics also narrate a relationship in which political supporters pledge to be loyal to their leaders until death. The line "I will follow Bustamante till I die" almost eerily foreshadows signs up held by West Kingston residents marching out in support of Dudus in 2010, proclaiming: "Jesus die for us. We will die for Dudus!!!" The twenty-first century declarations of absolute loyalty to dons, bolstered with religious references, have a clear precedent in the songs celebrating Jamaica's early nationalist leaders. This tradition of political music helped craft an emotionally powerful model of authority that celebrates individual personalities, but also legitimizes their rule by situating them within institutions—in the case of the early leaders not just within the new political structures, but also long-standing religious ones.

Beyond the personalist model of authority that became established within the new forms of political mobilization of the 1940s and 1950s, the JLP and the PNP also sought to educate the new electorate into their new status as franchised citizens through union activities. The middle-class, light-skinned ("brown") union and political leaders sought to instill a sense of political consciousness and political agency amongst the darker-skinned ("black") working poor.[16] The PNP and its union partners in particular distributed political literature and organized study groups throughout the island, with the aim of inculcating a nationalist desire for independence, a sense of the rights and duties of citizenship, as well as a socialist sensibility.[17] As in many other contexts where the labor movement and party politics were entangled, trade unions played a central role in brokering state-citizen relations.

While these political education initiatives were ideologically driven, centering on notions of uplift and emancipation, the entanglement of party loyalty and union benefits also fed a clientelist form of electoral politics from early on. From the JLP's landslide victory in 1944, with Bustamante as head of national and municipal government, and as leader of both the trade union and the party, public funds and employment opportunities were increasingly distributed in a partisan fashion.[18] It became clear to union supporters that they stood to gain access to employment and other benefits if their party won.

The relationship between electoral politics and unionism also meant that the BITU-TUC rivalry, which took on violent forms in the streets of Kingston in the 1940s and 1950s, quickly blurred into party-political violence. As identification with the interests of a trade union formed the basis for party-political identities, the willingness of labor activists to fight for the economic benefits associated with the dominance of their union became difficult to distinguish from a willingness to use violence to help their party win elections. Indeed, the earliest pre-independence elections were marred by violent and sometimes deadly conflicts between PNP and JLP supporters, and by the late 1950s, loosely organized political gangs with access to firearms had emerged on the scene in Kingston.[19]

Where historical accounts of this era tend to read economic gain and inter-community violence as key factors in the consolidation of party-political identities, less attention has been paid to how more pleasurable affects, such as excitement and fun, also work to cement political bonds. Chelsey Kivland's elaboration of the concept of "hedonopolitics" encourages us to consider the role of pleasure in constituting political leadership. Her work highlights the importance of "feelingful" events in generating pleasure and political power—the affective intensity that emerges at such events is a key political resource for those leaders able to harness it.[20]

In Jamaica, elections have long been such feelingful, hedonopolitical events. Beyond violence, if not fully separate from it, electoral campaigns are moments of pleasure. Music, jokes, and alcohol all contribute to affective atmospheres of festivity. In an interview with Mr. Douglas, an eighty-three-year-old gentleman from West Kingston, it was precisely this sense of excitement and fun that stood out in his account of Jamaica's earliest elections. We sat on his veranda, accompanied by our mutual friend, Keith, with neighborhood children running back and forth. Occasionally interrupting himself to caution the children if he felt they were getting too rowdy, Mr. Douglas began to describe the 1949 elections. He recalled the campaign vividly, recounting how he had left Kingston to attend an election rally in the rural parish of St. Elizabeth in support of the JLP incumbent, Cleve Lewis. Despite the rivalry between Lewis and his PNP challenger, Edward Vivian Allen, the competition was friendly and took the shape of musical battles rather than actual violence, while alcohol always contributed to the high spirits.

"I never forget it," Mr. Douglas declared, describing the rally and the JLP supporters' attempts to discourage their opponents through music. "They're running the election now, you know, big election, and they would sing a song." He began to sing, tapping his foot and swaying in his chair to the rhythm:

> *Tell them Lewis, no enter the election contest*
> *Tell them Lewis, no enter the election contest*
> *We have no gun, we have no revolver*

> *The JLP, the rock of Gibraltar*
> *Tell them Lewis, no enter the election contest!*

Recalling the moment, Mr. Douglas became animated, singing the lines again. The PNP loyalists would respond to the musical challenge in kind, Mr. Douglas continued. He sung their rejoinder twice in a row for us:

> *Old clothes government, a wah mi do yu*
> *Old clothes government, a wah mi do yu*

Like the first song, these lines were also sung to a cheerful tune. Rather than celebrating their own leader, this response was a derogatory song, its lyrics berating JLP politicians for seeking to buy votes by handing out second-hand clothing to their followers. "A wah mi do yu"—what have I done to you—the singers asked, to be treated in such a demeaning fashion by the "old clothes government." "We would get a kick out of it!" Mr. Douglas laughed. The antagonism between the two candidates and their followers was performative, he assured us: "And the two of them, after they finish the election, two men in the rum bar drinking, yes, and Labourites and PNP drinking, getting high."

The classic collection of Jamaican women's life stories, *Lionheart Gal*, includes a similar account of such a lyrical back-and-forth between two women doing their laundry on either sides of a tenement yard. "The PNP one" would sing:

> *Old clothes government*
> *A weh me do yuh*
> *Me no waan no saltfish*
> *Me no waan no weevil flour*
>
> Old clothes government
> What have I done to you
> I don't want any saltfish
> I don't want any weevil-infested flour

This disparagement would elicit a sung response from her JLP neighbor, who would "come out and find someting else fi sing and dem start throw word [make disparaging comments] and dem sing and cuss all day." While part of a different gendered sociality, this oral history similarly depicts early electoral competition as friendly lyrical banter, woven into the fabric of everyday life.[21] This longer version of the song also highlights how early election campaigns involved a negotiation between voters and elected officials. What kind of material support does a government owe its citizens? The refusal of hand-me-downs and substandard food conveys a classed and raced insistence on dignity, a rejection of political leaders who think they can obtain their voters' loyalty so cheaply.

Mr. Douglas clearly remembered these early elections as a form of political festivity, a feelingful event that offered Jamaicans a sensory, serious-but-fun form of engagement with the new political structure. While these recollections are mainly happy memories, the line "We have no gun, we have no revolver" in the Labourites' campaign song indicates that party-cum-union violence and intimidation were an unmistakable background presence during these early elections. Collective fun, economic interests, party loyalty, and violent antagonism were intertwined elements in the mid-twentieth century formation of political subjectivities.

During this period leading up to independence, then, a number of factors served to instill not only a national but also a party-partisan subjectivity in Jamaican voters. During the early pre-independence election campaigns, the newly formed political parties and trade unions used structured political education drives to mobilize colonial subjects to see themselves as rights-bearing democratic citizens and workers. While national sentiments intensified, the boundaries of party-political belonging also hardened, encouraged by the economic benefits that accrued to union members and party supporters, and solidified by the violent clashes between supporters. Beyond these economic and coercive factors, the festive atmosphere and embodied sensation of early electoral practices and performances were also conducive to the experience of both national and partisan belonging. Through the entanglement of the labor movement and party politics, and the intertwined mobilization of labor and the electorate, a new population of voter-citizens developed an allegiance to the emergent nation as well as to the party and the union. In the second half of the twentieth century, however, these entangled allegiances began to change, with dons taking over the role of union leaders in terms of political mobilization.

GARRISON POLITICS

The territorial antagonism that had begun to emerge in the 1940s and 1950s, as groups of violent enforcers sought to claim the space of their neighborhood for their political and union bosses, became more marked in the decades following independence. In the 1960s and 1970s, both the PNP and the JLP created party-loyal "garrison communities" by concentrating supporters in new government-built housing developments. There is a general consensus that the West Kingston neighborhood of Tivoli Gardens was the first garrison, constructed between 1963 and 1965. As part of a larger process of urban renewal, Edward Seaga, JLP Minister of Housing and Member of Parliament (MP) for West Kingston at the time, had the informal settlement of Back-o-Wall demolished. Seen as a hotbed of PNP support and as the home of disreputable, antiestablishment Rastafari, Back-o-Wall's self-built homes were destroyed and replaced with modern housing units, which were distributed to JLP supporters. The electoral consequences of this partisan form of urban development were unmistakable, and the PNP copied the model, developing its own housing estates and allocating units to party supporters in Arnett Gardens (more commonly known as "Jungle") and Wilton Gardens (known as "Rema").

Across Kingston's low-income areas, party supporters increasingly clustered together in politically homogenous enclaves. These housing developments provided the initial material basis for a broader system of "garrison politics": a form of communal clientelism in which politicians used state resources to secure votes, and to supply loyal communities with material benefits that extended beyond housing to include employment, infrastructural improvement, and general welfare.[22] The creation and maintenance of garrison communities not only involved rewarding political loyalty with these forms of material assistance, but also using violence to discourage electoral competition. Accordingly, such communities have been defined as spaces where "any individual/group that seeks to oppose, raise opposition to or organize against the locally dominant party would be in physical danger, thus making continued residence in the area extremely difficult, if not impossible."[23]

Homogenous voting within these political enclaves was not only achieved through the distribution of benefits and violence. It also resulted from an increasingly strong sense of collective, partisan identity known as "political tribalism." The two parties had both developed a range of visual symbols, or public identity markers, including specific colors and hand signals. Supporters of the PNP wore orange, called each other "Comrade," and signaled their party allegiance through a raised fist, while green-clad supporters of the JLP, known as "Labourites," made a V-sign. In garrison communities, political graffiti, party colors, and murals depicting politicians came to mark the physical borders of the neighborhood.

In short, a type of party-political subjectivity emerged in and through the space of the garrison. Anthropologist David Scott argues for viewing the clientelism that is central to garrison politics as a form of governmentality, as a rational principle through which behavior can be governed. This also entails attending to the spaces and processes of subject formation that support this mode of political rationality. Clientelism, Scott emphasizes, "works through certain kinds of space, the construction and deployment of certain kinds of subject, the inducement of certain kinds of motivations, and the shaping of certain kinds of desire, aspiration, and lifestyle."[24] Over the decades, in garrison spaces, the clientelist logic of garrison politics became inseparable from the subjectivities of political tribalism.

In establishing and maintaining garrisons, politicians relied on local brokers. It is these brokers—neighborhood strongmen initially often referred to as "area leaders"—who eventually became known as dons. They were central in ensuring that the distribution of state largesse was managed effectively, and that residents of these low-income strongholds voted for the "right" political party. In the early days of garrison politics, politicians from both parties enabled donmanship by surreptitiously sending both weapons and sums of cash to these emerging dons. In exchange, the dons ensured that their political bosses got their desired electoral outcome in three main ways. Within their neighborhoods, they pursued a form of party-political cleansing by ensuring that public housing units only went to party loyalists, and by forcing out supporters of the "enemy" party, threatening them with violence or actively burning down the homes of those who refused to leave. In addition, they would "encourage" those loyalists who remained to turn out to vote on election day. And, if there was still any doubt that the election might go the wrong way, they would steal and destroy ballot boxes containing less favorable votes.

A don I interviewed, whom I call "Richie Boom," explained his role in the elections to me. Back in the 1980s, when he was a teenager, he became involved in getting out the vote: "You call people out of their yard go vote. Old man lying sick in bed—you lift him out of bed, go polling station." In addition to mobilizing voters, he would target ballot boxes from polling stations in areas where party loyalty might not be guaranteed. "Mi go for the ballot box in 1985," he told me. "Politics nuh play in them time"—politics was not a game in those days. In addition to stealing ballot boxes known to be stuffed with votes for the opposing party, Richie would have to defend his own electoral turf by protecting the "good" ballots. "You haffi [have to] stand up for your turf," he explained. "Them come thief [steal] the ballot box, we haffi stand up for that. It's just so it grow, we haffi fight the struggle. It's not a game when you defend the ballot box, you can dead in the polling station. It's just so the system set up."

During the 1970s and 1980s, these electoral clashes had become increasingly violent as Jamaica's national political contests became entangled with the geopolitical and ideological conflicts of the Cold War. The PNP, now led by Norman Manley's son Michael, was embracing democratic socialism as the path forward, a position that involved strengthening ties with Cuba and left-leaning nations more broadly. Meanwhile, the JLP was aligning itself with the US-centered political project of free enterprise. This ideological polarization reinforced difference and legitimated violence between supporters, as the street-level competition over political territory and clientelist benefits became understood as part of a global battle between socialism and capitalism. Accordingly, the capacity of dons to shape election outcomes was not only of interest to Jamaican politicians but, increasingly, also to foreign intelligence agencies.[25]

During elections, Kingston's low-income areas became Cold War battlefields between armed PNP and JLP supporters. Electoral violence peaked around the 1980 elections, when these clashes resulted in the deaths of nearly eight hundred Jamaicans. The violence of the 1970s and 1980s was contested through popular music at the time. Multiple songs titled "Tribal War" were released, penned by artists from Gregory Isaacs and John Holt to Culture, all analyzing garrison politics and political tribalism as a political system set up to divide and rule Jamaica's urban poor.

From the 1990s onward, this history began to be narrated in dancehall lyrics, but not always through the critical lens that characterized the roots reggae of the preceding decades. Super Cat's "Ghetto Red Hot" (1992), one of the first dancehall songs to become a hit in the United States, is less concerned with condemning violence than with laying claim to place-based "rudeboy" authenticity. Super Cat asserts that he was there, on the scene, at key moments when Kingston "ran hot." Every verse begins by asking: "Weh dem deh when di ghetto run hot, when wi lookin' di food for di pot?" Where were others when the ghetto was "running hot" with violence, when Super Cat and his friends were seeking to earn a living? Unlike some would-be gangsters, they *were* there:

> *Kingston wi deh when Massop get shot*
> *Kingston wi deh when Copper get shot*
> *Kingston wi deh when Bird get shot*
> *Man a Kingston wi deh when Cow get shot*
> *Sandokhan when him lick down flat*
> *Natty Morgan lick down flat*

> We were in Kingston when Massop was shot
> We were in Kingston when Copper was shot
> We were in Kingston when Bird was shot
> We were in Kingston when Cow was shot
> Sandokhan when he was knocked down flat
> Natty Morgan, knocked down flat

Key historical episodes, in this song, are the deaths of dons: Claudie Massop of Tivoli Gardens, Dennis "Copper" Barth of Rennock Lodge, Glenford "Early Bird" Phipps of Matthews Lane, Wayne "Sandokhan" Smith of Olympic Gardens, and Nathaniel "Natty" Morgan of Riverton City. Super Cat's rhythmic recitation of their names, to the dancehall beat, adds sonically to the sensation that the song is writing—or rather, rewriting—a historical canon of Kingston's leaders. Several of these men played a central role in garrison politics, defending the borders of their politically aligned neighborhood. Yet the political dimension of Kingston's violence receives only a brief mention, in a later verse, where Super Cat positions himself as a protector of the poor amidst the "politics friction":

> *Weh dem deh when Kingston run hot?*
> *When wi looking di food fi di pot*
> *And guardin' poor people head-top?*
> *When di politics friction drop?*
> *When di bomb a drop on house top?*
> *And every mornin' a dead man on spot*
> *And di youth dem go school through shot*

> Where were they when Kingston was dangerous?
> When we were trying to earn a living
> And protecting poor people's heads
> When the political conflict started
> When the bombs fell on houses
> And every morning a man was found dead
> And the children had to dodge bullets on their way to school

Rather than distancing himself from this violence, it serves as a platform that allows men such as Super Cat—who refers to himself as a "don, die-hearted, dog-heart"—to affirm their status as powerful, authentic protectors.

Similarly, in Cham's international hit "Ghetto Story" (2006), which describes growing up in a low-income urban area, the electoral violence of the 1980s is associated not so much with ideological enmity, but more with big men seeking to "run road"—to take control of the streets. Like "Ghetto Red Hot," this song is a conscious act of urban memory-making, with successive verses starting with "I remember when . . ." or "I remember those days . . ." Remembering the 1980 elections and the explosive conflict it entailed, Cham namechecks a number of powerful men. However, rather than dons, he pays respect to Keith "Trinity" Gardner and Tony Hewitt, legendary police officers who were not afraid to use violence in their attempts to run the streets. "Ghetto Story" traces a lineage—again, an apparent canon—of notorious policemen, describing Trinity and Hewitt as the forefathers of infamous officers such as Isaiah Laing, Cornwall "Bigga" Ford, and Reneto Adams, who were still junior officers unfamiliar with "the road code" around 1980.

> *I remember 'bout '80*
> *Jamaica explode*
> *When a Trinity and Tony Hewitt*
> *Dem a run road*
> *Dat a long before Laing dem*

And even Bigga Ford
When Adams dem a corporal
Nuh know di road code

I remember about 1980
Jamaica exploded
When it was Trinity and Tony Hewitt
Who ran the streets
That was long before Laing
And even Bigga Ford
When Adams was a corporal
He did not know the law of the street

While paying respect to such police officers, Cham also positions them as antagonists, highlighting the excitement of young men becoming involved in various forms of crime and violence. "Ghetto Story" moves seamlessly from memories of a first successful robbery of a neighborhood shop, to detailing the thrill of electoral fraud:

I remember when we skip the poll clerks
And dump the ballot box 'pon Tivoli outskirts
And hold a plane ticket
And go chill over Turks
When mi come back, a still inna di hole mi a lurk

I remember when we ran past the poll clerks
And dumped the ballot box on the outskirts of Tivoli
And got a plane ticket
And went to chill in Turks [and Caicos]
When I came back, I still had to hide

Cham describes rather matter-of-factly how involvement in street-level conflicts enabled their international mobility: those stealing ballot boxes would be provided with plane tickets to lay low abroad until after the elections (although they still would face the risk of retaliation on their return). The song is relatively uncritical about the overall effects of the electoral violence, though it briefly disparages how politics manipulated young men, echoing David Scott's point on clientelism as a form of governmentality:

Jamaica get screw through greed and glutton
Politics manipulate
And press yutes button

But we rich now so dem cyaan tell man nutten
'Cause a wi a mek mama nyaam fish and mutton

Jamaica got screwed due to greed and gluttony
Politics manipulated
And pressed young men's buttons
But we are rich now so they can't boss us around
Because it's us providing mom with fish and meat to eat

In foregrounding the autonomy that gunmen gained as they found their own sources of wealth and came to eschew politics, "Ghetto Story" historicizes the shift many of those involved in electoral violence experienced. Moving into the 1980s, economic recession and neoliberal structural adjustment programs, which stressed cutbacks in government expenditure and public-sector employment, meant that the politicians' power to distribute material resources to their constituencies were diminishing drastically. The dons, their neighborhood-level armed enforcers, found other sources of income. In addition to identifying a lucrative niche in the transnational drugs trade, and expanding "taxation" activities within Kingston, their financial independence also grew as they developed formal business activities within the entertainment, construction, and private security industry.

As their financial autonomy increased, dons such as Richie Boom also became more skeptical about their role in electoral politics. In describing how his thinking had developed, the don told me: "We go through, we see it do nothing for we. You get a better overstanding." Eventually, as he developed this "overstanding"—the Rastafari term for understanding—he distanced himself from garrison politics as such. "Politics, mi haffi let it go," he stated. The trust he had placed in politicians turned out to be of little value: "Them win [the election], them nuh [re]member you, and send police, them call you terrorist. You find [out] who go to the morgue, who go to the penitentiary." As the bonds between MPs and their enforcers weakened toward the end of the twentieth century, the intensity of political violence also diminished. Although violent crimes more generally increased, "the rate of the politics drop," Richie Boom concluded.

DONS AS CORULERS

In the twenty-first century, garrison constituencies and their party-political boundaries have become so consolidated that the don's role as an electoral enforcer has become less urgent. Politicians still look to them to mobilize the vote, but this currently involves hardly any electoral violence. Indeed, much of the enmity associated with elections has disappeared. Spending time in Brick Town, historically a hardcore PNP garrison, around the 2011 election, friends recounted an episode to me that indicated how much had changed. "Rickie," a Brick Town resident, went to vote at the local polling station, which was located in a school in a "Labourite" section of the constituency. Dressed in full orange regalia, he crossed into the heart of JLP territory, electoral turf that had been defended and expanded violently during earlier decades. In response to this somewhat audacious act, the Labourites near the polling station took his orange PNP cap, put a green JLP cap back on his head and sent him on his way. On returning to Brick Town, he laughingly told my friends about what had happened to him, showing off his JLP cap. In this garrisoned part of Kingston, this kind of playful banter between Comrades and Labourites—reminiscent of how Mr. Douglas described the 1949 election—had been unthinkable, until very recently. To go into a "green" area dressed in orange during election time would be inviting trouble, to say the least.

Meanwhile, dons became less dependent on politicians for guns or money—they had acquired their own sources in the legal and illegal economy. This does not mean they no longer receive financial support from politicians. Influential MPs, with control over major political contracts, can direct significant amounts of government funding toward dons, who either receive compensation for acting as "community liaisons" or, if they have developed formal businesses, act as official contractors. Perhaps more important than money is the ability of politicians to use their clout to protect dons from prosecution and other forms of harm. A senior MP I interviewed, whom I call "Karen," described to me how she was called on to intervene in prison, in order to protect a convicted criminal from her constituency, "because when he was inside, somebody in there wanted to kill him." She called the Commissioner of Corrections, telling him: "Look, I know I'm not supposed to intervene in matters like this, but this young man's life is at risk. He's on this block, this cell, see what you can do for me please."

Notwithstanding the continued value of political connections, as the dons' national and transnational networks expanded and their financial independence increased, their negotiating power vis-à-vis politicians grew. As programs of deregulation and privatization diminished state ability to provide services such as health care and social and physical security, their role became less that of clientelist brokers, who could trade community votes for political pork. Increasingly, dons came to replace MPs as community patrons who could distribute largesse.[26] It is important to note, though, that the relation between state actors and dons is dynamic and varies in intensity across Kingston and other garrisoned urban areas. Certain state actors combat the power of the dons while others continue to rely on them and actively shield them from criminal investigation and prosecution.

In addition, dons' roles and impacts vary significantly across low-income communities, depending on, amongst other factors, their economic base, the nature of their organizations, their attitude toward politics, and their political, social, and business connections.[27] On the whole, dons continue to function as important gatekeepers for politicians, government agencies, and bureaucrats.

The more successful dons, however, have expanded their role beyond being brokers and local patrons to being partners-in-governance. They draw on their own funds and their access to the means of violence, and the residents of their communities rely on them for the provision of public services such as welfare, employment, and security. They provide residents with "irregular" access to basic public goods, such as free utilities, by intimidating electricity and water bill collectors or technicians sent to lock off illegal connections. But they have also taken on a more formal role in state programs: as dons became increasingly incorporated into the governance of low-income urban areas, their function expanded from mobilizing voters to realizing government objectives and projects. Dons do much more than just providing political parties with access to electoral blocs and distributing clientelist benefits—they have also become important governance actors in their own right, and state agencies and bureaucrats rely on them to ensure the successful implementation of government programs. From policing and welfare provision to solid waste management and the construction of public parks and other forms of infrastructural project management, dons take on governance roles effectively and efficiently.

This incorporation of dons into governance began in the late twentieth century, as the Jamaican government became less resourced and less of a developmental state, and dons became more resourced and more independent. In the twenty-first century, dons' connections have increasingly extended beyond politicians to state institutions more broadly. As following chapters illustrate in more detail, politicians, police officers, and administrators enter into partnerships with dons to achieve improvements in access or efficiency or to preempt violent conflicts in low-income urban areas.

As discussed in the introduction, leaders such as Jamaica's dons, with their involvement in criminal activities and organizations, have sometimes been imagined as heading "parallel states." However, the various unstable yet enduring coalitions between government officials and dons' organizations have made it difficult to separate formal state governance from donmanship. These developments necessitate an understanding of the entanglement of dons and state actors that goes beyond clientelism and brokerage. I understand the relationship between dons, bureaucrats, and politicians as central to a hybrid state, in which a range of state duties have been de facto outsourced to dons. In return, they claim a steady flow of state funds and a measure of political protection. These links to state agencies and bureaucracies have frequently been framed as public-private "partnerships," and been justified by state actors in the neoliberal terms of cost efficiency, decentralization, and community participation.

Rather than clear-cut strategic decisions, these transitions in governance are the unstable outcome of complex, historically structured negotiations, of ongoing power struggles between dons, politicians, and bureaucrats who are engaged in relations of collusion and competition, each with their own political and economic interests. However, as Anthony Harriott notes, "The collusion between the political parties and organized crime is not just the outcome of materially self-interested motivations; it is an adaptation to state incapacity that permits co-rulership of the communities of the urban poor."[28] In certain cases, the de facto outsourcing of government responsibilities to dons took place as a direct consequence of state retrenchment, with an emphasis on cost efficiency. In other contexts, a relatedly neoliberal emphasis on participatory development, decentralization, and community-based project management—promoted in Jamaica through World Bank loans, bilateral donors, and NGOs—has framed the dons' involvement in governance. Politicians and state actors use dons to pursue public goods as well as private interests while dons use officials, in return, with the same objectives, making it hard to discern personal gain from the common good.

The association of dons with the public good is often incomprehensible to outsiders. It is, however, a central theme in songs focusing on donmanship. There are very few songs that outright reject this form of leadership and a much more elaborate tradition of celebrating dons. The lyrics of such songs often emphasize the leaders' "badness," that is, their tough and fearless character. But the artists singing about dons generally take pains to show how this willingness to use violence or to skirt the law is directed toward the good of the people. This was especially clear in a spate of songs that emerged in the period leading up to Dudus's extradition, all of which were concerned with defending his reputation as a legitimate authority figure.

One prominent example was the song "Don't Touch the President," by Bunny Wailer, one of Bob Marley's original bandmates. With a catchy melody and instrumentation reminiscent of the roots reggae music of the 1970s, the song sounds like much of Bunny Wailer's back catalogue. Released not long before the Tivoli Incursion and Dudus's arrest, it urged the authorities not to touch "the President," as the don was commonly known, "'cause we confident, seh him [that he is] innocent." This assertion of innocence is at the heart of the song's chorus, but it is also immediately qualified—Bunny Wailer depicts Dudus as a Robin Hood-style social bandit, acknowledging "the bad" and "evil" involved, but insisting on the overall goodness and progress he has brought to his community:

> *Don't touch the Robin Hood in the neighborhood*
> *'Cause he take the bad and turn it into good*
> *Sometimes out of evil comes forth good*
> *Can't you see the progress in the neighborhood?*

The song continues to elaborate on Dudus's importance for the residents of Downtown Kingston, pointing to his role in generating economic activities and protecting the poor:

> *Them mash down Passa Passa and Fully Loaded*
> *Containers with the carrots and tomatoes*
> *Say mi sorry for the vendors and bend-down plazas*
> *For if them touch him, poor people a go bawl*

These lines refer to the don's status as informal guardian of "Passa Passa," a weekly dancehall street party held in Tivoli Gardens from 2003 until 2010, and associate him with the popular annual beach party "Fully Loaded." Bunny Wailer gestures toward Dudus's role in ensuring a safe and orderly market, expressing his sympathy with those selling in the "bend-down plazas," where fresh vegetables are displayed on the ground, concluding that if the authorities "touch" the don, poor people "a go bawl"—they will cry.

An explicitly historical take on legality and legitimacy in political leadership was evident in "Crime Minister," a dancehall song by comedic duo Twin of Twins released shortly after Dudus had been arrested and extradited.[29] A scathing critique of Prime Minister Bruce Golding's role in the extradition and Tivoli Incursion, the song directly contrasts dons and formal leaders, coming down in clear favor of the former:

> *Which one a dem man deh a di real crime minister?*
> *Which one a di leader dem people do this for? . . .*
> *Who is di real criminal inna di country? . . .*
> *The first Governor-General was a pirate*
> *A nuh Dudus send di bill dem with such a high rate*
> *Who make di nurses and di doctors dem out fi migrate*

> Which one of those men is the real crime minister?
> Which one of the leaders did people do this for? . . .
> Who is the real criminal in the country? . . .
> The first Governor-General was a pirate
> It's not Dudus sending the bills that are so high
> Who is making the nurses and the doctors migrate

Who is the real criminal, the song asks, Dudus or Golding? Rather than a prime minister, the song proposes viewing Golding as a "crime minister" and ties him to a longer, colonial lineage by pointing out that "the first Governor-General was a pirate," a likely reference to Henry Morgan, infamous buccaneer and seventeenth-century lieutenant governor of Jamaica. In contrast to this corrupted canon of formal political leaders, Dudus is heralded as a leader that people would sacrifice their lives for—a leader who provides for the people, rather than presiding over an economic situation in which the cost of living is so high that skilled Jamaicans see no other option than to migrate.

In contrast with the early twentieth-century songs in which politicians featured as heroes, in more recent political dramas they tend to be cast as villains. Notwithstanding, the songs released around Dudus's extradition in 2009–2010, pitting "the President" against Jamaica's formal prime minister, mispresent the level of antagonism between politicians and dons by disregarding their long-standing and continuing entanglement. Bruce Golding's initial reluctance to extradite Dudus cannot be understood outside of the close ties that Golding's party, the JLP, had to this don and his neighborhood of Tivoli Gardens, "the mother of all garrisons." When the Tivoli Incursion took place in May 2010, after nearly nine months of national and international pressure, the security operation shocked the Jamaican public, not only because of the level of state violence it involved, but also because it saw a JLP government attacking its first and most important garrison.

DONMANSHIP AFTER DUDUS

In the wake of the Tivoli Incursion, many citizens, politicians, and businesspeople saw the crisis as an opportunity to "dismantle the garrisons" and to fashion a new urban future without dons. In the early 2010s, a series of strategies were rolled out, including social welfare policies intended to convince garrison residents that they could rely on the state rather than on dons for their material needs. Despite urgent calls to tackle political corruption and the two parties' entanglement with organized crime, no clearly effective actions emerged aimed at fundamentally transforming the relationship between politicians and dons. And, in the years that followed, the emphasis shifted away from "softer" social strategies toward more punitive forms of intervention into don-led areas.

Rather than a radical political transformation, newly militarized modes of policing have emerged since the Tivoli Incursion. The State of Emergency declared in 2010 was followed by a series of emergency measures applying to parts of the country. In 2017–2018, the government passed the Zones of Special Operation Act and established a new State of Emergency in sections of the island, which was first extended and then succeeded by the declaration of additional States of Emergency. These acts involved a new series of spatially circumscribed curfews in areas declared "zones of special operation" or ZOSOs, where the security forces were granted legal powers to stop, search, and arrest persons without a warrant. These zones included Denham Town in the West Kingston area, but also incorporated new areas in the tourism hub Montego Bay, reflecting a concern with the recent rise of "lottery scammers," a relatively new form of crime with a political, economic, and geographical logic quite distinct from that of the dons.[30]

Despite a formal requirement that ZOSOs include social interventions, the rollout of these zones has primarily involved an emphasis on repressive policing and a turn away from "softer" forms of crime prevention and control. By mandating a military-police joint command to administer these special operations, the ZOSOs further normalized the use of emergency powers and the militarization of policing.[31] Ultimately, the developments that followed Dudus's extradition have done little to disturb either the dons' involvement in urban governance or the entrenched classed, raced, and territorial patterns that support their claims to authority within low-income neighborhoods.

In the context of these militarized crackdowns, a significant number of dons were removed from power. This removal involved the publication of lists of "Persons of Interest" who were summoned to police stations. These persons were alleged dons, who were sometimes listed by their real names and sometimes only by their aliases and general address, a practice of public naming and criminalizing that was not necessarily legal. It was also rumored that those Persons of Interest who showed up at the police stations would be warned to lay low, or else face the extralegal wrath of the JCF. In the months and years following the incursion, some dons were killed or imprisoned by the security forces, while others lay low or fled their neighborhoods in an attempt to avoid this fate. The Brick Town don, "Junior," who had succeeded his more popular father, left the neighborhood after he was listed as a "Person of Interest" and never returned to a leadership position, taking seriously the warnings he had apparently received.

The fear of being killed by police resonated more broadly throughout Downtown Kingston. In the Central Kingston neighborhood of Tel Aviv, the alleged don, Donovan "Pepsi" Ainsworth, had announcements posted through the area stating, "I Donovan Ainsworth, otherwise known as 'Pepsi' or 'Calla Danks,' write this notice to officially inform all politicians and members of the security forces who have classified me as a gang leader or a don that I am neither" (see figure I.1). Evidently, some dons were indeed "removed" from power and others kept a lower profile to avoid being targeted by the police forces. But rather than dismantle the system of donmanship, the removal of "kingpins" appeared to lead to more violent

1.1 Poster disavowing the status of don.

conflict. When one don is killed or leaves his neighborhood (for instance to settle in a foreign country), it is not necessarily the case that a noncriminal form of governance immediately envelopes his territory. Rather, in many instances, when a strong don dies or migrates, this is followed by internal power struggles between different men who wish to succeed him as don, or between different territorial factions that do not accept the authority of the apparent successor.[32]

In "Safe N Sound" (2021), a song centered on urban security, Chronixx reflects on these developments, connecting Jamaica's states of emergency to a proliferation of gunmen at the community level while also highlighting the absence of long-term political plans for economic development:

> *All of a sudden, everybody a gun man*
> *State of Emergency and a bag [a lot] of tension*
> *Politician don't have no development plan*
> *That's why every community need a one don*
> *One order, everybody fi [must] unite*

In the accompanying video clip, the singer stands alone in the streets of a garrison-like neighborhood, chanting these lyrics against a dystopian background of burning debris and abandoned vehicles. The eerie atmosphere is reinforced sonically by the song's dark symphonic sound, combining classical strings, synthesizer melodies, and a spare beat. The lyrics suggest that the State of Emergency is a key source of tension and conflict—shattering the equilibrium, it creates a situation in which "all of a sudden, everybody [is] a gunman." While locating the source of insecurity in such militarized strategies, the song also directs blame for conflict and deprivation toward politicians who prioritize policing over development plans. The conclusion that Chronixx draws from these observations is that every community needs "a one don," uniting everyone in "one order." The song evinces a political imagination that locates authority in the centralized order of a strong don, privileging this form of leadership as a source of unity, peace, and economic development.

CONCLUSION

The emergence and development of the system of donmanship, over the course of nearly a century, challenges conventional imaginations of where political authority is located. While the charismatic leaders of Jamaica's two political parties were once celebrated as heroes, in the twenty-first century, many citizens view politicians with, at best, a strong measure of skepticism. This is not to say that Jamaicans have fully renounced the pantheon of officially consecrated leaders—the formal canon of National Heroes still remains significant to many citizens. But for others, the politicians in this canon have been joined or even replaced by the most beloved dons.

In the years that followed the Tivoli Incursion, successive governments sought to "dismantle the garrison" and improve the relationship between low-income urban residents and the state system. After more than a decade of such discourse, changes seem negligible. Protoje's "Sudden Flight" (2015) suggests that the widespread distrust of politicians and party politics has grown stronger, if anything. Resignifying a famous hiphop line—Slick Rick and Snoop Dogg's "La-di-da-di, we like to party"—the singer insists that he "nah join no party," he won't join any political party. Like Super Cat before him, Protoje establishes a lyrical canon of dons, specifying the three Tivoli Gardens leaders of Claudie Massop, Jim Brown, and Dudus and pointing out that each of them was betrayed by politicians:

> La-di-da-di, nah join no party
> Look what di politician dem do to Claudie [Massop]
> Look what di politician dem do to Jim [Brown]
> Him son [Dudus] resurrect it and look what dem do to him

Other songs also chastise politicians, but express a yearning for the "wholesome" heroes of yesteryear rather than turning to dons. Queen Ifrica's "Times Like These" (2010) describes Jamaica's present-day "slackness" or moral decay, assigning responsibility to corporations and media houses but identifying electoral politics as a main source of conflict:

> People use the fist, hold the bell
> Beat promise till it swell . . .
> Go ask them, who put the crab in the barrel?
> PM, opposition, unno done [you all must stop] with the quarrel
> Unite, come together, teach the people how fi [to] chill

Alluding to the raised-fist hand symbol of the PNP and the visual JLP symbol of a bell, the song references a long history of unfulfilled political promises and divide-and-rule strategies in which poor people end up attacking each other like "crabs in a barrel." Calling for politicians to stop this conflict, the chorus of the song repeatedly contrasts the flaws of present-day leaders with the virtues of role models from earlier centuries, asserting: "It's times like these, I'm missing our heroes, times like these, I really wish they were around, shouldn't have to be like this." Queen Ifrica goes on to voice the canon of heroes she misses: Marcus Garvey, Nanny of the Maroons, and Sam Sharpe—three anticolonial role models found amongst Jamaica's official National Heroes—along with Bob Marley and Miss Lou, cultural icons in music and literature. "We need you," she sings repeatedly.

Writing on the role of visual art in public memory, art historian Petrina Dacres notes that "the building of monuments has been associated with changing political regimes in complex and often contradictory ways."[33] Reggae and dancehall songs, along with everyday discussions of political leadership past and present, play an analogous role in reflecting and supporting shifts in the configuration of power. They are sonic monuments, sites where political authority is imagined and re-imagined, where official celebrations of past rulers are reworked and alternative histories of political leadership are posited. Within such lyrical forms of political imagination and heroization, dons have come to feature prominently. They are often commemorated as righteous protectors of the poor, providing physical and economic security where politicians and police offer false promises and brutality. In the aftermath of 2010, the many pledges to fundamentally disrupt the system of donmanship, and the state violence that accompanied these declarations, do not seem to have shifted this imagination of the dons' authority in any profound way, as I show throughout the rest of the book. Notwithstanding, as the following chapters also suggest, seeds of doubt may have been planted that now have more space to grow into a broader questioning of these long-standing modes of leadership.

2
Geographies

The first don I met was Richie Boom. He was a so-called corner don: while a more powerful don was the leader of the larger neighborhood, Richie was in charge of a "corner" section. At the time, a friend of mine worked in a cultural institution with offices located in Richie's area, near the city's central business district. This organization was housed in a carefully renovated historical building with air-conditioned offices, and frequently hosted members of Jamaica's cultural elite. In the daytime, it was a little pocket of middle-class respectability. Nonetheless, it was clearly part of an "inner-city neighborhood" and as such could not fully escape the logic of donmanship. Any time the organization began to develop construction activities, Richie would show up and suggest, in a persuasive fashion, that they hire some of his men. He was also more than happy to offer his security services, should they be required. Still, he generally maintained a courteous attitude toward my friend and her colleagues, and she offered to invite him to participate in my research. Somewhat to my surprise, he agreed. A large man in his late forties, he showed up at the organization accompanied by his deputy, "Marshall." We made our way to a little table in the courtyard of the building, where we sat shaded by ackee and guinep trees while office workers passed by occasionally, casting slightly nervous glances in our direction.

Curious about his second name, I asked Richie why he was called Boom. In response, he brandished his arm, which had "BOOM" tattooed onto it in capital letters. "Mi get di name off di corner," he explained to me. "Yu associate with di corner, yu get di name a di corner. Mi have a tattoo says Boom, others will have a tattoo with 'Max' or 'Renkers.'" Like these other dons, he literally embodied the slice of urban space he represented. However, he confided, his territory had been slightly reconfigured in recent years. He was originally from Boom Corner, but the men there had shifted allegiances to "link up" with the PNP-aligned area that bordered his community. A JLP stalwart himself, and loyal to the larger don in his own neighborhood, Richie was unable to deal with that shift, he told me. Eventually, his base became the smaller section of the neighborhood where we were sitting. Men from the original Boom Corner had recently got into a conflict with another deputy of his, "Delroy," and shot him. But, Richie explained, they knew they could not get to *him*, because he owned guns, and had a large guard dog in his yard to protect him.

What are the political geographies of donmanship? While the borders of a don's turf may shift, as was the case for Richie when he had to move from Boom Corner, donmanship is always based on a territory, whether a corner or an entire neighborhood. Years may go by without major conflict, but dons must always have the means to defend this territory and its borders, whether they rely on guns, guard dogs, or other forms of violence. Yet their authority is rooted in urban space in ways that go beyond this capacity to police the borders of a territory. As Richie's tattoo suggests, dons also perform a close, embodied connection to the urban places they represent. Donmanship is inseparable from Kingston's sociospatial fragmentation, its classed, raced, and party-political divides. The legitimacy of dons' rule connects directly to their ability to claim a basis in the city's most marginalized urban areas—they must be able to suggest persuasively that they represent those who live in those spaces characterized alternately as "Downtown," "inner-city," "ghetto," or "garrison." At the same time, dons' authority is bolstered by their ability to forge alliances that go beyond their own territories.

In this chapter, I consider the spatial dimension of political authority. *Where* and *through which spatial relations* does power come to feel legitimate? Political authority is performed and recognized in an embodied fashion, but these affective processes take place within, and in relation to, specific sociomaterial landscapes. A perceived "fit" between rulers' bodies and the places over which they rule makes their claims to authority more robust. This corporeal fit may include a raced and classed "look," but more importantly, it involves sharing the sensorial experience of living in a Downtown neighborhood and demonstrating the embodied disposition of both toughness and care that is connected to this environment. Recent geographical work has suggested that authority relies on "relations of proximity, distance and presence, often through topological distortions of reach that make authority feel at once present and absent, both proximate and mysterious."[1] This is clearly the case for Jamaica's dons. In addition, I suggest, in contexts of trenchant urban inequality and sociospatial immobility, the performance and recognition of authority also depends on rulers' capacity to move and connect across borders—to be mobile themselves and to enhance the mobility of those over whom they rule. This chapter demonstrates the centrality of urban space, place, borders, and mobilities in the production of dons' authority.

In what follows, I situate donmanship within Kingston's geographies of inequality. I introduce, first, the broadly shared sense of the city as divided between

"Two Jamaicas," rich and poor, Uptown and Downtown, separate and unequal. As I go on to show, such spatial imaginaries, which map race and class onto the urban landscape, feed the notion that the don is the legitimate representative of "a community." Many people who live in a "ghetto" neighborhood identify strongly with this place-based community, their bonds shaped through shared experiences of poverty and stigmatization. Within this framework, it is near impossible for elected politicians—generally middle-class or elite outsiders—to truly "represent the ghetto." In contrast, as "sons of the soil," dons personify proximity, affinity, and loyalty to the urban poor. Next, I discuss how, in addition to this presumed rootedness, dons' effectivity and authority is enhanced through strategic forms of place-making and bordering. Their association with local sports and musical achievements encourages a shared place-based form of subjectivity with their constituents while they also engage actively in marking and maintaining neighborhood boundaries to establish territorial control. To be fully effective, dons need to balance this neighborhood-based bordering with their ability to transcend these same boundaries. As the concluding section of this chapter details, the most successful dons are those who have been able to network across Jamaica's urban divides, and to "link up" across the diaspora to form transnational connections.

WHAT URBAN INEQUALITY FEELS LIKE

Kingston is marked by a roughly binary sociospatial order, split between an Uptown and a Downtown. This broad binary is a spatial imaginary that maps Jamaica's racialized class hierarchy onto the urban landscape. While urban life encompasses other divisions than that between Uptown and Downtown alone, the distinction between these two realms has long been central to the lived experience of the city's residents. Roughly speaking, Uptown denotes the wealthier, hillier areas toward the northeast of Kingston, and is associated with an overrepresentation of "brown" Jamaicans of mixed or ethnic-minority descent. Downtown is the southwestern part of the city closer to the harbor, often glossed as "below Crossroads," a reference to a key transportation hub that functions as an informal border (see map 2.1). This part of the city is generally understood as those "inner-city" or "ghetto" areas where impoverished "black" Jamaicans of predominantly African descent live.

The ethnoracial categories of brown and black are not strictly phenotypical—they do not only or primarily reflect skin color. Rather, these categories are coproduced with class and urban space, with geographical designations—Downtown, or inner-city—used as adjectives that are taken to self-evidently mean lower-class and black. Besides skin color, an individual's positioning as either brown or black is based on class markers. These include clothing and hairstyles, but also the use

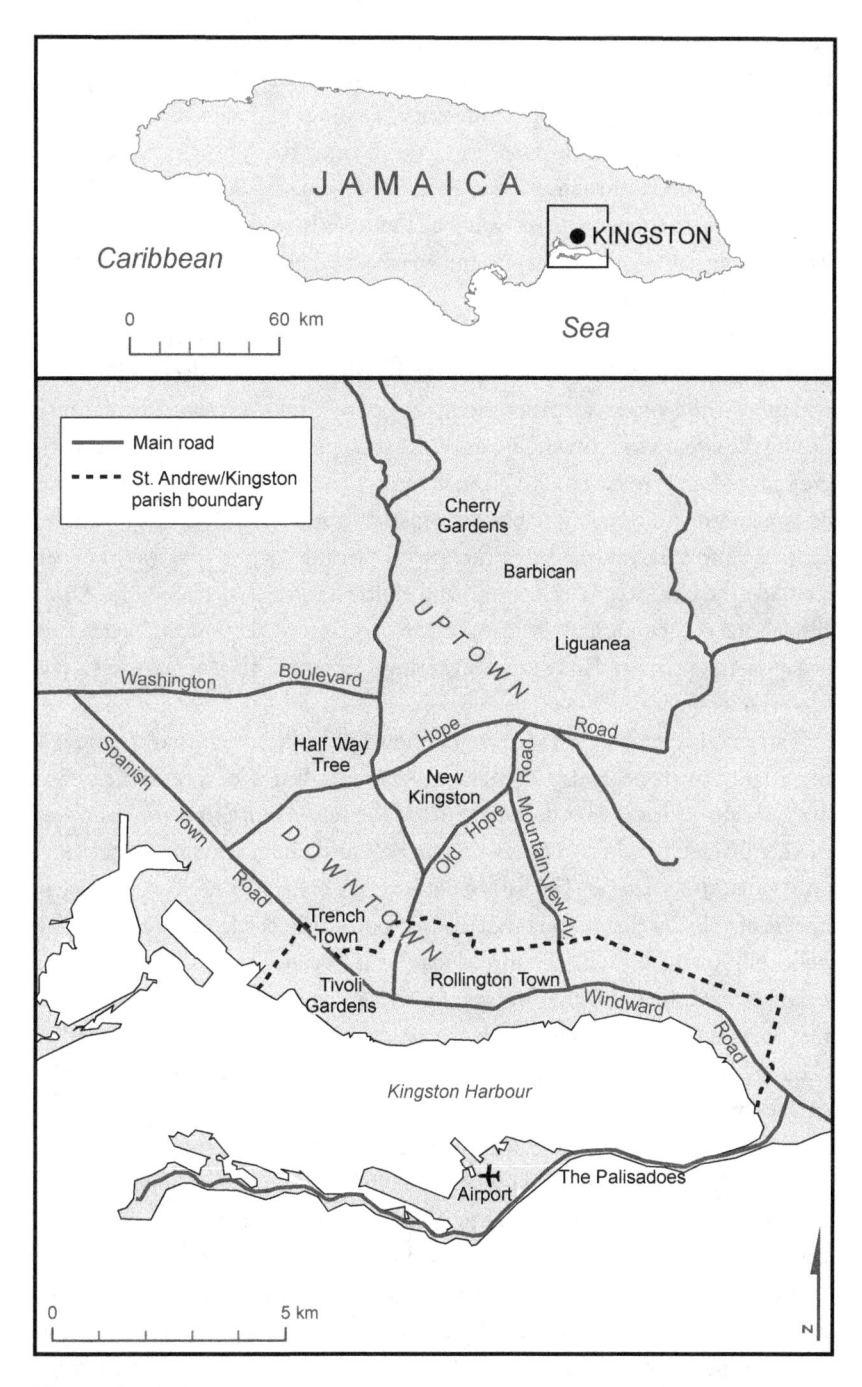

Map 2.1 Map of Kingston.

of language, specifically fluency in English versus the Jamaican vernacular of Patois. In addition to this entanglement of class and color categories, the Uptown versus Downtown binary shapes differential readings of bodies across the urban landscape; racial labels such as black and brown are assigned in part on the basis of spatial location.[2] For instance, a darker-skinned woman driving an expensive car into an Uptown shopping plaza would be more easily read as brown, while if she were making her way through a Downtown neighborhood on foot, many Jamaicans would identify her as black.

The post-independence era has witnessed significant social mobility amongst Jamaica's low-income black population, and analyses of census data indicate that Kingston's residential segregation along lines of skin color decreased significantly during the twentieth century.[3] Nonetheless, residents from a range of social backgrounds continue to narrate Kingston in terms of a combination of class and skin color mapped onto a largely bipolar sociospatial structure. Anthropologist Charles Carnegie also observes that this structure has remained a powerful way of understanding the city, despite the porous and elastic nature of its boundaries. "Even though the geographic and social markers of the Uptown/Downtown divide have always been inexact and have varied over time," he notes, "they nonetheless retain powerful metaphorical force."[4]

Party-political affiliation adds an additional dimension to this urban order, if one that is slowly becoming less salient. As I described in chapter 1, the system of "garrison politics" that developed from the mid-twentieth century onward further divided Downtown Kingston into politically homogenous "orange" PNP and "green" JLP enclaves. The party-political boundaries produced by this violent system of political clientelism mean that for Downtown residents, an adjacent but politically antagonistic neighborhood may be as foreign a territory as an Uptown neighborhood. Increasingly, however, for those who live in Kingston's marginalized areas, a shared identification based on the entanglement of urban location, class, and skin color trumps what is called "political tribalism," certainly outside of election times.

These interlocking forms of identification came out clearly during my conversation with "Roddy," a PNP politician based in Brick Town. Although the larger electoral constituency in which the neighborhood was located had become a solid JLP area over time, Brick Town remained a small but stubborn enclave of PNP diehards. While his attachment to the neighborhood was entangled with party-political loyalty, Roddy emphasized the extent to which classed and raced divides may be experienced as more salient. Discussing Kingston's divisions with me in June 2010, in the wake of the Tivoli Incursion, he demonstrated how deeply the city's patterns of inequality are *felt*, emotionally and sensorially.

Roddy had invited me to meet him on a street that bordered the JLP section of the larger area. One of the few urban politicians who actually lived in their constituency, his house was on this border while the PNP constituency office was a few streets away, in the heart of Brick Town. When I called him as I reached his address—the house with a poster of then PNP leader Portia Simpson-Miller in the window—he was still "on the road," making his way back home. A group of women sitting in the shade on the sidewalk urged me to park there. I did, and got out to wait. I told them I was looking for Roddy and asked them whether it was the house with the Portia poster. This started off a little discussion: one woman shouted "Portia! Wi love Portia!" while another, who was dressed all in green and was lying stretched back on a motorcycle, said "No, Bruce! Bruce mi love!" referring to Bruce Golding, the JLP leader and prime minister at that time. Evidently, political antagonism had not disappeared from the area, but it did not stop these women from being friends, or hanging out on what had been a tense border in previous decades.

I stood chatting with them, answering questions about visa regimes and joking with them about men. "Buy me a drink, nuh?" the Portia supporter asked me, telling me she'd "look after" my car in exchange. I said it didn't need looking after but I could buy a round of drinks, and we walked toward the nearest shop to get them. By the time we reached back with the drinks, Roddy had arrived. "Why yu mus' tax her?" he scolded the young woman, surmising that she had pressured me. I protested that it wasn't a "tax"; I had offered them drinks. Roddy ushered me off the street and into the walkway leading off from his residence. He pulled out a plastic chair for me and sat down on the stairs himself. Mosquitoes buzzed around us, nipping my ankles as we began to talk. Dressed in full PNP regalia—an orange T-shirt and baseball cap, as well as an orange campaign bracelet and an orange-and-yellow "Portia Time!" wrist watch—Roddy articulated slowly and spoke loudly as he answered my questions, relying on a mode of oration similar to formal political speeches. Avoiding my more direct questions about dons, he resorted to political rhetoric, explaining to me more than once that while the JLP was a party, the PNP was an institution.

Roddy became more animated as he began to discuss Kingston's class and color divide. He listed various examples of the differences between Uptown and Downtown. Under the State of Emergency at the time, all Downtown street dances had been shut down: "Alright, we have the State of Emergency in Kingston and St. Andrew, but Uptown can party. But Downtown Kingston can't party!" To him, this type of unequal application of rules and regulations amounted to a rejection of the poor, and a denial of their rights as Jamaicans: "So it's a thing, that society already reject us. And if society reject you, you don't care what you do, 'cause you are not a part of society. What government need to do is reach out to the people and make them know that we are a part of Jamaica."

He saw the State of Emergency as no more than a way of policing poverty. Perhaps presciently, given the often heavy-handed "urban regeneration" efforts that would target the area over the next decade, he linked the militarization of society to the displacement of the poor:[5]

> Because you see, what they are doing in a democratic country is a system like in South Africa within Apartheid. You drive the black people more and more into some suburbs, force them more into poverty, and then you use the military to control. And if you feel that them get out of hand too much, you order the military to shoot. And that quell them down for a while, because too much of them dead in one week. And then five years, or four years after, they rise up back to the same where they were, because you still don't change the poverty line and the system.

Slipping out of English and into Patois as he grew more impassioned, Roddy spoke of the need to enhance employment, not only to alleviate poverty but as a matter of self-esteem. His explanation, though rather gendered, underlined not only the importance of having the means to consume, but also how dignity—and indignities—connect to the segregation of Kingston's spaces of consumption: "When Friday, when a person get him pay and him come home, him can give him girlfriend or him wife . . . [together] with what she earns, she know that she can go to the market, and later on in the evening, she go to the *supermarket*. You know the proudest thing in a person life is when you can go into a supermarket and push a trolley." Doing fieldwork in other parts of Downtown Kingston, I had indeed heard residents, always women, speak yearningly of shopping in supermarkets, of piling up their groceries into a supermarket cart, and then taking a taxi home because that type of upscale trip could not be made by bus. Being able to escape shopping at "the wholesale"—small dry-goods stores where the owner, often a recent Chinese immigrant, slid your purchase through a small opening in the thick metal grill—could feel like freedom.

"No, no," Roddy emphasized, "the proudest time inna yu life is not to go to the wholesale and order something. Go up to the supermarket and take up a trolley where you can mingle with you goods, pick up, put in you trolley. If you even spending $2,000 [around US$20], but you feel . . ." He searched for the right language. "When you go to the wholesale, is like a *prison* you go. But when you go in the supermarket, the air condition, you feel free. You see the Uptown, you see different people, you interact and you can pick up you little things in your supermarket." As we sat in the walkway, various children and women passed through, making their way to and from the street, always greeting him and me with a pleasant "Eveling!," wishing us a good evening. To confirm his assertion that most people

Downtown dreamed of "going up" to a supermarket rather than shopping at a wholesale, Roddy called out to a passing lady, asking her whether it wasn't so. She agreed as she kept walking: "Yes, it make you feel nice—relaxed!" He continued, seeking to ensure that I understood the sensation such an Uptown space could confer. "It make you . . . It give you a sense of unity. And, and . . . a dignity, that every week you look forward to this supermarket."

Roddy's description of the feeling of *freedom* a shopping trip can evoke—in contrast with the prison-like atmosphere of the heavily fortified wholesale—underscores the everyday sensation of physical and social immobility that is a key component of "ghetto" life. While not every inner-city resident might express this experience in the same terms, I frequently heard similar discussions of feeling trapped in conditions of heat, poverty, and indignity while just a mile or two away, others lived in air-conditioned luxury.

Such experiences of humiliation and injustice, in which class, race, and space combine, are place-based sensations that residents feel dons can understand more readily than outsiders, including politicians and other representatives of the Jamaican state. For many Downtown residents, the city's unequal order—its geography of dignity and indignity—is evident, and painful, in how they are perceived by their Uptown counterparts.[6] They are acutely aware that those living "above Crossroads" tend to speak of them with fear or disdain. This feeling that "ghetto" residents are not regarded as full citizens is exacerbated when agents of the state treat them disrespectfully, or as criminals, based on their place of residence.

"Monique," a Brick Town resident in her early forties, felt this keenly. She was a regular churchgoer and was pursuing a university degree—I had been introduced to her by one of her fellow congregants and we met after a lecture on her university campus in early June 2010, just a week after the Tivoli Incursion. She was clearly shaken by the recent events, and explained to me that if she could get a better job with her degree, she would leave Brick Town even though she wanted to contribute to its development. "Yes, I am planning to leave," she told me, "because what happen last week really push me. I want to leave. And if I get the opportunity now I would leave. I will come back and work in the community, but for living, it's a no-no."

Still, given the choice, Monique would rather move to a rural parish rather than to Uptown Kingston. "I'm not a person who really have this Uptown culture," she explained. She did feel comfortable moving around other Downtown areas, including JLP neighborhoods. Although she generally supported the PNP, she was not politically active, and she felt safe crossing party-political borders. While she stressed her commitment to Brick Town's development, living there felt like too much of a risk—neither her education nor her faith could remove the stigma that accompanied an inner-city address. She voiced a common sentiment amongst Downtown residents, that only certain types of crime received attention: "Our society has been focused like when 'below Crossroads people' are stigmatized of being criminals. It won't change until people start to look on a person who lives Downtown and a person who lives in Cherry Gardens [an elite Uptown neighborhood] as being the same color blood. Because people out there commit crime. What they call those crimes? White color crime. And they are treated differently by security forces." The linguistic slippage—"white *color* crime"—in Monique's explanation suggests the extent to which crime is also understood through a racial lens. Many low-income, black Kingstonians have a lifetime of evidence supporting their conviction that the security forces, and other state agents, care less about them than about their wealthier, lighter-skinned counterparts, and the Tivoli Incursion brought this home powerfully.

In addition to pointing out persistent hierarchies of class and race, residents such as Monique and Roddy also underline the geographical dimension of this differential treatment. They understand it in terms of territorial stigmatization, a phenomenon that involves what sociologist Loïc Wacquant calls "a blemish of place." Such a place-based stigma adds an extra layer of disadvantage to the negative associations that frequently accompany poverty and blackness, to which this form of stigmatization "is closely linked but not reducible."[7] In Kingston, territorial stigmatization centers on widespread assumptions that Downtown is marked by a type of place-based deviance, with residents prone to crime and violence. Having a "wrong" address—a postal code such as "Kingston 12," referencing so-called ghettos such as Trench Town, rather than an Uptown address such as "Kingston 6"—can be a major obstacle to finding employment, or even love.

The classed and racialized spatial order that Roddy and Monique described has its roots in a history of colonial urban development but has persisted after Jamaica's independence in 1962, if in a reconfigured form.[8] A broadly shared understanding of urban inequality and exclusion shapes how many Downtown residents perceive "government," whether Uptown politicians or bureaucrats. Government policies, social interventions, and security operations are easily interpreted as acts motivated by raced and classed hostility. This understanding also feeds the contrast they make between these officials and informal leaders such as dons. As Roddy's account emphasizes, the experience of Kingston's divisions also informs how residents may come to recognize dignity or even freedom. A shared, place-based sense of indignity, rejection, and confinement makes it all the more important to be treated with respect, to have the freedom to party, to have formal employment, or to temporarily escape the neighborhood just to do groceries in a space of consumerist comfort. As I detail below, and in the chapters that follow, dons can also mobilize such shared indignities and associated aspirations strategically. These geographies of inequality, then—this spatialization of dignity and indignity—is a critical element in understanding how donmanship comes to be seen as legitimate.

SONS OF THE SOIL

Unlike many political representatives, dons tend to have direct roots in Downtown communities. A large measure of their authority is rooted in their status as "born and raise in the ghetto." And preferably not just any ghetto—ideally, they should have a family history in the neighborhood where they are in charge. They should be a "son of the soil." This status suggests a source of allegiance based on birth. Where Uptown politicians may claim to represent the same constituency, many residents see their outsider status as signaling a lack of affinity or loyalty. In contrast, dons' local roots and their shared experience of "ghetto life" confer them with a measure of representativeness that transcends that of formally representative politics.

"Roshawn," a corner don from West Kingston, explained to me why he felt that men like him were more effective representatives than formal politicians. He was part of a meeting I organized in the summer of 2012, together with a conflict-resolution NGO. Groups of men from across the city, many of them affiliated in some way or another to criminal organizations, had gathered to discuss transformations in community leadership. I sat in a small group with Roshawn and a few other men from his community as they discussed different types of leaders. In clarifying his conviction that politicians—those he described as "put in place"—were not effective, he emphasized the importance of physical proximity in knowing the people of the community:

> The roles of the politician are not effective, based on my side [in my opinion], 'cause them nuh know we [they don't know us]. So, in order to know the people of the community, you have to come in the community more often. Them just in them A/C every day and feel like everything is alright. 'Cause our leader, according to who is put in place, is Omar Davies [the MP at the time]. He's not playing an effective role, based on my behalf. To me, he's not a leader. 'Cause if you a leader, you have to communicate with the people on a day-to-day activity.

Representing an inner-city neighborhood means literally placing your body in the same physical surroundings as your constituents. Being *in* the community makes it easier to communicate with residents, but it also shapes a common experience, one of deprivation. Urban heat, and the ability to tolerate it, is an important marker of difference.[9] You cannot be "in your A/C every day" if you want to represent the ghetto. If you do not share this sensory experience of hardship, how can you claim to *know* us? If you do not suffer the same heat, Roshawn's remark suggests, you will be under the impression that "everything is alright." But it's not.

Representativeness, then, is a corporeal phenomenon. Dons' embodiment of authority involves visual elements—it helps to "look" like you belong Downtown. But at least as important is a type of embodied sensibility that is based on proximity and copresence, and developed through a shared sensory experience of deprivation. This results in what is recognized as a classed, raced, and gendered form of "toughness" that is associated closely with "the ghetto." Politicians are well aware of this perception, that they may be considered not quite black enough, or Downtown enough—in fact, not *tough* enough—to represent an inner-city constituency. Sometimes, they acknowledge this perception explicitly. For instance, in seeking to represent St. Andrew Southern, a political constituency that includes various "ghetto" communities, PNP politician Mark Golding insisted that his "Uptown boy, softie tag" was undeserved and "that his privileged background and pigmentation [would] not prevent him from managing a constituency that has been stigmatised as one in which 'Don' rule is common." While recognizing his own elite upbringing and Oxford education, he averred that "I have been exposed to the life of the inner-city through my family connections," referring to his wife's roots in the low-income neighborhood of August Town.[10]

Those politicians who can claim a more direct, intimate knowledge of Downtown life—not just through their in-laws, but through their own upbringing—will generally seek to use this to their advantage. This can be a delicate balancing act. Former PNP leader Portia Simpson-Miller, for example, was not only Jamaica's first female prime minister, but also the country's first and only head of government with an urban working-class background. This background was the focus of much negative media attention. Such portrayals were generally "in line with stereotypes of Black women of the Jamaican ghettos," as political scientist and gender scholar Maziki Thame highlights: "Simpson-Miller is seen to be vulgar, low-class, lacking in proficiency in the English-language, and incompetent given her low educational achievement."[11]

Yet simultaneously, Simpson-Miller's positioning as a black woman from Downtown Kingston was an important source of her popularity amongst low-income voters and women in particular. They warmed to "Sista P" (or as she grew older, "Mama P") precisely because of her willingness to speak Patois, her tendency to enfold voters in spontaneous hugs, but also her capacity to display verbal aggression when challenged. Brick Town resident Monique, who had earlier described the effects of territorial stigmatization, also recognized the gendered prejudices Simpson-Miller faced: "When I look at Portia, I think of the struggles she have been [through], to be a leader, how men . . . they stigmatized her because of gender. I think she's a strong woman." Unlike many of her colleagues, Simpson-Miller could code-switch from middle-class respectability to an embodied performance of toughness. Her capacity to personify "the ghetto," to come across as street-smart and tough but tender, is rare amongst politicians.

Perhaps it is even harder for middle-class male politicians to embody such a tough but caring persona. The contrast between Uptown and Downtown is not just classed and raced but also gendered.[12] While Downtown women are often seen as "unladylike," Uptown men struggle with classed understandings of masculinity. If men from low-income areas are often associated with aggressive, hypersexual forms of masculinity, those from Kingston's wealthier areas—like politician Mark Golding—need to contend with the feminized "Uptown boy, softie tag."

For dons, it is much easier to personify a type of classed, racialized masculinity that maps directly onto urban space. In Brick Town, the General's reputation for toughness, including a willingness to use violence when warranted, was part of his appeal. Yet his authority relied on his ability to combine this toughness with a reputation for humility and compassion. This combination came out in how "Andy," a young man who had grown up in Brick Town, described the General. While his father had had a serious conflict with the General, Andy still felt loyal to the don.

I had met Andy while interviewing another resident, "Mikey," in front of one of the neighborhood's smaller streetside cookshops. Andy was obviously interested in striking up a conversation, interrupting Mikey's answers and taking an interest in my voice recorder, telling me: "You know the Feds use these!" Startled, I responded: "But I am not the Feds." Given the history of American intelligence agents in Jamaica, it felt urgent to clarify that I had no connections to the FBI. "I know, but I'm just saying . . . they use these." Apparently, he was not very concerned, as when I left he asked me: "When are you going to interview me?" A few days later, I ran into him and we sat down to talk. We were discussing how the General set norms in the community, a role discussed in more detail in chapter 4. I asked Andy if there were any residents who still harbored resentment at being sanctioned by the don for transgressing such norms. "Nuff people round here," lots of them, he responded, but rather than siding with them, he launched into an approving account of the General's response to being disrespected:

> Like you had a Rastaman up the road, him did call up the General's name and disrespect him when the General was still around. One day, the General and his men were down here and he heard somebody come tell him that the Rastaman up the road was calling up him name, accusing him of things he never did, disrespecting him. So anyway, him go round there, the General grab him inna him head and say: "How you call up my name so?"—*Boop!*—and kick

him inna him face. And him drop against the side of a shutter, in between it. Them start kick him up.

Andy's face lit up as he reenacted the kicks. While he had described the incident to me as an example of residents who had not been happy under the General's rule, it was clear that to him, the assault only enhanced the don's standing. Such a readiness to defend your reputation violently, in the face of even a minor slight, is an important element within the classed, racialized, *and* gendered performance of authority. Because this type of tough masculinity is associated so closely with "inner-city" areas—the same association that forms the basis of territorial stigmatization—a don who is "born and raise" in such an area can perform it more easily than an outsider MP with an air-conditioned lifestyle. Even when dons may actually have moved Uptown themselves and send their children to elite schools, as the more powerful ones generally do, they can mobilize a type of spatial capital, so to speak, that politicians rarely can.

As Andy continued to describe the General to me, his account moved to highlight that a don's authority is rooted not only in a common sense of proximity and presence, but also in the quality of transcendence that the don is able to convey—the sense that these leaders are larger than life, that their existence is somehow elevated above that of normal people. A don cannot *only* be a tough guy. The most successful dons are mythical personas who combine great strength with great humility, a combination that positions their rule within religious discourses. In explaining to me what type of leader the General had been, Andy drew very directly on this framing:

> Like Jesus is how the General would behave. Serious! He was a born leader. Like, people see him and say that it's him who should be the don. Picked him. In fact, you yourself can never pick yourself to be a don, it's the people who have to pick you. He was almost like a prophet, what he said happened—he told us before he left this place [when he went to prison], that this place would get worse. He said: "You know this community is going to be one of the worst when I'm gone."

Monique, the Brick Town resident introduced above, was more skeptical than Andy in her assessment of donmanship, emphasizing to me that her community was trying to "move away" from this system. She was not especially enthusiastic about Junior, the General's son, who had more or less taken over as the don after his father was imprisoned. "He's just an alright guy," she told me. "He's around in the community and talk to people. . . . He's okay." When she described the General himself, however, her admiration shone through: "A brilliant person, a person if you get to know him he is creative. He has a human side, deep human side some people wouldn't know. If you get to talk to him a deep, a compassionate person, deep human side... He has a deep human side. I can tell you that, I have spoken to him, he is a nice person. So there are many positive things about him." A don like the General was able to cultivate a sense of being simultaneously ordinary and extraordinary: like Jesus, humble but also a born leader, deeply human but also brilliant. Dons' authority is based largely on social and geographical proximity, but this closeness is not enough on its own—even though Junior was around Brick Town, talking to people, he was still not necessarily more than an "alright guy." A successful claim to authority is supported by a performance that combines familiarity with exceptionality, immanence with a type of transcendence.

This transcendence is perhaps conveyed most clearly in the public murals that commemorate deceased dons. The late William "Willy Haggart" Moore, leader of the Black Roses Crew in the West Kingston community of Arnett Gardens, is depicted in one such wall painting that declares: "Though you are gone your memory live on" (see figure 2.1). Willy Haggart was known for his love of partying, and the bottle of liquor he is holding reflects his reputation as a "party don." Yet the earthly symbols that surround him, including the black roses referring to his crew affiliation, are balanced by religious references. Haggart appears to be floating above the clouds, suggesting an iconographic reference to the Ascension of Christ into Heaven, a subtle evocation of the image of a martyr who has died for his people. The cross around his neck, his elevated depiction, and the use of the color blue trigger associations with religious images more broadly. They reference the glossy memorial programs commonly distributed at Jamaican funerals, which also tend to superimpose pictures of the deceased against images of blue skies with clouds and doves.

We see similar iconography in the murals commemorating Cha Cha Don (figure 2.2) and Roundhead (figure 2.3). Cha Cha Don—a godfather, neon green font proclaims—is simultaneously elevated and grounded. His wings, combined with the background of blue sky and airbrushed clouds, suggest that he has ascended to heaven, and indeed has become an angel himself. Yet this mural also clearly depicts a leader who is at home in a Downtown neighborhood. Cha Cha Don's outfit, while stylish in its color-coordinated combination of cap, shorts, and sandals, is much more casual than Willy Haggart's, and his relaxed pose, resting on an improvised seat made out of a car tire weighted with concrete, evokes a man who feels comfortable lounging on the street corner. This godfather is both godly and very much of this world.

Roundhead's mural concentrates on his face, but shows a similar combination of transcendence and worldly concerns.[13] Here too, the don's portrait floats against the background of a blue sky with a dove. This peaceful, heavenly background,

2.1 Willy Haggart memorial mural. Photo by Donnette Zacca.

2.2 Cha Cha Don memorial mural. Photo by Tracian Meikle.

however, is marred by the framed text above his head, spelled out in red paint and fringed by a spray of drops reminiscent of blood spatter: "Mi know dem fear mi," I know they fear me. Staring straight at us with an unflinching gaze, these words allow Roundhead to address viewers directly, asserting his capacity to act violently even as additional text—"Love, we miss you"—conveys the affection and grief of those who commissioned the mural. Along with the diamond studs in Roundhead's ears, the image of a motorcycle, its exhaust fumes indicating that it is in motion, signal the don's wealth. In addition, I suggest we read the motorcycle as an expression of his capacity for mobility. Many memorial murals portray dons alongside motorcycles, cars, and helicopters or alongside skylines of evidently foreign cities. In the context of the experience of physical and social immobility that characterizes "ghetto" life, these various symbols of mobility reinforce the dons' reputation as men whose movements are not restricted by borders.

These murals are what performance scholar Jack Santino calls "performative commemoratives"—even as they mourn individual deaths, they are expressive public displays that make the absent present and perceptible, and invite participation from a general audience.[14] The memorials are aimed to affect spectators, attuning their attitudes toward bodies in which authority is located. This visual performance of authority works topologically, bridging proximity and distance: beyond allowing the departed to remain present in the community, the murals position dons as simultaneously transcendent and rooted in the urban landscape, with all of its pleasures and its perils.

GEOGRAPHIES   65

2.3 Roundhead memorial mural. Photo by Tracian Meikle.

THE POLITICS OF PLACE-MAKING

Dons' ability to gain authority through their positioning within the urban landscape not only works at the more generic level of being able to convincingly claim toughness and affinity based on being "born and raise in the ghetto." The connection between territory and authority also involves being able to craft a connection with residents centered on their identification with one specific, neighborhood-level community. At the level of individual neighborhoods, a don may become a key element of the area's identity, a local icon, as was the case with Dudus and Tivoli Gardens, and arguably also for the General and Brick Town.

Kingston's residents do not necessarily identify strongly with the city as a whole. Low-income residents in particular will often root themselves by referring to one of its neighborhoods. Where wealthier neighborhoods are known as "residential areas," the poor live in "communities." It is these communities—often characterized by tight social networks and local support systems—that often inspire a strong sense of place attachment. In the face of strong territorial stigmatization, many Downtown residents demonstrate fierce loyalty to their own neighborhoods. In garrisons, such neighborhood loyalties will incorporate a political color, with residents collectively identifying as either JLP or PNP. In addition, a specific don or a longer lineage of dons may be an important feature of these identities.

Such positive identifications with one's neighborhood frequently find expression through music and sports—two domains that have become entangled with politics and donmanship. The walls of Kingston's Downtown communities feature murals of their most famous progeny, the sports stars or reggae musicians who hail from the neighborhood but went on to achieve international fame—the connection between Bob Marley and Trench Town is perhaps the most well-known example. Many present-day celebrities will "shout out" their communities of origin, even if they now live in luxury Uptown apartments or hillside mansions. Dancehall superstar Beenieman, for instance, still frequently refers to himself as a "Waterhouse Man," while Olympic medalist Shelly-Ann Fraser-Price similarly speaks proudly of her humble origins in the same Waterhouse community. Sports and music inspire local pride, but also spark competition between neighborhoods. Which neighborhood football club will win Jamaica's National Premier League, Tivoli Gardens or Arnett Gardens? Which weekly street dance is most popular, Rae Town's Old Hits or Waterhouse's Nipple Tuesdays? Such competitions generally take the shape of a friendly vying for reputation, but they are not entirely separate from organized crime and politics.

In many cities across the world, football is enmeshed with both place-based identities and various forms of politics.[15] In Kingston, neighborhood football teams represent a clear domain in which community identity, donmanship, and garrison politics intersect. Tivoli Gardens Football Club trains in the Edward Seaga Sports Complex—the JLP leader founded the club in 1970 and was its president until his death in 2019. Tivoli's archrival has its home in Arnett Gardens, the neighborhood more commonly known as "Jungle." Its stadium, the Tony Spaulding Sports Complex, is named after the politician who founded the club and who developed Arnett Gardens as a core PNP garrison. Arnett Gardens Football Club's longtime manager George "Pepper" Phang is not only famous for his successes as a reggae producer; he has also frequently been named as the area's PNP-affiliated don. Jamaican newspapers refer to him alternately as "community leader," "gang leader," "reputed don," and "Arnett Gardens FC manager." During the 2010 State of Emergency, the Police High Command published several lists of "Persons of Interest" whom they described as gang members or leaders. Phang's name was amongst the first list of thirteen.

Just as Tivoli Gardens and Arnett Gardens clashed during elections, so the football supporters saw each other as their natural enemy. During the 1980s the political tension was such that "those who lived in Tivoli Gardens dared not venture into Arnett Gardens, unless they had already affixed their signatures to their death wish certificates," Jamaican journalist H. G. Helps observes. "Even members of sports teams were having a hard time putting their best on display without having to be consistently looking over their shoulders to see if danger lurked."[16] In the 1990s, the violence associated with Tivoli-Arnett matches had escalated to the extent that the Jamaica Football Federation threatened to expel both teams from the National Premier League. Faced with this threat, George Phang announced to his team that he intended to make his way into Tivoli Gardens to broker a peace with Dudus. As Phang described it, the players refused to believe that he was serious but in the end, two brave team members insisted on accompanying him into what they saw as the lion's den. They were recognized as they neared the JLP stronghold, and a Tivoli football player came out to meet them and to escort them to safely to the community center. According to Phang, Dudus received him with honor and they soon agreed that the violence should cease. Following this "peace treaty," the two teams played friendly matches in each other's stadium, and the clashes between supporters came to an end.[17] Both the "war" and the eventual peace between Tivoli and Jungle worked to strengthen the association between the two areas and their respective leaders.

Dudus's reputation as a dangerous force *and* an honorable peacemaker also played a part in his neighborhood's reputation for hosting dancehall events. Under Dudus's rule, Tivoli Gardens' Passa Passa, a weekly street dance held from 2003 until early 2010, gained national and international fame. Attracting Jamaicans from across Downtown and Uptown as well as tourists, its popularity was frequently connected to its reputation for being a very *safe* dance. Writing on the "Passa Passa phenomenon" in its early days in 2003, the Jamaican journalist Balford Henry celebrated "the safest, friendliest atmosphere one could imagine for an area which only two years earlier witnessed the mass killing of 25 civilians and two members of the security forces"—a reference to the deadly 2001 security operation in the area. He cites a Tivoli Gardens elder who describes how safe the dance is: "People from all over come. Dem park dem vehicle or dem bike or dem bicycle knowing that nobody will touch it. People wear any amount of jewellery without fear. . . . A man can mash a man 'pon him corn [step on another man's toes] and him doan even pay him no mind."[18] This quote depicts the dance's security as so effective that people come from *all over* (not just from Downtown areas), knowing that their expensive cars and jewelry will be protected. In fact, a man can even "mash a man 'pon him corn" without it escalating into a conflict. Although Dudus did run an entertainment business of his own, called Presidential Click, he was not formally involved in the organization of Passa Passa. However, the subtext of such descriptions of safety was that dancehall patrons were protected by Dudus's zero tolerance policy in Tivoli, a protective role I describe in more detail in chapter 4.

Dudus's reputation enhanced the popularity of Tivoli's dancehall party. In turn, Passa Passa made both the neighborhood and the don look good.[19] Through such associations, distinct but interconnected elements—dons and politicians, athletic prowess, and dancehall innovation—can come to form core parts of a neighborhood's identity, connecting residents to both the place and its leaders. These are important processes of political place-making, in which pride in local musical achievements, or support for a local football team, may become hard to separate from allegiance to the local don.

BORDERS

In addition to fostering place-based forms of subjectivity that help normalize their rule, dons also establish forms of territorial control that enable them to govern their neighborhoods effectively. Historically, this territorial basis was tied closely to the ability to control a homogeneous voting bloc within the borders of a political constituency. Defending the border meant defending your party and your politician, and with it access to continued clientelist benefits. Increasingly, defending and expanding turf relates to extortion practices more than to voting behavior. In contrast to the United States, where conflicts over criminal turf generally center on controlling drug retailing on specific "corners," clashes between Jamaican dons and their organizations have often been fueled by contestations over extortion turf.[20] As I describe in chapter 5, "taxes"—as extortion is commonly known—are a key source of income for those dons whose territories include significant commercial activity, for instance an open-air market, clusters of wholesales and other stores, or a transportation hub. In addition to "taxing" vendors, business owners, or minibus drivers, dons may also find a key source of income in controlling street parking in busy Downtown commercial districts, charging motorists for curbside parking at rates similar to those of official state-run and private parking lots, even issuing formal receipts. Tivoli Gardens, located between Kingston's central market district and the freeport zone, occupies a key site in this regard, and Brick Town, likewise adjacent to a commercial district, offered similar opportunities.

This shift in the meaning of borders, their transformation from political to economic boundaries, was explained to me by "Second," formerly part of the Brick Town leadership, but now retired and leading a quieter life in a suburban area outside of Kingston. We had met at Brick Town's annual West Side Posse dance in April 2010, a few weeks before the Tivoli Incursion. At the dance, I ran into "Roger," the General's relative, who had first introduced me to the neighborhood. He was standing with Second and urged me to take his number to get to know more about the neighborhood's history. A few days later, I went to visit Second out in the suburbs. We sat on a wall outside his two-story home as he explained how the logic of territorial control had shifted over the decades, a transformation in which he had participated actively himself. "We grow up typically garrison, with war between the two sides," he said, referring to the political antagonism between Brick Town and its JLP neighbor. "So, you know, election war, violence. In the inner city everybody haffi stand them own ends because is war. If you nuh stand up on your own ends, the other man them will come across and kill you 'cause of election politics." He explain that standing up on your "own ends," your own area, meant defending your life: "It's like you haffi stand guard for your own life. That is how the inner city work." I asked him whether this system had remained the same since the 1980s and he was quick to acknowledge the changes: "Typically now, the politics thing kind of change. Typically now, it's more turf." He explained what he meant by turf: "It's how a man can . . . like, if a man responsible for an area that him know, probably him can get a little hustling. What little hustling is there round him, he stand up for his hustling. So him nuh allow another man to come across and take away him food."

Back in the days, the animosity between Brick Town and its rival garrisons, which included Tivoli Gardens, was strictly political. As a young child, Second could cross the political border. "But when you reach certain age, you haffi stop. 'Cause if you go cross, they will kill you. Both ways it used to be." Brick Town would consider its JLP neighbors to be killable, just as they themselves would be seen as enemy intruders if they crossed the border. I asked him at what age these territorial boundaries would become impassable. "When you turn fifteen. 'Cause everybody know everybody. So they see you start grow up and brand you. They say: 'you are PNP' and 'you are Labourite.' So typically you have to hold your own ground." With political identity ascribed from birth, holding your ground meant remaining within the borders of your political garrison, adhering to borders created by the politicians. "That's the way they set it. Borders. And they influence youth. But it kind of not much like that again." Now, Second confirmed, politicians no longer drew these lines. The borders were more economic than political. "Most youths realize, all of that, it was just tricks. So most youth now, as I've told you, have turned to the extortion, yes tax, to survive."

As he acknowledged again that, yes, there had been a move away from political antagonism, he emphasized that the system of taxation, discussed in more detail in chapter 5, still involved a strict policing of territories and their borders. "It shifting to every man defends and controls turf. And anywhere them can extort, them control it, border it out. Them responsible for here, another man responsible for over there. Over here is their food grounds, over there is the other's. So them won't allow you to come impede in theirs, understand?"

The borders of a given territory—whether understood as a political garrison or a "food grounds" for extortion—may not be visible to outsiders. But to those who live there, the borders are marked and maintained clearly. In Trench Town for instance, several blocks of empty terrain known as No Man's Land mark the border between Arnett Gardens and Federal Gardens, two political garrisons within the larger neighborhood. In the 1970s, the area was home to tens of thousands of residents. As a politically mixed area, it was a site of concentrated electoral violence, forcing all residents to abandon their homes. Writing in the early 1980s, geographer L. Alan Eyre described the border zone as follows: "Few individuals—some politicians excepted—would be rash enough to risk crossing this frontier . . . although a city map indicates that twenty streets traverse the divide. Each of these streets has a visible 'no-pass' point like a wrecked automobile, a pile of logs, a group of burned buildings, or a strip of waist-high grass in the middle of the roadway. Polarization is total."[21] Decades later, much of this desolate scene remains recognizable. The emptiness of the stretch of land still acts as an everyday reminder of this history, and continues to mark a clear border between the different sections of larger Trench Town.[22]

Elsewhere, borders may be marked by more subtle interventions into the landscape. In Brick Town, graffiti on the walls bore out the neighborhood's leadership. In addition to various murals commemorating deceased residents, including members of the West Side Posse, the General's name and that of his son, Junior, were scrawled across the neighborhood walls, while PNP graffiti left no doubt regarding the area's political allegiance. Like in other neighborhoods, the entrance roads were "gated" in various ways. For instance, at various key intersections along the border, drain covers had been removed. This created deep trenches, forcing cars to slow down, preventing outsiders from speeding through to commit drive-by shootings. In other parts of the neighborhood, like in Trench Town, an abandoned car or old fridge would similarly work as a roadblock, allowing strategically positioned men to check out anyone entering the neighborhood.

Of course, these infrastructures of protection do more than keep outsiders from coming in. As Second pointed out, they also deter residents from venturing outside the borders of their own community. For him, Tivoli Gardens had become off limits from age fifteen. Decades later, he would not venture there, not even for its famous Passa Passa dance. "But isn't it supposed to be the safest dance of all?" I asked him. "So them say," he answered. "But as mi know how them stay, mi nuh go there. I know what they give, so mi nuh give them the chance. Them know me, we used to rival against one another both ways. So mi still not trusting, because both of us were involved inna things." Even if those things happened many years ago? He shook his head. That didn't matter. It also made no difference that he had left Brick Town for the suburbs in the late 1990s. Jamaica is small and memories of violence do not fade quickly.[23] He didn't want to be at a party and to run into someone on their home turf who would recognize him and connect him to enmities, no matter how long ago.

Despite the endurance of antagonisms, territories and their borders do change over time. The death of a long-term or powerful don can lead to the splintering of a previously consolidated territory, especially in instances where there is no clear successor, such as a second-in-command or a respected family member. Within a larger community, "hotheads"—younger men in particular—may regroup into factions and become embroiled in violent competition over the former don's turf. In various cases, such violence has resulted in the atomization of power, and a splintering of the previously unified territory. As borders proliferate, new contiguous mini-territories emerge, each controlled by a different leader.

This was more or less the situation after the General was imprisoned. Initially, his son Junior was the heir apparent. Although he did not garner the same respect as his father, his status was not contested openly either. However, during the State of Emergency that followed the Tivoli Incursion, he was marked as a Person of Interest and detained by the police. I was told that officers warned Junior that if he valued his life, he should not show his face in Brick Town again. He did not appear to have fully followed this advice, but he laid low for a significant period. In the meantime, without a clear leader in charge, tensions within Brick Town that had previously been suppressed came to the surface. As the State of Emergency destabilized the status quo, a group of men began to establish their section of the neighborhood as independent from the General's family.[24]

In the summer of 2012, this escalated into a series of violent "flare-ups" between the two factions. In July, my friend Keith described this as "a little war between two sets of youth" from different sections within the larger neighborhood. One section was associated with Junior and his family, the other with a rivalling set of men. The little war involved nightly attacks by Junior's men on his rivals, in an attempt to reclaim the entire neighborhood. During my visits to the neighborhood that summer, sitting on the side of the road with Keith around the corner from the General's former headquarters, the conflict was the topic of many conversations. Passersby exchanged the latest news on the flare-ups, often in slightly hushed tones.

At first, people discussed who had been shot in the other part of the neighborhood. Then, a few weeks later, a man was murdered close to our regular hangout, in Junior's territory. These acts of violence always took place at night and information became a little muddled. Keith, generally in the know about the most minute shifts in power dynamics, was not quite certain what was going on—he was keeping out of things to stay safe. However, it was someone from the set around Junior who had been murdered, and it was clear that "a little power thing a gwaan," a minor power struggle was going on, if not yet a full-blown war.

Walking off to buy lunch, I found the cookshop owner, "Lion," discussing the details of the same murder with two other customers. They were describing how many times the person had been shot, and that he had been killed by shots to the head. "Do you think the thing will escalate? Or is it going to cool down?" I asked Lion. He said he didn't think it would escalate, but he did look a bit worried and annoyed. "Them boys too stupid," he muttered. Near the General's former headquarters, I passed the posters announcing a dance in honor of the West Side Posse, the larger organization associated with his family and the neighborhood. The posters announcing this dance—an annual event prior to the State of Emergency—had been plastered on walls across Brick Town for weeks. I asked the young men outside the headquarters whether the dance was still on. They referred me to another member of the General's extended family, who told me, "No, I don't think it's going to keep . . . It's not going to keep, because of the . . ." She trailed off and waved her hand, gesturing at the general situation. "Yeah, because of the thing," I suggested. For the conflict to cancel such an important neighborhood dance—a highly popular event reinforcing allegiance to the neighborhood and its don—meant that it had become more than a "little power thing."

A few weeks later, men loyal to the General's family shot and crippled a man in the other section of the neighborhood. With long periods of peace in between, the flare-ups and reprisal killings continued over the years that followed. The episodic nature of the violence meant it was not experienced as a full-blown "war"; the intensity of conflict was not such that it brought neighborhood life to a standstill. Yet each act of violence inscribed a clearer border, dividing what was previously one neighborhood unified both by party-political affiliation and by a strong don. Eventually, two clusters of leadership emerged, each section becoming a new territory in the absence of a single don strong enough to quash competition and "unite" Brick Town as a whole. New borders had emerged where there were none before.

LINK-UPS

As Brick Town's recent conflicts and longer history demonstrate, dons war over borders, and may be loath to cross over into a neighboring area even decades after a feud has ended. This does not mean they are confined to their own community. Their authority also derives from their ability to "link up," to make connections beyond the boundaries of the neighborhood. While the system of donmanship is tied tightly to the space of the neighborhood, it operates across different scales. For instance, various noncontiguous don-led territories may be "linked up" through loose alliances. Most often, these alliances between dons will have taken shape through a shared history of political tribalism, although in some cases, dons will make connections that transcend the boundaries set by garrison politics. The networks connecting don-led territories work to protect gunmen and their weapons. During police operations or targeted searches, Persons of Interest can keep a low profile by moving to an affiliated garrison on the other side of town, returning when the pressure diminishes. Like men, firearms also circulate, either to neighborhoods where they are needed but in scarce supply, or away from neighborhoods where the police might link them to a specific shooting.[25]

The most powerful dons, however, are those who not only demonstrate a capacity to cross urban and international borders themselves, but who also enhance the mobility of residents. This is exemplified by dons who were able to broker "peace treaties" within Kingston, dissolving borders created by party-political enmity and turf wars. At another scale, the ability of dons to develop transnational networks through illicit trade, connecting their neighborhoods to a range of locations in the United States, the United Kingdom, and Canada, consolidates their authority.

Over the past half century, there have been a few instances when formerly warring dons linked up across criminal-political enemy lines to forge peace treaties. This was the case in 1978, when Tivoli Gardens' Claudius "Claudie" Massop and Matthews Lane's Aston "Bucky" Marshall called a truce, signing a treaty at the intersection of Oxford Street and Beeston Street, the border between JLP and PNP territory.[26] To cement the deal, they invited Bob Marley to come back to Jamaica from London to headline the One Love Peace Concert, where the singer famously convinced political rivals Michael Manley and Edward Seaga to come on stage and clasp hands in peace. In a less publicized parallel gesture that took place earlier on during the peace concert, reggae singer Jacob Miller invited Massop and Marshall on stage as well, as he celebrated their role in his song "Peace Treaty Special":

> *Jungle, Rema, Tivoli, Matthews Lane*
> *Tivoli-ites is moving on, hurrah, hurrah*
> *Peace treaty is going on, hurrah, hurrah . . .*
> *People can walk free again*
> *No more tribalism, yeah yeah yeah . . .*

The truce came to an end the next year, when Massop was shot in ambush by the police. The animosity between JLP-affiliated Tivoli Gardens and PNP-affiliated Matthews Lane resumed, flaring up around elections. It took nearly two decades until a new détente was achieved: in the late 1990s, Tivoli was ruled by Dudus and Matthews Lane by Zeeks, and the two dons agreed to a new peace treaty, dividing access to the lucrative extortion turf of Kingston's central market district between them. Government officials were happy to take credit for the steep drop in homicide rates in West Kingston, but it was generally acknowledged that the break in fighting had resulted from negotiations between Dudus and Zeeks, rather than from any government intervention.[27] Again, reggae artists praised dons for ending the violence. In "Peace Treaty," for instance, Cutty Ranks sang:

> *You know how long Jamaican people want the love and the unity in the community?*
> *Boy, mi haffi big up the Father [Zeeks] and the President [Dudus] . . .*
> *When I see Spanglers and TG sign the peace treaty*
> *The youth get wise and them share the same street*
> *So mi know corruption must get defeated*

Like the 1970s peace treaty that allowed people to "walk free again," when Zeeks's Spanglers organization agreed to a truce with Dudus's men in "TG," this temporarily dissolved the borders between Tivoli and Matthews Lane, allowing residents to "share the same street." This unity held to the extent that when Zeeks was arrested in 1998, men aligned with Dudus joined in the riots, marching out to the police station where their former enemy was being detained. This peace began to falter in 2004, when a former Matthews Lane lieutenant defected to Tivoli Gardens. Nonetheless, it held to some extent even when, in 2005, Zeeks eventually received a long prison sentence, and only began to unravel after the Tivoli Incursion deposed Dudus in 2010.

In addition to these various types of connections across Kingston's boundaries, the most successful dons have been able to work across international borders, linking up Jamaicans across the diaspora as part of their involvement in illicit trade. Watching foreign crime documentaries with Brick Town residents, I came to appreciate the type of transnational intimacy such networks could yield.[28] One of the cookshops I frequented had a television and a DVD player, and I often joined the customers who gathered to watch movies, from recent blockbusters to kung fu classics. A research assistant I had worked with in the context of a survey conducted across Kingston had given me a disc with the title *Lords of the Mafia Jamaica* scrawled on it, and I asked the Brick Town residents who frequented the shop whether they would be interested in watching it together.

On the day I showed up with the DVD, various regulars grouped around the TV to watch it with me. The crowd included market vendors who had stopped by to take a break and employees coming off of their shift at a nearby government institution. Most ate our cooked lunch from styrofoam boxes while the regulars had their rice served into their own bowls made from calabashes. Together, we crowded onto wooden benches and improvised seats to watch the show. The DVD turned out to contain a series of documentaries, starting with a BBC show from the 1980s on the so-called Yardie gangs, interviewing many different people in Downtown Kingston. This was followed by a series of American cable TV shows focusing on Jamaican criminals in the United States, especially New York. The final set of programs appeared to be a Canadian series, linking Jamaican gangs in Toronto to Kingston.

Some parts of the DVD, especially the American shows, were quite sensationalist, with dramatic voiceovers, spectacular shots of guns, drugs, and squalor, and scenes in which armed law enforcement figures hunted down alleged criminals in suspense-filled chases. I wondered whether the men with whom I was watching these documentaries would be offended at the ways in which Downtown Kingston, and Jamaicans more generally, were being represented internationally. However, they did not really seem to be watching it this way: they were more interested in recognizing and commenting on the various individuals and places featured in the DVD.

For instance, the 1980s shows featured Chubby Dread, a prominent don from the central Kingston neighborhood of Southside, who had died in the 2000s. Watching these scenes, the viewers all started pointing to the people they recognized: "Chubby that!" "Chubby right hand that!" A little later, a female politician appeared in the show and one of the men exclaimed: "She did mawga them time deh!"—she was skinny in those days. Spotting many people they recognized from decades ago, they commented on what had happened to them in the meantime. Recognizing Delroy "Uzi" Edwards from the Renkers Crew, for instance, one of the men informed the others that Uzi was now in prison in the United States. A man called Broomie came up on the screen, and someone explained to me that "Oh, he's from Tel Aviv [a Central Kingston neighborhood], he got shot in his belly." It was almost like watching old family videos and reflecting on how relatives' or friends' appearances had changed, and what had become of them in the meantime.

The comments were also quite critical, as people started talking back at the television screen. One of the documentaries featured a don explaining how he and his men would take up weapons in election time, to get out the vote for the politicians. "And what you get in return?" someone shouted back, implying that it had all been for nothing.

While the men were critical of the way dons and "shottas" let themselves be used by "politricks," they also reproduced some of the attitudes intrinsic to the rule of the don, such as the prohibition on "informers" who spoke openly about illegal activities. When Tony Brown, a don from the East Kingston community of Rockfort, appeared on the screen and started explaining how some aspects of the illegal economy worked, various people started shouting at the screen: "A informer ting that!"—that is the behavior of an informer—"Informer!" Overall, the men viewing the DVD with me were not concerned with denying any of the illegal acts being portrayed in the documentaries. One scene included an exposé of passport forging after a whole set of passports disappeared from the US embassy in Kingston: "Dem times deh did nice! Yu cyaan do that again . . ."—those times back then were nice, you can't do that anymore . . .

However, the crime and conflict were not their main focus. As we watched a DEA raid in Brooklyn, with heavily armed security forces knocking down a door and running through a brownstone building in order to arrest Jamaican drug dealers, Keith, who was also watching, started smiling. "A my likkle corner that!" he exclaimed. "Your corner?" I asked. I knew he had lived in the UK but I did not know that he had been in New York as well. "Yes man, that is where all the West Side Posse men ended up," Keith answered, referring to the Brick Town gang, which had had a prominent presence in New York in the 1980s. He wasn't watching the documentaries to learn anything new about raids, drugs, and guns. Nor did he seem particularly annoyed at the rather lurid ways in which Jamaicans were being depicted. Rather, he was engaging intimately with the people and places portrayed in these quite sensationalist shows, and it made him happy to see faces and streets that he hadn't seen in a long time. One of the younger viewers was also quite enthused and began to make arrangements with a friend who had access to a copying device, insisting that "mi must get a copy of this."

Oddly, these documentaries turned out to have something in common with both the memorial murals that foreground the mobility of deceased dons and the reggae songs celebrating peace treaties between dons. These forms of expressive culture establish a visual and sonic historical-political record of authority, recognizing leaders for their ability to be mobile *and* to create a new freedom of movement for others by linking up across entrenched urban divides. When viewed and discussed collectively in the way they were, these crime shows also enable an everyday archiving of authority. They inscribe and rework social memory, highlighting the transnational reach of supposedly "local" leaders and their men, even as they also bring home the injuries and imprisonment their trajectories involved. Considering how the Brick Town audience viewed the documentaries against the grain, might we understand their engagement with these foreign films as constituting a counterarchive? Following anthropologist Deborah Thomas's conceptualization of the counterarchive, might we recognize in this engagement "acts of reconstruction [that] are oriented toward the creation of an historical consciousness, one that often stands in opposition to forms of state memory"?[29] The circulation of such documentaries across Kingston's low-income areas and the eagerness of residents to access a copy suggest a desire to engage with a visual archive of their neighborhoods and their transnational connections, but on their own terms.

While shot through with strands of sadness and frustration, the affective atmosphere that emerged most clearly during the viewing was one of intimacy, of connection across oceans and across decades, inserting the audience into longstanding networks that transcended the neighborhood, and understanding those connections not through the lens of crime, but through that of community. The authority of the men who established those networks and ruled those communities is strengthened by their capacity to move across borders and to enhance the mobility of others. Being reminded of this capacity for urban and transnational mobility—whether by a documentary, a reggae song, or a mural—has a powerful effect, precisely because a sensation of immobility is one that so many residents of Downtown Kingston experience so frequently.

CONCLUSION

The performance and recognition of political authority are *spatial* processes. Achieving authority involves enacting spatial relations between rulers and ruled that normalize the political arrangement between them. These are relations of proximity and distance, and of mobility and immobility. A leader's rule is more likely to feel right when he can claim a "natural" connection to a territory and its people—when he can mobilize a shared place-based subjectivity. Yet his authority is generally strengthened if his relation to those over whom he rules is experienced not only as one of proximity and presence, but also as one of distance and transcendence.

In this chapter, I have sought to demonstrate how dons' authority relies on such spatial relations, emphasizing that their power comes to feel right through their embodied positioning in Kingston's sharply divided, highly unequal urban landscape. The support dons receive is rooted in a sense of closeness, derived from shared attachment to a "ghetto" neighborhood. In a city where social positioning is informed by an entanglement of spatial location, socioeconomic attributes, and skin color, the place-based subjectivities that dons mobilize draw simultaneously on classed and racialized forms of belonging. The bond between dons and the populations over which they rule is strengthened by their shared sensorial experiences of urban poverty and racialized exclusion. For many residents, dons' association with, and pledged loyalty to, the neighborhood suggest that they have more authority to represent poor, black Jamaicans than politicians do. Balancing this sense of familiarity, dons' authority is also enhanced by their ability to suggest a certain distance from other residents, a type of social or even spiritual separation from the masses.

In addition to this combination of closeness and distance, the dons' authority is also strengthened through what we might understand as different types of border work: their capacity to mobilize, navigate, and reconfigure urban and international borders and, in so doing, to control residents' mobilities. Part of this work involves restricting residents' mobilities by marking and defending the borders of a don's territory, through aesthetic interventions into the urban landscape, and through forms of surveillance aimed at preventing outsiders from coming in. But border work also involves performing the ability to *cross* borders, and enhancing others' ability to do so too, by inserting their neighborhood into national and international networks of aligned locations. This border work is a material process that involves physically marking and defending urban space, but it is also an emotional one associated with embodied sensations of fear but also of comfort and freedom.

Kingston's many borders, then, are not only limiting—within the city's geographies of inequality and immobility, dons can more easily utilize place-based bonds, while their capacity to move and connect across borders presents an additional form of spatiality that can buttress their authority. The most successful dons are those who are adept at deploying flexible forms of territoriality and inserting their neighborhood communities into translocal networks.

3
Electoral Politics

"Karen," the MP for a constituency that included several "volatile" urban areas, was happy to talk to me about how she dealt with the dons who ruled the communities she represented. But she had several errands to run, so we would have to talk in her car as she drove across town. She picked me up at the University of West Indies, where I had been visiting former colleagues, and where she was pursuing a graduate degree. As I hopped into her car, she began to explain the difficulties she faced representing a constituency suffering high levels of violent crime. Over the past years, there had been several murders in the area, and she had spent significant time and energy ensuring that the violence did not escalate further. "It really took a lot of my time to be on the ground, and keep things level, and then keep doing that over and over again."

These peacekeeping efforts, which frequently involved negotiating with dons, formed an important part of Karen's work as a politician. At the university, she found that her classmates, many of whom held senior positions in government agencies, preferred to ignore the existence of criminal organizations altogether. "Their whole attitude is, as if, 'Well, this thing don't exist. And if you are talking about it, it means *you're* involved,'" she said, with some exasperation. As government officials, her classmates found it unseemly to recognize criminal leaders. "One girl asked if you must talk to the dons. I said, 'How are you going to engage the community? They're a stakeholder.'"

In contrast to her classmates, Karen was convinced that politicians needed to work with dons strategically. "The more you ignore it, the deeper it becomes. And then those of us who use that, meaning that we foster them . . ." She interrupted herself to clarify why she would foster dons. "Because those people are natural leaders. If they weren't, people wouldn't follow them." Working with them could encourage them to use their force for good, she continued. "What I found is that when you have a different set of conversations to the man, you change their attitude of what they're doing. They begin to ease down on the stuff that they're doing. Because they naturally want to be in charge, and get some things done, and have acknowledgment for it."

Karen took a pragmatic approach to dons, recognizing that anyone who wanted to get work done in low-income urban areas would have to deal with these authority figures. Yet as an elected politician, her description of dons as "stakeholders" and "natural leaders," as people who "naturally want to be in charge," also conferred legitimacy on their role in these neighborhoods. As I discuss in this chapter, such "horizontal" recognition by politicians is a critical element in dons' performance of authority.

Pausing frequently to answer her cell phone, which rang incessantly, Karen continued to relate her experiences representing her constituency. The larger area included different communities, some aligned strongly with her party, the JLP, and others affiliated with the PNP. Each of these communities had its own don, second-in-command, and shottas, and there were frequent clashes—"war"—between the different sections. In discussing her engagement with these various men, it became clear that her feelings toward them were ambivalent. She expressed a variety of sentiments, ranging from pity and compassion, to respect and even fear. When she spoke of the entreaties for help she received, for instance from convicted criminals, it was clear that she felt sorry for these men, if also a little perplexed at the types of requests they would submit to an MP: "People call you. And the things they call you about: 'We're in jail and there's a little football league in here, can you send some material for we to make shorts and a shirt?' Serious, those things I get called for: 'Well, we need some socks.'" A confident woman in her forties, Karen struck me as relatively fearless. Many of her constituents, including those involved in crime, evidently respected her. As we zigzagged through Kingston traffic, she described various instances where the JCF had called her to "come down" to her constituency and help curb an escalating conflict.

In one instance, a child had been killed during a shooting in one of the PNP sections of Karen's constituency. Angry residents were taking to the street, threatening revenge. "It was 10:30 at night, the police were calling me to go back down in there. And I had to say to their assistant commissioner [of police], 'Commissioner, do you realize what time of night you're calling me?' 'Yes! The only person they're going to listen to is you.'" She questioned whether she would be the most effective mediator, referring to the party-political divisions, telling him: "Commissioner, those are not my people." While the police official recognized that he was asking her to enter opposition turf after dark, he told her he felt she was the only one who could calm down the situation at that point.

Karen described driving to the area with her security detail: as she reached the access road, she met a police vehicle. Tasked with carrying the mother and the grandmother of the child who had been killed back to the community, the police officers were afraid to drive the women all the way to their house. They feared that their car would come under attack on their way back out of the area. She offered to take the women in her car instead:

> "Alright, come, I will take you down." My security looked at me like I'm crazy. I said, "No, we're going down there." So I put them in the vehicle, I put them in and we went down. I spent about maybe half an hour with them, and the great-grandmother, the mother of the mother of the mother, was on the step with some of the same youth who was causing the problem and I reasoned with them, just talking about the child. And we work it out. And we left. And there was no demonstration the next day. I said, "Look, it hurt bad, you can come out and make everybody know, you know? But you can't come back out and hurt other people because someone hurts you. Then who is going to be the result of the reprisal for that, when you're hurt? It just goes on and on and on, when does it stop?"

While the residents from that section eventually did take to the streets to express their anger, the incident did not lead to direct reprisal killings, and the other section of the constituency that was seen as responsible put out a collective apology for the child's death.

Karen went on to tell me about another occasion, when a police officer's car had turned over in her constituency. In the commotion that followed the accident, men in the community had managed to steal the officer's service weapon. She knew that the JCF would crack down mercilessly in retribution if the firearm was not returned, so she went down to the community to make sure that this message was clear. Not long after, she received a call on her private landline at home. The men who had the gun let her know that they were willing to return it, but they would only give it to her, not to the JCF. Wanting to discuss the situation with someone before agreeing to this, she called her campaign manager. "He told me: 'Karen, the boys are telling you that they trust you. It's a hell of a ranking [a sign of respect]. But call the police before you go and tell them what you're doing. And give them a time frame. And let the men in the community know, that if you're not out of there by X time, the police is coming to look for you.'" So that was what she did. She went down to the community, where a room of some twenty men—"from the little fifteen-year-old, to the big sixty-year-old men"—had been waiting for her to arrive:

> So they carried me to this spot, and I stand up there and waited. Oh man, it was drama. They went for the gun and they bring it to me, but they bring me this gun with no magazine in it and just handed it to me. "Do you expect me to

walk out of here with this gun in my hand? No! Where is the clip and where is the spare? I mean, I ask you for the ammunition, give me back the two clip then! And plus, bring it in one scandal [an opaque plastic bag], I cannot walk out of here with this thing in my hand." They went and they got a little black scandal.

Relating such negotiations, Karen sounded entirely unafraid. Yet it was evident that she never took her safety in the constituency for granted, especially not outside of the JLP enclaves. She described a Friday evening visit to one of the constituency's PNP garrisons, to show her face at a sports event she had sponsored. As an MP, she had a security detail assigned to her as a standard procedure, but this evening she had decided to travel alone. However, she had assumed that the event was at the entrance to the neighborhood, rather than "down inside" it. "When I got to the front and I heard that it's down inside, I said 'No, I can't. Ask for them and then turn back, because it's inside, we're going *down in there*.'" She stopped the car and asked residents to call the don for her. "I said, 'Yeah man, call him, tell him JLP is here.' Yeah, and I said to him, 'Boss, my safety you know. . . .' 'Alright, everything cool,' and he hung up."

With the informal leadership aware of her presence in the community, she was able to make her way to the event safely. This don was a relatively young man—in addressing him as "boss," Karen mobilized a popular Jamaican term of respect. At the same time, it communicated her recognition that *he* was in charge, and that even as the area's formal political representative, she still needed him to guarantee her safety.

As Karen's stories suggest, encounters between elected leaders and dons are frequent, even though this engagement may be highly ambivalent, in part due to the dynamic balance of power between the two types of leadership. Sometimes a politician must seek to de-escalate a conflict between warring dons; at other times, she must mediate between gunmen and the police. Sometimes convicted criminals will beg her for material support; at other times, she will need to seek permission from a don to enter his territory.

In this chapter, I explore how dons' authority connects to Jamaica's system of electoral politics. Political authority relies on the recognition of a ruler's rightness by both the ruled and by other rulers. How does recognition conferred by elected politicians contribute to dons' positions as legitimate political figures, and how do dons' enduring ties to political parties make their rule feel more natural to residents? When politicians actively recognize dons' ability or even right to rule— their role as "natural leaders," as Karen put it—this strengthens dons' authority. And, despite a widespread distrust of politicians, in garrison communities where neighborhood histories and identities are entangled with electoral politics, dons' party-political allegiance can enhance their standing as legitimate leaders. While the connections between dons, political parties, politicians, and voters have often been read as primarily transactional forms of clientelism, the chapter emphasizes the aesthetic, affective dimensions of these relations.

In the next section, I start by discussing how elected politicians confer recognition on dons, actively authorizing the dons' position by framing them in terms of participatory democracy—as leaders and representatives of "the people" who should be respected as such. Kingston's tradition of street murals, in which politicians and dons are presented as analogous and compatible types of political heroes, does similar authorizing work. However, these forms of authorization would have little effect if they did not resonate with broader understandings of democratic representation including, concretely, what party politics and elections mean to residents of "garrison" neighborhoods. In the second half of this chapter, I show how low-income urban residents recognize donmanship as a legitimate system based on dons' direct relation to Jamaica's party-political system. In and beyond garrison communities, dons' ties to party politics remain strong and their authority continues to be bolstered through their connection to either the JLP or the PNP. Where politicians describe dons as representing "the people," for many residents, their support for a don is entangled with their support for "the party." This three-way relationship between the electorate, the party, and the don comes out clearly at election time. Elections, and the practice of voting, are aesthetic and affective performances through which people come to recognize themselves as political subjects. These performances foster a political subjectivity in which loyalty to the political party, and to the larger ideals it may claim to represent, is hard to separate from allegiance to the neighborhood's don.

RECOGNIZING REPRESENTATION

How might we conceptualize the relations between dons and politicians, two different types of rulers who draw on similar models of heroic leadership, mirroring and mimicking each other's style over the decades? Earlier analyses represented dons' position vis-à-vis MPs as more or less subservient clientelist brokers, locating their authority primarily in their ability to mediate in the hierarchical relationship between politicians and the residents who depended on them. This power balance has clearly shifted as dons managed to develop autonomous, often illicit sources of income and weapons. Some scholars have suggested that, in Jamaica's garrisons, dons have displaced politicians as patrons, at least in part.[1] Yet this process of displacement has by no means been unilinear or uncontested.

As discussed in chapter 1, while relations between dons and politicians are highly variable, with significant differences across constituencies and throughout time, this relationship is characterized less and less by a clear hierarchy. In the twenty-first century, these two types of leaders provide each other with implicit or explicit expressions of recognition, what we might call the "horizontal" recognition of authority. Both dons and politicians also require a more "vertical" form of recognition, from their followers, which could take the form of protests, votes, or reggae songs.[2] Later in this chapter, I focus on this vertical relation, in which "the people" perform their recognition of authority. In this first part, though, I am interested primarily in the horizontal expressions of recognition between politicians and dons, in the narrative or performative acknowledgments by politicians of other leaders' rightness to rule. In which ways do politicians recognize dons as leaders, and how does this institutional recognition enhance dons' authority?

One important way in which politicians authorize dons is through framing them discursively, not just as "natural leaders," as Karen did, but as *representative* leaders. This came out clearly in an interview with "Bryan," a cabinet minister with responsibility for local government. His portfolio had become progressively important following a global wave of decentralization programs starting from the 1990s, as development aid and loans became conditional on local government reform. For decades, donors and international financial institutions such as the World Bank have promoted political and fiscal decentralization as enhancing democratization. In Jamaica, local government reform has emphasized community participation and empowerment, a vocabulary that Bryan applied in justifying government engagement with dons.[3]

I drove to Bryan's government agency together with "Patrick," a colleague from a Jamaican university who was conducting research on community development. We settled down for the interview in an air-conditioned office as Bryan explained to us that dons should be seen as just one iteration of local leadership in Jamaican history, as leaders who were representative even if they had not come to that role in a formally democratic fashion. "The area leader, don, is not a negative," he told us. "Because they provide what the formal structure cannot provide, that microleadership." Even the smallest local government units, each represented by a Councillor, contained multiple smaller communities, and, he asserted, "It's normal, natural human nature to have leaders, so you have little-little leaders." These naturally occurring microleaders included, in his narrative, the dons.

Discussing rural districts, Bryan pointed out that elected leaders of small community organizations, such as the popular Citizens Associations, could, in fact, hardly be considered democratic. "Let us be honest, you will have a community council, you have a meeting, thirty people turn up and you elect this person as the president of the Citizens Association for District X. . . . It's not democratic, many times it is the only meeting that ever happen, and the president is the president for the next forty years and he speaks on behalf of the community." He went on to list various historical examples of nonelected representatives. "Many times, historically, the only man in the district who could read was the leader in the district. And many times the teacher or the parson was never elected, but—sometimes by consensus and sometimes by default—he becomes leader. How much more different is he than an area don Downtown?" Becoming increasingly animated, Bryan continued his analogy:

> Is the area leader different from the MP or the Councillor? If the community is comfortable with this person, who am I to put an outsider to tell the community . . . ? I mean, what you're trying to propose is counter to the principles of good governance and local democracy. We must accept the community's leadership and if the community says "It is Tom," it is Tom—I must leave it. It should not be that I should bring my own standard to the table, to say: "Tom did not measure up to my standard, therefore Tom can't be your leader."

As the minister responsible for local government reform, his argument was that accepting area leaders—a polite term for dons—was directly aligned with principles of good governance and local democracy because these leaders had the community's support. I began to suggest to him that it was hard to know whether a leader was truly representative. He interrupted me: "Is the Prime Minister truly representative of every Jamaican? You will never find Barack Obama is truly representative of every American. Your King is not truly representative . . ." "Not at all," I agreed, though adding that the Dutch monarch was, at that time, Queen Beatrix. He continued to elaborate this rather apt analogy between donmanship and monarchy: "Beatrix, she is the Queen of the Netherlands and I am sure at least 30 percent of the citizens of the Netherlands don't really recognize it, but yet she is the head of state and she has the army. So how different is she than an area leader with a gun in his waist? She has the army so if you don't like her she's going to throw you in jail and if you dare speak against her you are charged for treason." I asked him how he felt about government officials who stated that they never interacted with dons. "These are people with their head in the air, or their head stuck in the sand like an ostrich!" he exclaimed. "So you're saying it's impossible *not* to deal with them?" I asked. "It is impossible! For example now: Hamas is elected by the people, the Palestinians. Why should I not deal with Hamas? If I am saying 'democracy,' there was an election, Hamas was elected ... I am duty bound, if I believe in democracy, to speak to Hamas." "Right, but Hamas *is* elected democratically," I suggested, trying to point out a difference. Bryan countered that not every election was fully democratic, implicitly referencing Jamaica's garrison politics: "Yes, but how? What yu call 'democratically'? Yu live inna Hamas control area, yu betta go vote fi Hamas."

He summed up his position on elections:

> Is an election representative? When you have an election and 20 percent of the people come out and vote, what happen to the other 80? What are they saying, how do you canvas the other 80? Is it that they are in support, or is it that they are against it? Or is it that they are in fear? What is the ideal measure? I'm saying: whether it is by birth, whether it is by force, whether it is by free will, it is the representative of the people that has come forward and you're duty-bound to deal with that person.

I asked him in what contexts he would deal with dons. "Whatever context. I would invite them to any table," he responded. "Because when I go into a community, into a parish, and we are speaking of an issue to affect the parish, these people represent a substantive block of citizens. Should we ignore them? How do I go in? We are told to have stakeholders consultation, are they not a stakeholder? Do they not represent people? Because people will still stand up and say: 'That is my leader.' So what am I going to do? Insult the voice of the people?" Through a series of analogies, Bryan sought to trouble dominant understandings of "truly representative" and "democratically elected" leadership. Comparing dons with a range of other political figures who might not be democratically elected, or who relied on violence, yet were recognized as legitimate leaders, he emphasized that dons had to be dealt with as representatives of the people.

Bryan's views on representation—his assertion that "the voice of the people" manifested itself in other contexts than elections alone—resonate with the arguments of scholars who seek to conceptualize democratic representation "beyond the ballot."[4] Why should we assume that an elected leader is automatically a legitimate representative, and why should outsiders get to determine which nonelected leaders are viable stakeholders? As a cabinet minister tasked with enhancing local participatory government, though, Bryan's recognition of dons as nonelected but legitimate leaders had direct implications for their authority. I read his narrative recognition as a speech act that normalizes—indeed, authorizes—dons' leadership. Through such speech acts, politicians position themselves in a horizontal relationship to dons, a position from which they recognize dons' leadership and their right to rule.

PAYING RESPECT

Bryan was by no means the only politician to speak of dons as legitimate representatives of the people.[5] In addition to such explicit references to the democratic will of the people, politicians have frequently conferred recognition on dons by bestowing them with quasi-formal party titles such as "party activist," "staunch JLP supporter," or "PNP stalwart." Beyond such verbal forms of recognition, certain dons have been invited to participate in official political events at the invitation of party officials. In the 1970s, Winston "Burry Boy" Blake and George "Feather Mop" Spence—two of the PNP's top "enforcers"—joined the PNP prime minister Michael Manley on a state visit to Cuba.[6] More recently, in 2016, the PNP chairman Paul Burke invited George Phang—"former Arnett Gardens strong man" and alleged don—to the political party's National Executive Council.[7]

A similarly concrete expression of recognition of dons' political significance is seen when prominent politicians attend a don's funeral. Despite the controversy that tends to follow such acts of respect, this practice has continued over the decades. In 1975, shortly after returning from the Cuba trip, Burry Boy was killed in a drive-by shooting. His funeral at the Holy Trinity Cathedral was attended by some 25,000 mourners, with Michael Manley, his wife, and a number of his ministers leading the funeral procession.[8]

The criticism that the presence of these PNP politicians at Burry Boy's funeral evoked did not deter JLP leader Edward Seaga and other prominent party members from attending the funeral of Lester Lloyd "Jim Brown" Coke, in 1992, after the Tivoli Gardens don died in what is commonly called a "mysterious fire" while in prison awaiting extradition to the United States. Lauding Jim Brown as a protector of the urban poor, Seaga helped lead the funeral, which also attracted tens of thousands of mourners.[9]

In 2001, the funeral of William "Willy Haggart" Moore, don of the PNP-aligned Black Roses Corner in Arnett Gardens, attracted a similarly prominent set of politicians. The funeral itself, attended by thousands of other mourners, was a rather spectacular event held in the National Arena, which had been "converted into a colourful shrine of orange and white balloons," reflecting Haggart's political affiliation.[10] The *Jamaica Gleaner* described the attendees—politicians, well-known sports figures, dancehall stars, and businessmen reputed to be PNP-affiliated dons—in the manner of a social event, noting not only their function but their attire:

> Heading the list was Finance Minister and Member of Parliament for South St. Andrew, Dr. Omar Davies, who arrived accompanied by the Arnett Gardens Premier League football team, all decked out in black blazers and red under-

shirts. Member of Parliament Horace "Oliver" Clue of East Rural St. Andrew was dressed in similar fashion. Minister of Water and Housing, Dr. Karl Blythe, had on a grey suit with orange undershirt, while Minister of Transport and Works, Dr. Peter Phillips, wore a grey suit and white shirt. Paul Burke, the chairman of the People's National Party Region Three also attended, as did East Kingston businessman Danhai Williams, Kenneth "Skeng Don" Black of Clarendon and George Phang of Arnett Gardens. . . . Popular deejays, Moses "Beenie Man" Davis and L. A. Lewis were among the entertainers who paid musical tributes before the start of the service.[11]

While the presence of politicians and the "quasi-state funeral"[12] in the National Arena led to much debate, they also emphasized Willy Haggart's importance to the PNP, the ruling party at the time of his death. The *Gleaner* report does authorizing work of its own. The leading newspaper's extensive listing of well-known men confirms the national significance of a leader such as Haggart, establishing him as a man whose death is lamented across social strata. The colors these men wore—the red and black of the Arnett Gardens Football Club and the orange of the PNP—root him firmly in a garrison neighborhood and the party it supports. More broadly, by listing other reputed dons and grouping them alongside politicians, sports heroes, and musicians, the *Gleaner*'s list actively positions dons as Jamaican leaders whose presence at a funeral is a noteworthy sign of respect.

WALLS OF HONOR

A similar equivalence between dons, politicians, and other leaders is produced visually, in the murals found on the walls of many low-income neighborhoods. Such art includes the memorial murals discussed in previous chapters, which commemorate the deaths of individual community members, including dons. In addition, many neighborhoods feature walls of fame, murals that showcase the portraits of multiple individuals. Being included in such an assemblage mural attests to an individual's local, national, or international importance.

These artworks can be understood in relation to a longer tradition of murals, often painted close to a neighborhood school, that depict Jamaica's National Heroes as an explicitly pedagogical statement. This canon of seven heroes includes figures who struggled against colonialism and slavery, such as Nanny of the Maroons, Paul Bogle, and Marcus Garvey. Alexander Bustamante and Norman Washington Manley, the founders of the JLP and the PNP respectively, are also National Heroes. Over time, less official heroes have been added to this canon. Depending on a neighborhood's political affiliation, the walls may be decorated with former prime ministers, such as the PNP's Michael Manley and Portia Simpson-Miller, or the JLP's Edward Seaga. Many murals spotlight Olympic champions and other sports heroes, reggae singers such as Bob Marley, or other musicians with roots in the community, and the poet and cultural activist Louise "Miss Lou" Bennett-Coverley. In addition to national and neighborhood heroes, a range of international public figures appear frequently: Rastafari icon Haile Selassie is portrayed across neighborhoods, as are internationally known Black political leaders such as Nelson Mandela and Barack Obama.

Dons, too, figure in these assemblages. By depicting dons in the same visual style and directly next to elected politicians—and other cultural and political icons—these murals show different types of leaders to be compatible, or indeed equivalent.

The authorizing work of visual culture can be seen, for instance, in a mural from Black Roses Corner in Arnett Gardens (figures 3.1 and 3.2), Willy Haggart's former territory. On the wall to the left of the gate, we see the don's visage, while the wall to the right features portraits of P. J. Patterson, Bob Marley, and Michael Manley. The territorial marker "Roses," in large black letters, adorns the center of the mural while a smaller text to the right marks this as a "Wall of Fame."[13] The inclusion of Patterson and Manley, two former PNP prime ministers, not only indicates Willy Haggart's allegiance with their political party. These combined images, positioned at a central location within the neighborhood, work to visually constitute authority. They are part of what visual culture scholar Nicholas Mirzoeff calls "complexes of visuality": sensorial complexes that "for[m] a life-world that can be both visualized and inhabited," in which visuality is the key element in making authority feel self-evident.[14] The visual juxtaposition of don and politicians in this Black Roses mural makes them legible as similar types of heroic leaders. Importantly, it does not suggest an antagonistic relationship between dons and democratic leadership. Rather, it visualizes an order in which legal and extralegal rulers can coexist peacefully as part of the same system.

Not far off, along Collie Smith Drive, the main entry road to Trench Town, another wall of fame spotlights local, national, and international figures (figures 3.3 and 3.4). "Sons of the soil" including musicians Alton Ellis and Dean Frazer and football coach Carl Brown share the wall with Marcus Garvey, Barack Obama, and Winnie Mandela. Also featured is Damian Brown, a reputed "badman." This centrally located assemblage mural replaced an earlier version, sponsored by the Bob Marley Foundation and titled the "Wall of Honour," which did not feature either politicians or any apparent dons; at that time, murals featuring dons and political graffiti signaling partisan allegiance were located in less conspicuous locations.[15] Not long after the wall was painted, somebody expressed their disapproval of Brown's presence amidst these other heroes, disfiguring his face by splattering it

3.1 Wall of Fame, Black Roses Corner.

3.2 Wall of Fame, Black Roses Corner.

3.3 Wall of Fame, Collie Smith Drive, Trench Town.

3.4 Damian Brown mural, Collie Smith Drive, Trench Town.

with black paint. This apparently "bottom-up" unsettling of the sensorial-political consensus that naturalizes the dons' authority had its counterpart in a more formal, nationwide "anti-mural campaign," led by the JCF and aimed at disrupting the visual order of donmanship, discussed in more detail in chapter 4. While unhappy residents or police officials may seek to challenge such visual manifestations of authority, the longer tradition of murals including both politicians and dons suggests that these two types of rulers feel that sharing the wall can be mutually beneficial. They do not view murals' aesthetic power as a competitive, zero-sum game that benefits *either* politicians *or* dons. Such murals can be a site for depicting the relationship between dons and politicians as one of mutual, horizontal recognition. Part of the everyday urban landscape, the men grouped together in these murals gaze at passersby from the walls, sometimes benevolently, sometimes sternly. Rather than dons replacing politicians, they *share* this aesthetic site of authority.

These assemblage murals can be understood as a form of institutional recognition although they cannot always be tied directly to individual politicians. It is not always clear who has commissioned or funded a specific mural—it could be a politician, but more often family and friends of the deceased organize these visual tributes.[16] Accordingly, the murals present a more indirect connection to electoral politics than those instances when politicians demonstrate their respect publicly by attending dons' funerals or other social events. Those performative acts of recognition are highly significant but also more transient. In contrast, the murals are part of the neighborhood fabric, a constant reminder of who is in charge within the neighborhood, and with which rulers—and which party—residents' allegiances are expected to lie.

ELECTORAL FEELINGS

The murals are an important site for visualizing a horizontal relationship between dons and politicians and inscribing these political alliances within the territory of the neighborhood. More broadly, such artworks make manifest the long-standing ties between that neighborhood territory, its residents, and the political party. Within the context of garrison communities, murals depicting political leaders, symbols, or colors reflect and reinforce the strong allegiance that many residents feel toward their party. This loyalty to either the PNP or the JLP, often referred to as "political tribalism," precedes and transcends support for individual leaders, whether politicians or dons. Yet this party-political loyalty is critical in normalizing the "vertical" relation of authority between residents and those individual leaders.

Garrison politics has generally been understood as a type of communal clientelism, a transaction brokered by the don: he ensures that the politician gets their votes and, in exchange, residents get housing, jobs, and occasional handouts. Yet the ways that residents relate to the party are by no means merely instrumental. The affective ties known as political tribalism are what make garrison politics more than a neighborhood-based form of collective clientelism. Many Jamaicans—whether wealthy or poor, rural or urban, black or brown—experience party affiliation as a key form of belonging, as an identity you are likely to inherit from your parents. You are born into a PNP or a JLP family, or your parents might have a "mixed marriage." For many people, then, this political identity is for life. In garrison communities, with their histories of electoral violence, this deeply felt identity also has a strong territorial dimension and is entangled with donmanship. In these neighborhoods, being a "die-hearted" party loyalist is a form of political subjectivity that is experienced as both an embodied and a territorial condition: being a "Labourite" or a "Comrade" involves powerful emotional ties to the party, to the neighborhood—*and*, in many cases, to the don.

As residents are socialized into political partisanship, the colors, hand signals, and sounds of the political party generate positive sensations. The affective impact of party-political aesthetics was brought home to me during fieldwork in the mid-2000s, on urban pollution, in Rae Town, a PNP-affiliated community in Central Kingston. I had become friends with a group of women in their twenties and thirties, and we would often hang out near the cookshop that one of them owned. During one of our conversations, the topic turned to elections and political rallies, events they discussed with great enthusiasm.

Like many other Downtown residents, I had previously heard these women speak disparagingly of politics. "Sharon," the most outspoken of the set, had explained to me that the problem with politicians was that they built up people's hopes, and encouraged people to depend on them, yet would forget all about their constituents as soon as election time was over. She felt her MP was useless in helping his constituency and held "his people" on the ground to be corrupt: "After the MP win, him nuh memba nobody. Him come shake hand, but mi nuh wan' shake him hand, 'cause him nah do nuttin' fi wi. His people get money and give it to dem friends." She was particularly vehement in her assessment of the local Councillor, who represented the opposition party: "She's a bitch!"

After those comments, I was surprised to see Sharon and her friends wax poetic about electoral rallies, especially as they emphasized the potential risks of participation, describing how JLP loyalists had coated a road with oil in an attempt to get a campaign bus full of PNP supporters to skid and crash. Trying to explain to me why they loved going, Sharon described the affective experience of singing the party anthem at the political rallies held during election time: "When dem play the party anthem, shivers just run down yu spine. Yu put yu hand over yu heart and everyone a sing . . . it's so beautiful!" She demonstrated this by singing the first lines of the PNP anthem, "Jamaica Arise," together with two of her friends, sitting up straight to indicate the solemnity:

> The trumpet has sounded, my countrymen all
> So awake from your slumber, and answer the call
> The torch has been lighted, the dawn is at hand
> Who joins in the fight for his own native land?

As they reenacted the embodied experience of singing the anthem together with hundreds of other Comrades, the song—and Sharon's description of how its beauty sent shivers down her spine—drew my attention to the potential of music to move people, to produce political subjectivities through emotional impact and bodily sensation. Like party anthems, party colors, logos, and hand signs can come to work in a precognitive fashion to produce sensations of affinity, intimacy, and familiarity. The atmosphere of exhilaration, the "vibes" that characterize these rallies or party conferences, are on the one hand "just fun." For people who might not have the money to go on a bus trip, this is an outing with free food and drinks, where you can go out and enjoy yourself, for free. But it is more than that—it is also a ritualized format in which even the most skeptical participants cannot help but feel one with the other people taking part in the festivity. These regular performances of party-political belonging generate a form of "collective effervescence," those intense experiences of joyousness, excitement, and energy that encourage a feeling of shared belonging.[17]

Party-political identity has an everydayness to it, not unlike the experience of racial and class identities. At the same time, it does, of course, become more salient at specific moments, specifically around elections, as Sharon's account of political rallies indicates. Voting is an important expression of political identity that reinforces the tight connections between the political party, the neighborhood, and the don and his organization. As a range of anthropological studies have emphasized, voting is so much more than the free, individual expression of political opinion that it is generally held to be within liberal political philosophy. Challenging such assumptions, these "electoral ethnographies" show that voting always involves more than individual interests and that the expression of political preferences and opinions is rarely free and autonomous. For many marginalized citizens, voting is not necessarily a way to endorse a specific political ideology or to express support for specific policies, but neither is it a fully instrumental votes-for-goods transaction. Rather, the act of voting can be meaningful in itself: participation in elections is often experienced as a dignified means of asserting belonging to a large political community, of narrating and performing a relationship of mutual recognition and obligation.[18]

In Jamaica, despite widespread disenchantment with the political system, elections similarly involve a range of emotions and loyalties that include individual interests and opinions but also exceed them. Elections continue to evoke the promise of postcolonial political freedom, and in this sense they do resonate with liberal notions of democracy: the vote still entails the promise of being a politically sovereign citizen within a politically sovereign nation. In addition, while the ideological difference between the PNP and the JLP is hardly discernible in the twenty-first century, party supporters—especially older ones—may still feel a residual attachment to the ideals mobilized during the Cold War era, to the political promise of socialism or of the free-market economy. Yet at the same time, in an apparent paradox, voting can feel less like a political right, and more like a duty: an obligation to the party, the neighborhood, and the don. This obligation to vote for "the right party" may be enforced violently, but oftentimes it is fulfilled voluntarily, as an expression of an unassailable political bond.

"NAH SWITCH!"

The way that garrison politics has produced electoral subjects whose voting behavior may be less instrumental than it is affective became evident to me during a discussion with a group of corner dons and other gang-affiliated young men from a PNP garrison neighborhood.[19] Explaining their relationship to their MP to me, they sought to highlight how garrison politics ultimately worked to their disadvantage. They expressed a feeling of being what they called "shortchanged." By this they meant that while they were one of the PNP's core garrisons, they received very little in return for their vote. One of the men, Roshawn, explained how this lack of reciprocity had become even more patent when their MP was appointed to a cabinet position from which he could easily wield his influence to ensure that his voters were rewarded for their loyalty. As the Minister of Works, this MP was responsible for infrastructural development, a prime position for directing economic benefits in the form of construction work toward his constituency: "He's at Ministry of Works right now, that's where more [construction] work should come into the communities. So that means he's still not effective, he's not doing an effective job. Because if he's changing one point to a next point where he's Minister of Works, that means more work should a gwaan [be happening] in his community. And there is no work going on!" Another young man, "Damion," joined in: "On a community basis now—he's our representative—we're getting shortchanged. We not getting the real results from him, the help that the community need: employment, sanitary convenience. And all of them things affect we." To clarify the point, I asked the men whether, given that they had been a PNP area for a long time, they were wondering why the community was not in a better state. Damion explained that it was actually disadvantageous to be known as a fully loyal PNP community; neighborhoods that were known to be contested electoral turf received much more attention: "Let me stick a point, one point that is very critical. Die-hearted: that's when they get shortchanged, that's the only way them get shortchanged. If you reside on a battleground where it can go either way, you will get the full support of either party. But we are predominant PNP stronghold. We are gonna get shortchanged, owing to the fact that they know that we won't change our political allegiance." He mimicked the politicians who knew they could satisfy these die-hearted supporters with small handouts: "We don't need to do anything, just check them Monday when them pocket broke." A third man, "Barry," now spoke up, explaining that it was precisely *because* they were known to be loyal that the MP could ignore them: "Through [because] him know that, him just abuse the situation. Through him know we are die-hearted PNP."

As these men narrated it, it was exactly because they were a hardcore PNP area that they were *not* receiving any attention in terms of jobs or development projects. Contested areas could expect a lot of attention from politicians whereas the electorally safe garrison areas would vote for the right party anyway. I asked them whether they could leverage their vote a little more to get the MP's attentions by threatening that they were going to vote JLP next time. Would switching parties mean more attention, more jobs, more money? This suggestion was rejected immediately. "But that is something that is impossible!" Damion exclaimed. The other men cut into the conversation, "Impossible!," the volume and intensity of the discussion increasing just at the thought of voting for the other party. Damion continued: "He knows that we could never vote JLP. We just couldn't do it, we are PNP to the bone. Plus, if we were even to suggest switching, it would cause too much tension in the community."

Even as these corner dons and other inner-city residents are fully capable of understanding how garrison politics work to their disadvantage, their loyalty to the party, developed from birth, keeps them tied unhappily into the same system. For "die-hearted" supporters, voting—for the right party—is not so much a political right as it is a political duty. As their expressions of unconditional support suggest, they experience partisan belonging as something absolute and involuntary. Being PNP is a form of political subjectivity that is experienced as an embodied condition—to the bone, die-hearted—and that cannot be separated from the territory of the neighborhood. For those who have grown up in a PNP garrison, just thinking of voting for the JLP can be a hurtful proposition. In addition, as Damion's reference to "tension in the community" underscores, party loyalty is entangled with the continued threat of violence.

"YOU VOTED ALREADY!"

While electoral violence has diminished dramatically since the 1980s, it has left lasting scars on the urban landscape and shaped experiences of voting for many current and former residents of garrison communities. For some, voting remains a partisan duty. For others, such as "Marcia," a JLP politician in her thirties, the context of coercion ended up alienating her from the party she had been "born into." I met with Marcia after having been introduced by a more senior politician. She told me about her first experience with voting, which she described as the moment "when I knew I was definitely going into representational politics." She had grown up poor—in a "lane," rather than on a street—in a PNP garrison, and had just reached legal voting age when an election was being held. "Eighteen years old and I'm going to vote now, and I said, 'Yes, I'm going to exercise my right to vote!' I felt so excited." She clapped her hands to convey to me the physical thrill she had felt going to cast her first vote:

> And I got up early in the morning and I said to two ladies that lived in my lane, 'cause I lived in a lane at the time: "I'm going to vote, you coming with me? I'm going to exercise my franchise to vote." And I'm not going to lie to you, I didn't know who I was going to vote for, I just knew that I was going to vote. And I went up to the polling station. And some men in orange asked me where am I going, I voted already . . . I never forget it.

She explained that the "men in orange" telling her that she had voted already were there to ensure that the PNP won the election—this was garrison politics in action. I asked whether the men knew her personally. "Well, yes, I guess. They say I vote already so I say, 'What, no, I haven't voted!' He say, 'Yeah man, go to your yard, you vote already.' I was so angry that the women that I came with had to physically take me out and say 'No, Marcia, no.' Because of course you know it could get ugly. And I cried. It was tears of rage." Two decades after the fact, Marcia relived her distress at being robbed of her vote. "Even now," she told me, "I'm talking to you, I'm getting upset, I'm thinking about how somebody chose to speak for me. You can't speak for me!" This embodied memory, along with her description of her initial excitement at being an eighteen-year-old exercising her right to vote for the first time, illustrate the strong affective and performative meaning attributed to elections. Voting inaugurates a young person's relationship to the state as an autonomous adult.

In garrison communities governed by a party-affiliated don, this relationship is reconfigured. The "men in orange" mediated citizens' relationship to the state by channeling it through the party and the party-affiliated criminal organization, disciplining neighborhood residents' political preference. In Marcia's case, this disciplining backfired as her frustration with garrison politics fed her desire to become a politician and align herself with the forbidden green party, the JLP. In many other cases, however, the don-mediated partisan loyalty that garrison residents are taught from birth is extremely strong.

"SHOWER! SHOWER!"

The *nah switch* (won't switch) mindset expressed by many party loyalists was also evident during the campaigns leading up to the December 2011 national elections, the first to be held after the Tivoli Incursion. One of the main issues during the electoral debates was the incumbent JLP government's handling of Dudus's extradition. The party—and in particular Bruce Golding, who had stepped down as prime minister and party leader shortly before the elections—had come under attack for first trying to prevent the JLP-affiliated Dudus from being extradited to the United States, and then for ordering the security operation that led to the deaths of sixty-nine citizens, many of whom were, based on their residence in Tivoli Gardens, presumably JLP loyalists. Nonetheless, the JLP still had many passionate supporters.

The morning after a major Labourite rally where the new party leader and incumbent prime minister Andrew Holness had made an appearance, I met "Keesha," a JLP supporter. She had attended the all-night rally and was still dressed up in a green shirt, sporting green hair extensions and green nails. We got into a discussion about the position of the JLP and I asked her whether she felt comfortable voting for the party in the wake of the Incursion. She vehemently rejected the idea that this could influence her voting behavior: "Mi love mi party *bad*! Mi a go vote Andrew!" She loved her party terribly and was going to vote for Holness. But she didn't really care which individual was on the ballot: "Mi woulda vote Bruce! Even if [it were] a rat, mi woulda vote Labour!" Like Roshawn and his die-hearted PNP friends, Keesha described her voting less as a choice, and more as an expression of unconditional love, an enduring affective relation to the political party.

The evening before, I had bumped into a cavalcade of buses waiting to leave for the JLP campaign rally. Green-clad female campaigners leaned out of the bus windows, waving green flags and leafy green branches at passersby, shouting "Shower! Shower!" and making the V-sign. Outside on the street, masked men in green lounged about, drinking white rum (figure 3.5). I asked one of them why he was hiding

3.5 JLP supporter during election campaign.

his face. "Don't be afraid," he told me, "It's just a style, just an election thing. . . . Normally you can't do this because 5-0 [the police] will come catch you!" Later that night, I saw the buses rush past on their way to the rally. They were quite a spectacle in the otherwise quiet night as they flew by, horns honking and lights blinking, with people leaning out the windows, ringing bells, and again shouting "Shower! Shower!"

Electoral campaigning demonstrates the entanglement of criminal–political forms of authority and political belonging. "Shower!" has become the uniform slogan associated with the JLP—the shout rings out from buses, at campaign rallies, as a greeting between green-clad supporters on the street. It is as much a core Labourite symbol as the color green, the V-sign, and the bell. However, the word refers directly to the Shower Posse, the international criminal organization that was run by Dudus's father, Jim Brown, often referred to as the "don of dons." The Shower Posse members were JLP stalwarts, acting as criminal–political enforcers in and beyond the party's "mother garrison" of Tivoli Gardens. While the etymology of the political rallying cry "Shower" is undisputed, these origins do not inform its use directly or consciously. When I asked people about the use of the term, both JLP and PNP supporters would acknowledge its posse roots, but tell me that "when we say 'Shower' now it just means JLP."[20] However, as the symbolic link between a criminal organization and a political party, can the term "just" refer to the JLP? In repeatedly shouting out a gang name in a range of contexts, these green-clad supporters produce and reproduce their allegiance to party leaders and criminal organizations, to political authority both in and beyond the state.

As discussed above, such campaign rallies are important political moments; they are key rituals in many parliamentary democracies. In addition, they are "feelingful" festive events that can produce sensations of joy and even euphoria.[21] In this sense they bear a strong resemblance to the public dancehall parties organized to celebrate or commemorate dons. A famous one was Tivoli Gardens' Jim Brown Memorial Dance, held on the date of the death of the "don of dons," every February 23 through the 1990s and 2000s, until 2010. Before that, Tivoli Gardens held an annual Claudie Massop Memorial Dance to mark Jim Brown's predecessor's death. Other annual dances have included Matthews Lane's Original Spanglers Dance, which followed the Early Bird Memorial Dance, and Roses Corner's Willy Haggart Memorial Dance.[22] A majority of residents, even those who may be unhappy with the way their community is being ruled, will attend these important annual events. By dancing and socializing in this context, and by responding to the "big-ups" the DJs give to past and present dons, participants legitimate the rule of those leaders. The annual character of many of these dances suggests that they are standardized institutionalized sites for experiencing collective belonging and for affirming a don's authority. While focused directly on a specific don or criminal organization, party-political ties may filter into these events as well, for instance, when politicians attend memorial events or when Edward Seaga held a dance in Tivoli Gardens to celebrate his fortieth anniversary as an MP, at the same site and with the same sound systems as the Jim Brown Memorial Dance.[23]

Like these street dances, political rallies such as those held in the run-up to national elections generate powerful affective atmospheres through their use of party slogans, songs, colors, and hand signs. Both types of political festivity involve organized, repeated patterns of interaction that not only engender a feeling of collective belonging, but also normalize the authority of specific leaders. Even skeptical residents can temporarily suspend their misgivings and be part of this community, performing the recognition of elected politicians—or nonelected dons. Such political festivities, these spaces of music and dance, are easy-access ways to participate in the political process. They are fun, they produce moments of euphoric connection to others, and they have an immediate but short-lived effect of allowing you to believe in the don, believe in the party, believe in Jamaica: these are transitory performances of hope that the powers-that-be *do* have your interests at heart. In the aftermath of those moments, however, you may find that you are more emotionally entangled than you would like with the same system you recognize as divisive and counterproductive.

DONS AND REPRESENTATIVE DEMOCRACY

As this chapter highlights, dons do not stand "outside" the institution of electoral politics. In contrast to some readings, the accounts and experiences of both politicians and low-income urban voters do not position dons as antagonistic to a system of representative democracy. Beyond the historical roots of donmanship in Jamaica's garrison politics, twenty-first century dons continue to be associated with politicians, elections, and party-political identities in various ways. While their claims to authority sometimes involve performing a fundamentally *different* type of leadership from elected politicians, most dons still maintain ties to those same politicians and tend to share some form of party loyalty with the residents over whom they rule.

Focusing on the three-way relationship between residents, politicians, and dons, this chapter has emphasized the relational aspect of political authority. When individual leaders make claims to political authority, these claims need to be recognized both by other rulers and by their political subjects. Here, I have emphasized first the horizontal recognition of dons' political authority, discussing the various ways in which politicians, from MPs to cabinet ministers and prime ministers, acknowledge dons as legitimate political leaders. Politicians enable donmanship through practical forms of support and protection, sending business contracts their way or helping them evade arrest. But they configure dons as legitimate political figures in more subtle ways. They do so through speech acts, through a narrative framing of dons as stakeholders, natural leaders, and representatives of the people. They also enact this recognition in a more performative fashion, by inviting dons to political meetings or by attending dons' birthday parties or funerals themselves. Such forms of copresence are signs of respect that indicate a type of political equivalence between leaders. This equivalence of political authority is also made manifest visually through murals and street art that feature dons and politicians together.

Beyond this horizontal signaling of the legitimacy of dons' power, residents also confer or deny individual leaders with recognition in more vertical relationships. They may commission murals and attend street parties that celebrate dons. Or they may express their displeasure with such forms of iconization by vandalizing the mural of a don. These relationships between residents and don are, as this chapter has emphasized, mediated through shared party-political belonging. The political identities that consolidated during the garrison politics of the Cold War era remain salient long after the decline of electoral violence and ideological distinctions between the JLP and the PNP. The transactional dimension of clientelist relations continues to be important to low-income residents, but their voting behavior is shaped as much by deeply felt partisan identities. Dons' long-standing allegiance to a political party can strengthen their bonds with residents—their claims to authority do not stand outside of these shared forms of political belonging, which have an embodied, affective dimension but are also connected directly to the territory of the neighborhood.

The emotionally meaningful connections between dons, electorate, and parties are shaped and reactivated through aesthetic forms and practices: through murals conjoining dons and politicians, through voting policed by "men in orange," through campaign rallies where shouts of "Shower!" intermingle with the sights and sounds of the party's colors, hand signs, and anthems. Over time, these aesthetic forms become associated with shared sensations: they generate a sensorial-political consensus, a commonsense understanding of political subjectivity and political authority that is rooted in electoral politics, yet exceeds the formal organization of representative democracy.

4
Law and Order

To those unfamiliar with Downtown Kingston, its neighborhoods often appear to be chaotic, dangerous, and lawless areas. If outsiders cannot avoid travelling through such neighborhoods, they drive through as quickly as possible and with their windows closed, to preclude any interaction with residents. Precisely to prevent ill-intentioned strangers from speeding through and committing drive-by shootings, the drain covers at the intersections of the streets have often been removed. This creates deep trenches that force cars to slow down to a crawl, allowing strategically placed observers to check out any outsiders entering the neighborhood. Elsewhere, careful arrangements of urban debris—a burned-out car chassis, an old fridge—serve a similar purpose. The various aesthetic forms that outsiders associate with violence and poverty, such as political and gang graffiti or potholed roads without drain covers, may in fact be interventions intended to produce a bordered space of safety for residents.

My first visit to Brick Town, in 2010, was to meet Roger, a close relative of the General, the neighborhood's former don. I had no car at the time, but my former student "Joshua," who worked at a government agency nearby in Downtown Kingston, was willing to give me a ride. While he wanted to help me, Joshua felt uncomfortable driving into the neighborhood alone as he had never been there before, so he convinced "Flynn," a coworker who lived in an adjacent low-income area, to join us as an "escort." Joshua's nervousness was contagious, and I also began to feel a little jittery as we stepped into his expensive car. Flynn indicated the direction Joshua should drive, away from the busy market area. We moved through narrow, potholed streets and past dilapidated housing covered with graffiti referencing the General, his son, and the political party with which they were aligned.

In addition to negotiating Downtown Kingston's improvised speed bumps, unfamiliar drivers also need to contend with its one-way streets. Cars will turn down one of the many narrow streets without traffic signs, only to find themselves forced to reverse in the face of an oncoming vehicle. Joshua drove just a little too quickly, and I tried to convince him to slow down as I studied a paper map of Kingston, trying to figure out which streets were one-way and which were not. Flynn chuckled at my concern with how the government had designated a street: "Dem nuh observe one-way inna dis yah part a di world," he commented drily. They do not observe one-way in this part of the world.

His depiction of "this part of the world" as anarchic put me in mind of my first fieldwork in Jamaica, in 2000, when my overwhelming impression of the city had been one of disorder. Returning to the Netherlands after three months in Kingston, I felt a physical relief as my plane landed and the neat, orderly grid of the Dutch agrarian landscape came into view. While I had enjoyed my fieldwork, I experienced Jamaica's urban sensorium as chaotic and disorienting—its streets packed with people, cars, handcarts, goats, and lined with hand-painted stalls and signs advertising all manner of goods; people shouting at each other over the loud music blaring from vehicles, stores, and CD vendors' speakers; the smells of exhaust fumes, rotting garbage, and jerk chicken; my movements through its dust and heat on foot, or in crowded minibuses and route taxis pressed up against other sweaty passengers.

As I returned over the years that followed, and as my access expanded to areas only accessible by private car, I discovered, first, that Kingston also included many middle-class spaces with a style resembling the "orderly" aesthetics I had projected onto Dutch landscapes. More importantly perhaps, I realized that the public spaces of Downtown Kingston were actually organized in a very tight and controlled fashion. The underlying social and political logic of these low-income areas, as well as the orderly colonial grid plan that Downtown streets follow, were not evident to me initially, distracted as I was by what I perceived as chaos.[1] It took me a significant period of time to be able to recognize the normative order—the de facto "law"—according to which these streets operated.

To many wealthier Kingstonians, life in "ghetto" neighborhoods has a similarly foreign quality, and Flynn's remark on one-way streets resonates with their sense of Downtown Kingston as a different world, a chaotic area where national laws do not apply. However, those who live there do take the official one-way traffic rules seriously. Precisely because the traffic signs are often unclear, when unfamiliar drivers accidently turn down a street in the wrong direction, pedestrians will quickly signal for them to reverse: "One way! One way! Turn back!" Belying Flynn's comment, and counter to popular opinion, residents invest considerable energy in correcting transgressions. Areas such as Brick Town are by no means lawless—their social life operates according to strong norms of appropriate behavior, including rules about who can go where. They are characterized by a system of order in which dons such as the General play a central role, but which often complements rather than clashes with state law—one way *is* observed in this "part of the world."

In this chapter, I discuss how dons derive authority from their role in providing "law and order," maintaining community norms and public security. Seemingly ironically, given their engagement in criminal activities from drug and weapons smuggling to extortion, to many residents, dons represent a more trustworthy form of justice and law enforcement than state institutions do. In light of their experiences with a legal system that they perceive as ineffective, corrupt, and biased against poor black Jamaicans, the violently enforced "community justice" system centered around dons may appear not only more accessible, but also more legitimate. The dons who enjoy the most legitimacy are often lauded above all for their capacity to "set the order," to establish social norms, and to punish transgressions swiftly and effectively, whether through violent retribution or through banishment. In contrast, neighborhoods without an effective don may suffer from higher rates of crimes, perpetrated by both locals and outsiders.

Concentrating on this system of community justice, I approach dons' neighborhood-level practices of crime control and conflict resolution in relation to the law. These practices could easily be glossed as vigilantism, as extralegal, "outlaw" acts. Here, I draw on concepts from legal anthropology to conceptualize such practices differently. I suggest that the dons' system of community justice should not be understood primarily as extralegal, or even as a form of legal pluralism that operates in parallel to the Jamaican state's police and court systems. Rather, it can be understood in terms of legal hybridity, as the entanglement of multiple legal systems. In addition to highlighting this entanglement, I seek to understand what law and order feel like, discussing how material and aesthetic interventions can work to produce a place-specific sense of justice and security.

The next section reflects on how we might understand the law as involving nonstate institutions, to establish how the formations of law and order associated with donmanship are positioned in relation to state institutions. This is followed by two sections that concentrate on, respectively, perceptions of state law and of community justice, discussing how many Jamaicans experience the state legal system as unjust in practice, and how this contributes to making community justice appear as a plausible alternative. Next, I propose an understanding of these normative systems as increasingly hybrid, as the JCF and the state justice system enable and incorporate elements of community justice. I end the chapter by analyzing the aesthetic and sensorial dimensions of dons' "law enforcement," reflecting on how the affective atmospheres that emerge within dons' territories help to reinforce their authority, normalize their rules, and make people feel safe.

LAW BEYOND THE STATE

While "the law" is often held to be the exclusive domain of the state, there is a long-standing tradition within legal anthropology and sociolegal studies that understands state law as just one amongst many normative systems—a phenomenon termed legal pluralism. This scholarship has questioned the taken-for-granted distinction between "the law" and other types of rules or norms. It emphasizes that a norm becomes "law" when it is backed by powerful political institutions, whether the modern nation-state or other systems of governance.[2] At the same time, through a circular type of logic, the authority that representatives of such political institutions claim is generally strengthened through their references to "the law."

Focusing on colonial and postcolonial contexts, studies of legal pluralism have generally analyzed the coexistence of precolonial legal orders in Asia, Africa, Latin America, and the Pacific with legal orders introduced under European colonialism.[3] Colonial legal orders are stark examples of the disjuncture between "the law" and "justice." Laws established by colonial regimes often worked to legalize the dispossession of colonized populations while allocating rights in ways that produced and reified difference. This was certainly the case in the Caribbean, where, for centuries, colonial law undergirded the system of slavery. In territories such as Jamaica, colonial rule was based on a legal reality that differentiated between enslavers and enslaved, establishing one category of humans as subjects with rights who were entitled to treat another category of humans as property.

Yet colonial legal systems were rarely absolute. Where it suited their purposes, colonial administrations recognized existing conflict resolution mechanisms, harnessing them to the colonial project. In various territories, colonial regimes crafted systems of indirect rule, relying on "traditional" rulers, courts, and laws to manage populations and extract resources more efficiently. This coexistence of legal orders offered advantages, first and foremost for the colonizing forces. In addition, if generally to a lesser extent, it presented opportunities for colonized persons or groups to engage in "jurisdictional politics" or "forum shopping."[4] Those who were able to maneuver strategically between multiple legal orders could prevail in disputes over property or political autonomy by selectively appealing to one system over the other.

Through such interactions across multiple legal orders, over time "coexistence" and "pluralism" may cease to be the best terms to describe the normative worlds in which people dwell. Legal orders are porous and dynamic rather than self-contained and static. Rather than coexisting separately, side by side, such orders evolve and thrive precisely through contact with each other. This dynamism may in due course lead to formerly distinct legal orders becoming entangled to such an extent that we can speak of legal hybridity rather than legal pluralism.

In Jamaica, legal hybridity is evident, for instance, in the system of land tenure. After the abolition of slavery, formerly enslaved people managed to gain land titles within the colonial legal system. Rather than reproduce the laws of private property and primogeniture that characterized the colonial plantation system, however, they often transformed these legal freeholds into inalienable family land or common land. These became "customary" freeholds, imbued with spiritual meaning through burial practices, that no individual could claim to own or sell but all descendants had the right to use. After independence, these forms of land tenure, or "folk law," began to influence the official legal order, as political leaders abolished primogeniture and began to recognize squatters' rights to land on the basis of use rather than title. Such articulations, appropriations, and innovations between previously distinct normative orders evidence legal *hybridity*—or creolization, to use a Caribbeanist term—rather than legal pluralism.[5]

Discussions of legal pluralism and hybridity have tended to focus on intersections of state and "customary" legal orders. Much less attention has been paid to the role of armed political actors such as guerilla, paramilitary, or criminal organizations in developing codified normative systems.[6] Perhaps this connects to the implicit or explicit distinctions we make between forms of rule rooted in law and those rooted in violence. As discussed in the introduction to this book, our analyses of armed groups such as mafias, guerillas, and paramilitaries tend to privilege violence. The idea that violent "outlaws" could be invested in legality, or even be lawmakers themselves, feels counterintuitive.

Yet many forms of violence are legal, and many laws are violent. As the philosopher Walter Benjamin noted, violence plays a central role in all forms of law.[7] Benjamin distinguishes between lawmaking violence, which involves the exercise of power over life and death that is the origin of law, and law-preserving violence, which is intended to reproduce a visible form of legitimate order. The first form aims to produce a legal order through violence while the latter involves the legitimization of a violent order through law.

States rely on both lawmaking and law-preserving violence, but so do other types of rulers—including dons and other "outlaws" who take on a governance role. We can recognize this in the Jamaican security forces' use of violence in attempts to establish state power, which stand in tension with the invocation of the law to legitimize such violence, from the consistently high rates of police homicides to the near-constant States of Emergency declared in the post-Tivoli Incursion period. Dons' violence, I suggest, is similarly bound up with a legal order, if a different type: their use of force is productive of, *and* legitimized by, locally accepted rules and regulations. Over time, as I discuss later in this chapter, the JCF and the state justice system have absorbed elements of the dons' "laws" and conflict resolution mechanisms in a legally hybrid fashion.

EQUAL RIGHTS AND JUSTICE?

To understand how dons are able to make their violence appear "legal," it is necessary to take into account how the workings of state law are experienced and perceived. In Kingston's low-income areas, many residents make direct and unfavorable comparisons between Jamaica's state justice system and the rules, regulations, and dispute resolution mechanisms that have been established by dons. I repeatedly encountered the conviction that law enforcement is corrupt and that the courts are biased toward wealthier, light-skinned Jamaicans with access to high-powered lawyers. Both poor and rich Jamaicans tend to consider the police to be at best unreliable, and at worst actively engaged in large-scale organized crime themselves. The JCF has consistently been associated with systemic corruption and extraordinarily high rates of extrajudicial killings.[8] The institutionalization of illegal and violent practices on the part of the police amounts to a clear form of state crime, complicating straightforward understandings of outlawry. Likewise, extensive formal reviews of the Jamaican justice system have confirmed popular understandings that the courts favor the rich, emphasizing the "lack of equality between the powerful, wealthy litigant and the under-resourced litigant."[9] Over the course of my research, recurrent media scandals drew attention to the apparent impunity that the country's elites appeared to enjoy, as prominent individuals managed to evade sanctions for lawbreaking, either through bribing the police or by drawing on their connections to influential politicians.

A chance meeting with one of these privileged Jamaicans gave me insight into some of these dynamics—into how police officers may feel the urge to demonstrate to wealthier citizens that no one is above the law and into how these elites can nevertheless leverage their connections in the course of such encounters. I was sitting in an Uptown café, working on a conference presentation, when a close friend, "Rachel," came in with one of her colleagues, "Celeste." They drew up chairs to join my table, asking me what I was working on. "Is your research on politics?" Celeste asked. It turned out that her uncle was a prominent MP for the JLP. The way her uncle's supporters would throw themselves into election campaigns was crazy, she told us, laughing. They would block the road hours before her uncle was due to visit a JLP rally. "I had to call my uncle and ask him, 'Can you get these people off the road, because I need to get to work and these carnival people are blocking the road!'" The JLP supporters would recognize Celeste as the MP's niece, calling out to each other that "A daddy dawta dis!"—this was "Daddy's daughter."[10] After identifying her as such, they would allow her car through, but not before berating her for not wearing green: "We know you're a Labourite, so how come you're not wearing your colors?" She would explain that she was going to her work at a government agency, so she couldn't show any political bias.

The mention of political bias launched our table into a discussion of the scandal dominating the headlines at that time. On his way to the airport, a prominent businessman, Bruce Bicknell, had been pulled over by police, who proceeded to issue him with a ticket for speeding. Slipped in with the motor vehicle documents that Bicknell handed over to the JCF sergeant was J$2,000, about US$20 at the time. Surprisingly to many Jamaicans, the sergeant took offense at what he assumed was a bribe meant to avoid being issued a speeding ticket. The sergeant alerted a senior officer, and the businessman was arrested and taken to a nearby police station. After the involvement of various high-ranking police officers, however, Bicknell was released. The real scandal began after a well-known JLP politician, Daryl Vaz, was found to have made multiple appeals to the sergeant to drop the bribery complaint while mobilizing his connections to the highest levels of the police to "take care of the matter."[11]

Celeste shared her take on the matter with Rachel and me. First of all, she said, the amount of money Bicknell had slipped in his papers was much too low. "He's so rich, how could he bribe someone with just $2,000?! He has to know that's not enough. A girl like me, I could get away with $2,000 . . . but not him." However, she defended Daryl Vaz's actions. *Everyone* knew that Bicknell was PNP, she told us, so it shouldn't have been a problem. It wasn't like it was political bias, because it was a JLP politician coming to the aid of a PNP supporter. If Bicknell's brother, a known JLP supporter, had been in the same position, she explained, it would have been a problem for Vaz to help him. But since Bicknell himself was a PNP supporter, the affair was clearly free of political bias. I found this emphasis on political bias an interesting take, as I had read the affair more as an instance of two elite Jamaicans—both wealthy and light-skinned enough to be read as white—helping one another out.

Becoming even more animated, Celeste sought to justify Vaz's actions further, sharing one of her own encounters with the JCF. She had been eating starfruit while driving, and had just thrown the seeds out the car window when a police vehicle pulled up alongside and an officer reprimanded for her littering. "It's a starfruit, it's biodegradable!" she retorted. This displeased the police and they made her pull over, telling her: "You were littering and that's an offense." "No," she told them, "It's biodegradable, and it's worse for the environment, actually, if I put it in a plastic bag and send it to the dump, because then it would take longer to rot." Evidently unpersuaded, the police drove back, found the starfruit seed in question and returned with the evidence. "It was already rotting away!" Celeste exclaimed. "And they didn't know what a starfruit was!" Gesturing to show Rachel and me how she had held up the fruit, she sought to demonstrate the officers' environmental and linguistic ignorance. "I told them twice, 'It was a starfruit!' And only when I said 'jimbilin' [the Patois term for the fruit] did they understand. I said, 'Really officer, this wasn't a bad thing and I need to go to work.' But they said, 'No, littering is an offense, and we're going to arrest you for littering.'" The officers asked her for her name, and on hearing it noted that her uncle was a well-known MP. Having located her within Jamaica's landscape of power, Celeste felt that they were even more set on punishing her, to bring home the point that nobody was above the law. In the midst of these exchanges, she had managed to call a prominent criminal lawyer, who told her the situation was ridiculous—the police could not arrest a person for littering but could only issue a ticket. "Why don't you give me a ticket?" she asked them. "We don't have a ticket book with us," they responded, "so we have to take you to the police station." Seeing that they were not going to let her go, she convinced them to let her park her car at her nearby office, where she could drop off her things, let an employee know that she was being taken to the police station, and ensure that a friend would quickly come get her out on bail.

By the time they reached the station, with Celeste having been uncomfortably sandwiched in the back between two male officers, a friend was there to bail her out. However, he did not have sufficient proof of address on him, so the police refused her bail. Next, she called her ex-boyfriend, who worked nearby—one of the required documents was a letter from a Justice of the Peace, an honorary position that his father happened to occupy. "I told him, 'I'm here in jail' and he said, 'Oh, I'll be right over there and I'll get Dad, who is here with me, to sign off for you.'" This ex was familiar with the long list of requirements involved in getting someone released from a police station on bail, including not only money and proof of address but also passport pictures. When he arrived, the second person attempting to bail her out, the police told him in an apparently spiteful move that they could not accept the passport pictures, as they were too old and he would have to get new ones taken.

After he left, her brother called her phone. "'What, you're in jail?' 'Yeah, but I have it covered,' I told him." His response seemed very nonchalant, but he must have been worried because immediately after that, the phone rang again and it was her politician uncle: "What's this I hear, you're in jail? How come you don't call me yet? What's wrong with you!?" Again, she reassured him that there was no need for concern, she had it covered with her ex working to get her out on bail. But as she hung up, she began to worry that he wouldn't be able to get the pictures in time, and that she might have to spend the night at the station. Also, in between these calls—which she was apparently free to make—one of the policemen who had arrested her pulled up a chair close to her and started telling her she needed a good man like him in her life. "Move away, now!" she snapped and he retreated. But she was starting to feel uncomfortable.

At a certain point, Celeste asked to use the bathroom and a female police officer was called to escort her there. On reaching the bathroom, Celeste found there was no toilet paper—an all too common occurrence in public buildings—and insisted that the officer go find her some. The officer went to locate a roll of toilet paper. On her return, it was evident that she must have heard about Celeste's political connections. She started telling Celeste that the police station was very undersupplied. They didn't have many of the things they needed, from toilet paper to pens. Couldn't she do something about it, the officer asked. Could she help them see that they get supplies? "And I was like, wait a minute, you want *me* to help *you*? You just arrested me, I'm supposed to go out and ensure you have toilet paper and pens?"

Soon after, her phone rang again. This time it was a JLP senator, apparently also marshalled by Celeste's brother, calling to ask what was going on and whether she needed help. At this point she said, yes, she needed help. The senator turned up quickly, accompanied by an assistant, and started trying to persuade the police officers that they should let her be bailed out. This time, the officers maintained that he was not allowed to bail Celeste out because he was a politician. She argued that this rule did not apply in this case because senators were nominated rather than elected politicians. "I told them: he's a senator, not an MP, so he is allowed to bail me out. But they wouldn't let him." Undeterred, the senator called the Minister of National Security, who called the police superintendent in charge of the station where she was being held, and she was released soon after.

"Fortunately, we were in power at that time," Celeste concluded laughingly, her use of "we" a reference to her party, the JLP. To her, this story served to explain why Daryl Vaz would go to the station to help Bruce Bicknell. The police could be unreasonable and vindictive and it made sense for Vaz to want to check whether his friend was being mistreated. In her own case, she was relieved to have been able to mobilize her own political connections, but she also recognized that she was an individual who could hold her own, even when surrounded by unfriendly—or overly friendly—police officers. "I have this air about me, a don't-mess-with-me type of air, so people tend not to cross a certain line. For somebody else, who doesn't know how to act . . . it might have been difficult."

She followed up with another story about her sister and brother, who had borrowed their uncle's car to drive to a party. On leaving the party, they found that the car had been broken into and their uncle's possessions stolen. Seeking to report the theft, they were given a bit of a runaround, with two police stations each directing them to the other station, claiming that the report should be filed there. Back at the first station for the second time, Celeste's brother, who was both drunk and angry, began to curse. Taking offense, the police arrested him for cursing. Their sister, who had been waiting outside, came inside to see what was taking so long. "My brother told her: 'I'm under arrest for cursing!' So my sister, who was also drunk, started laughing and said 'What kind of bad word did you curse? Was it like pussy-raasclaat-bumbohole?'" Hearing her utter this string of colorful curses, which included some of Jamaica's most offensive expletives, the police arrested her too. Her siblings called her uncle, who told them that he couldn't come for them because then it would obviously be a "political thing." It sounded like it was already political, Celeste told us, in that the police wanted to show her siblings that they knew who they were and it didn't matter to them: "You're not above the law—you can't curse in here, so we're going to arrest you." Their uncle called Celeste and said "*I* can't go down there but you should go down there and get them out." So she went to the station where, she told us, the police officer in charge took a liking to her. After flirting with her for a bit—no bribes or higher-ups were involved—he was willing to release her siblings, and that was the end of that mix-up.

What do Celeste's droll accounts of her encounters with the JCF tell us about the workings of the law? In part, these are the types of narratives that a member of the Jamaican elite develops to make sense of an unpleasant incident and to justify her own actions. They shed light on how an individual with class, race, and political privilege presents herself as a protagonist who will not be intimidated and who is able to maneuver her way out of tricky situations with poise. But even as these stories favor her perspective, they also offer insight into the multiple logics that structure encounters between police and citizens.

One logic that Celeste's accounts highlight is that of legality. Both police officers and citizens understand what is happening in legal terms. There are rules and regulations that must be followed: the police insist that lawbreakers should be punished regardless of their social status and connections, that bail can only be granted if all procedures are properly followed, and that their status as law enforcement officers should be respected. Wealthy citizens, in turn, feel that their rights should be respected and that it is unjust for them to be arrested for minor offenses such as littering or cursing, or to be punished precisely because they are privileged. They also recognize that an MP cannot meddle too closely in police affairs as this might have the appearance of perverting the course of justice.

Despite such recurrent references to legality, such encounters are also indubitably shaped by the logic of classed and raced hierarchies. Jamaicans like Celeste have grown up secure in the knowledge that people like them don't spend the night in jail. The feeling of security this gives them is evident in what Celeste called her "don't-mess-with-me type of air." Encountering this aura of untouchability, some low-ranking police officers—predominantly darker-skinned Jamaicans from working-class backgrounds—may slip into a supplicating demeanor, hoping that this person's political connections can help procure supplies to improve everyday working conditions at the police station. But others may become especially indignant and tempted to abuse their power if they feel patronized or disrespected by a light-skinned, wealthy woman from a prominent political family. Their resentment is unlikely to diminish when they realize that, in the end, despite all the anticorruption regulations, a few phone calls will still allow such well-connected persons to bypass legal procedure. Such encounters also involve a confrontation between two types of impunity: the police quick to use their powers of arrest in apparently unwarranted contexts and the wealthy class mobilizing their "links" to avoid prosecution.

Residents of Kingston's low-income areas are aware of both types of impunity, and it informs their perception of the state legal order as working against the interests of poor black Jamaicans, rather than protecting them. Many of my interlocutors felt that the police viewed them as criminals rather than as citizens with rights, and they saw the court system as favoring Jamaica's light-skinned elites.[12] "John," one of my Brick Town friends, vehemently rejected the idea that the law was applied equally: "Because the police do crime and get away with it! The rich man do crime and get away and buy it out, through him have money. But me and you do crime . . . The government do crime and get away with it. All [even] the Prime Minister himself. So the law nuh work fi everybody. The law is a one-sided thing. Mi nuh know which one of them say, 'the law is not a shackle.' It *is!*"[13] To John, the law did not represent justice, and law enforcement did not represent protection. He explained to me why many people in communities like Brick Town were reluctant to talk to the police. "Because sometime you talk to the police and the police make crime leap 'pon you and make more problem fi you. Nuh go to *them* with a problem, go to the don." Speaking to the police could get you killed, he stressed: "You go to them and relay a information, and them go round the back, go to the man [that you accused], and set the man 'pon you and make you dead."

Despite such readings of the law as a shackle and the police as a source of risk, I did not necessarily encounter a uniform "anti-police" sentiment. In discussions on the police, Downtown residents would often note that they also knew of good police officers and that they were often "just doing their job"—even when they used violence. What many found especially upsetting was the lack of respect with which police coming into their neighborhood treated them, shoving them aside as they moved through the streets, or insulting grown men and women by addressing them as "bwoy" or "gyal," as if they were children. Their attitude toward the JCF was not exclusively antagonistic, but their own experiences with the force had shaped their perception that in practice the police did little to protect them from harm or to deliver justice.

COMMUNITY JUSTICE

It is in light of such experiences and perceptions of state law and policing that we can understand the legitimacy of the dons' system of law and order. In the 1990s, mob killings of thieves were a regular occurrence in Jamaica. Many understood these collective acts of violence as an expression of disillusionment with an overburdened and ineffective justice system. Over the past decades, this type of spontaneous vigilantism has disappeared almost entirely. It appears to have been displaced by more organized if still often violent forms of dispute resolution in low-income urban neighborhoods. Centered around dons, this normative order is commonly known as "community justice," or more disparagingly, as "jungle justice."

Dons and their men function as important local policing agents, organizing an effective system of surveillance and setting and enforcing norms within the neighborhood territory. A reputation for punishing transgressions swiftly and violently enhances a don's claim to authority. I encountered a written expression of such community norms and the sanctions for transgressing them along a through road bordering a garrison community. Not far from the local police station, someone had scrawled in large red letters: "No stealing in our community" (figure 4.1). A little farther down the road, the edict continued: "All thief will be killed" (figure 4.2). In practice, dons may rarely punish theft with death, but the gist of this public message is clear. How does community justice work as a legal order? Dons play a central role in enforcing norms, maintaining public safety, and resolving conflicts at the neighborhood level. Residents may report normative transgressions—from theft and domestic abuse to rape—to the neighborhood don, who will seek to identify the guilty party and assign an appropriate punishment. These punishments may range from a verbal warning to banishment from the neighborhood to various forms of physical violence including, in extreme cases, death. While variations exist amongst different neighborhoods, there appears to be a significant measure of codification, with standardized punishments for certain crimes, and in some cases a local court system with groups of elders presiding along with the don.[14]

The workings of the system were explained to me by Second, a man who had worked under the General as part of Brick Town's leadership but had since moved to a suburban area to lead a more peaceful life. He started off by noting that a don's security role had two dimensions, external and internal. External policing involved

4.1 Community justice rules.

4.2 Community justice rules.

"defending your area" against violators from neighboring communities. Perhaps more important, however, was a don's internal role of "splitting justice" in an impartial manner. "You have to split justice. You have to deal with justice, because everybody comes to you for justice. Because in the area you have people who will dis[respect] other people. But you can't take sides, even if it's your friend. Where the right is, you have to lay it out. It's a serious position. If people find that you are not giving justice, you're taking it up for your friend . . . it will be unbalanced." Second emphasized that in addition to residents, local businesses also relied on the dons' role in deterring and punishing crime. Any problems they had with thieves, they would come to the don. "You have to go find [the thieves] and warn them, or make them bring back the people's things that they steal."

I told him about a friend of mine, a foreign PhD student, who had experienced something similar. Someone had stolen his backpack at Papine, a busy transport hub. We told a friend who lived in that area, who put the word out to the don in charge of the area, and within a day, they had retrieved the backpack. Referencing two of Kingston's most prominent dons, Second nodded: "When they do that, they go to the same man like Zeeks or Dudus and he sends out his men." "But how do they know who did it?" I asked. "Everybody know everybody and know all the thieves," he explained, and when the thieves realized the news was out, they would return the stolen goods. "So once the word goes around, they hear, they bring it back. They know what will happen, so they send it back, or . . ." his sentence trailed off.

What would the consequences be for those caught stealing, I asked. Second laughed. "Typical penalty? We have some man will beat them." He allowed that, in other neighborhoods, the penalty might be harsher: "Some place, some man will do all kind of things." However, if the thieves were first offenders, they would get away with a warning: "They talk to you and warn you, sometime them warn you. You get a warning, then you do it again? They punish you."

I was curious whether people also turned to the don to resolve domestic disputes, for example, if a male resident was beating his female partner. Yes, Second said, "Sometimes all those things the leader have to deal with. Family life . . ." After listening to both parties, he explained, the don—"the man"—would instruct the aggressor to stop abusing his spouse. "Once they go to the man, and the man says 'Mi want it to be done,' it have to done"—it has to stop—"or else they come beat you, if you are the aggressor." Verbal warnings always preceded physical punishment, he maintained: "They warn him—'don't put your hands back on her'—based on how both of them explain themselves. Their rules are more stricter than the police. The man is the man, his words stand out, no matter what. You might not like it, but the system is—whether you like or don't like it—what he says is how it goes." He did acknowledge that this autocratic jurisprudence did not always feel fair. "Sometimes it not right to you, you *know* it's not right to you. But still, whatever him say, a so it go"—that's how it goes. "Do you feel there were a lot of people who didn't like it?" I asked. "Yeah," he answered, "A lot of people really don't like it, because sometimes they take away all your justice, as you probably can't explain yourself the right way, over the other person." I suggested that this sounded like the regular courts, where some people or their lawyers might be able to talk their way out of a guilty verdict. He agreed that it was similar: "Typically then, him right, but the one who wrong explain himself better." But even if the don made the wrong decision, you would have to accept it, he continued. "From the man say 'Yo!' is so"—that was it.

The responsibility of splitting justice equally weighed heavily on a don, Second emphasized. "It's a burden. It's you that everybody come to and 'ray ray [blah blah blah].' Domestic problems . . ." Being called on to intervene in disputes between people you knew well could be a headache, he explained. "You end up in the middle sometimes. Sometimes people hate you. It make you think and stress you out sometimes. The people put you in that position, you know!" Delivering justice could be especially difficult when it meant confronting your own friends:

> As you par [hang out] with your friends and them do people some things . . . People come to you, and it's your friends, and you have to tell your friends . . . sometimes man will box up [slap] some of their own friend. The people looking for that. If you don't do that, they don't feel justified. They watch to see how you're going to react to your friends. If you don't balance the thing and make them feel like . . . they going back with their hearts full. But if them feel they get justice, they won't say anything to no police.

To make people "feel they get justice," to help allow them to "feel justified," then, could require a leader to use violence, to slap his own friends across the face in public. However, Second asserted, Brick Town penalties were relatively mild. "Tivoli punishment is more harsher," he claimed. They were more likely to kill transgressors. This was how they did things there, from Claudie Massop's time in the 1970s, through Dudus's father Jim Brown into the early 1990s, and Dudus himself had been even harsher, "more crosser," than his father. In Brick Town, in contrast, now that the General and people like himself were no longer in charge, the system had become loose: "The strong order and one order thing not there. From the General gone, now, people don't confident in anybody like that, or who they would look up to, people like me, who not there." Those who had taken over from the senior figures, the "bigger heads," were hotheads: "The bigger head originals left, so it's pure little youths gangster, little shotta, there now. They disrespect the elders, them do anything they feel like."

Notwithstanding the various flaws that Second himself identified in the day-to-day workings of community justice, I still found that many residents viewed this don-based, violently retributive system as more efficient and fairer than that offered by the JCF or the courts, and as rooted in broadly shared norms. In Brick Town and other Downtown neighborhoods, residents confirmed that a strong don could maintain a level of security and order that was difficult or impossible for the police to achieve. Various Brick Town residents described the important role that the General had taken in keeping their neighborhood safe and orderly, before his imprisonment. Echoing Second's assessment that there was no longer a "strong order" in place, they complained about the poor level of security following the General's imprisonment.

Andy, a young man from Brick Town, described to me what the neighborhood was like when the General was still in charge. "Normally thieves could not come and break into a store or anything when the General was here," he told me. "Mi nuh know why them want a man like that put in prison. But it's always like that, you know, it's always the honest man and the good people who ever do go down." A strong don, he felt, was important in ensuring community safety. "Every community should have a don." Although violence might be involved in maintaining community order, he tried to explain to me, it had to start with love: "When you're a don, it's certain things that you do [that] let you become a don. You have to love—the love that you have for the whole of the community people and children . . ." A don could not use violence with impunity, he stressed. "You can't just decide 'I'm going to murder this person' and expect that people will support everything you do." Andy spoke of the General as an ethical leader, who could protect residents from theft and rape. I asked him what a resident would do if, say, their daughter had been raped. "You go to *him*," to the don, he answered. When I asked him to explain, his answer echoed Second's account: "In a situation like that he would talk to [the perpetrator] to ask how you had reached into the people's house. Talk to them at the same time, so he would listen to this one first and then listen to that one. So he would tell who was wrong from who was right. And if you had got a first chance already, like if the first time you had got away, then you can get in trouble. Probably you would get a few slap ups and one of your legs might get broken." Other residents shared similarly positive, even nostalgic, recollections of the level of neighborhood security under the General. The importance of not only maintaining a strong order, but doing so in a fair fashion, came out clearly in a conversation I had with Mikey, a Brick Town resident who ran a small business in the neighborhood. Before the General went to prison, he told me, "If the leader say 'no stealing,' it's no stealing, you understand." Mikey spoke highly of the evenhandedness with which the General would deliver his verdicts: "That man split the justice right down the middle. Everyone is equal, no matter where you're from, whether you're inner-city, country, poor, rich. 'Cause you know that man is straightforward. Equality for everybody. If me and him [gesturing toward a man sitting nearby] have a dispute, then you're not supposed to take him side, though you and him might be cousin or family. You just know say: justice is justice." To my mind, Mikey's emphasis on fairness and equality—on splitting justice "right down the middle"—is the key to understanding the appeal of community justice, more so even than its efficacy. While the legal order associated with donmanship was certainly imperfect, many residents contrasted it favorably with a state system that they experienced as fundamentally unfair and unequal.

Dons also regulate public order outside of direct conflicts or "crimes." Ensuring that young people from the neighborhood behave appropriately is part of this responsibility. Reminiscing about how he grew up in Brick Town, Second noted that the big men, back in the day, would make sure that children attended school. "Every morning we have to go to school," he recollected approvingly, "and if we don't go, the big men beat us. If we don't have money to go to school, they give us. If we don't have school shoes, they find it for us—but we have to go to school . . . or we have to go hide until evening." This role of providing guidance to young people remained in place decades later, as I found during one stay in Kingston, when I volunteered at a homework club at a Downtown community center.

Tutoring high-school students from nearby low-income neighborhoods, I was surprised at the frequency with which the students, all between thirteen and sixteen, would talk about the dons and their system of law enforcement without any form of prompting. For instance, the very first day I gave a homework class, the teenagers began to discuss what to do if you found someone else's phone. One student, "Lee," suggested that people might become angry if you tried to return their phone because they would think that you had stolen it. When I asked him why anyone would think he had stolen it if he was giving it back, it came out that he would ask them for a little reward, such as a drink or some money, which could anger them. It was unclear to me whether this was a real or hypothetical example, but I suggested that such a request would be unfair: "How would you feel if you lost your phone and you had to pay someone to get it back?" Another volunteer suggested that if you were afraid, you could find someone else to give the phone back to the owner. A second boy, "Winston," agreed that the best thing might be to take the found phone to the "bigger heads" in the community, to which a third student, "Raheem," suggested you could take it to the don.

This discussion prompted Lee to tell the story of how a group of boys from his neighborhood were playing football and had put their phones to the side, with only two boys there to watch them. At the end of the match, one of the phones had disappeared and no one could find out which of the two boys had taken it, so they took the matter to the don. Both boys still refused to say who had stolen the phone. The don then took a big piece of cane and took them out to the road, telling them he would beat them both. After he hit the first boy, this boy confessed, telling the don that it was he who had taken the phone. This course of action was presented by Lee as a good solution.

In another homework class, teenagers from two adjacent neighborhoods spontaneously began to list and compare their respective dons' rules. In the first neighborhood, the don did not allow smoking under the age of fifteen whereas in the second neighborhood you were not allowed to smoke in front of adults. Other rules included curfews for children: those under the age of twelve had to be off the street by 8:00 p.m., while teens aged twelve to fifteen could stay out until 10:00 p.m. These curfews resembled the youth curfew that Dudus was said to have organized in Tivoli Gardens. In fact, Dudus referred to this as one of his achievements in a letter he wrote asking the US judge presiding over his case for leniency, writing that "I am a founding member of a Parent Association Committee . . . the members of the Committee would walk the street of the community to make sure the children between the age of six (6) years old to the age of sixteen (16) years old are off the street by 8 p.m. from Sundays to Thursdays." Like Dudus, the teenagers in my homework class and various parents I spoke to appeared to support such rules, and to understand their enforcement as an important positive contribution a don could make to his community.

LEGAL HYBRIDITY

While many Uptown Kingstonians might consider the residents of neighborhoods like Brick Town to be "lawless," the rules enforced within the dons' system of community justice are institutionalized to such an extent that we can understand it as a legal order, one that establishes collective norms and issues penalties when they are violated. It is tempting to read such an institutionalized normative system through the lens of legal pluralism. Yet the don-enforced alternative legal system described here does not function as a parallel system, separate from Jamaica's formal legal system, nor is it necessarily at odds with state law. Some of the acts that dons identify as transgressions do clash directly with state law; this is most marked in their ban on "informing," passing on information to the police—an act punishable by death. This prohibition on talking to the police is reinforced by the many reggae and dancehall songs that condemn informers, from Dennis Brown's "Wolves and

Leopards" to Vybz Kartel and Tommy Lee Sparta's "Informer." Beyond this anti-informer decree, many other norms, regarding the behavior of children or the use of violence to punish transgressions, overlap largely with either Jamaica's state legal order or with more general societal norms.

A closer look at recent strategies employed by the JCF and the Ministry of Justice (MOJ) suggests a reading in terms of legal hybridity rather than pluralism. What we see is, I propose, the entanglement of multiple legal systems, as various state actors either enable the dons' community justice system in a nonofficial form of "indirect rule," or have developed approaches that mimic and incorporate elements of this don-led system.

To start, the dons' community justice system is often actively enabled by members of the police force, who direct both victims and perpetrators of crime to the dons.[15] While giving a lecture at the University of the West Indies, I met a high-ranking police official, "Harry," who was pursuing a degree there. It turned out that Brick Town was part of the police division where he had had a senior role and he agreed to speak to me about his experiences. Because this was a garrison, he told me, any encounter between a community member and the police would be seen as suspicious by other residents, as a sign of informing. Harry admitted to only having visited Brick Town a few times: "It's not a community that you just get up and go to," he explained, referring to the improvised roadblocks at the neighborhood borders: "It is not an open community, it is a place where you have to remove barriers to go in."

I asked him how he saw the role of the JCF in areas like Brick Town, whether he saw the police as serving a different function there than elsewhere. He emphasized the slow process of gaining access: "You're trying to get the guns, trying to make the place accessible. As you would have known, many of these communities you have barriers, they actually put a thing across the road that they have to lift to let you in. So we're trying to move all kinds of barriers—physical, political barriers—and at the same time build trust and partnership, because you know decades of hostility towards the cop won't be removed in a night or day." Harry situated the distrust of police in longer histories of state violence: "You have to understand their hatred towards you, because you seldom meet somebody from the community that has not been affected by some acts of violence by the state, even against himself or against a relative, so that is not something that disappear overnight." The trust-building he engaged in involved investing in community relations: helping residents in financial need, helping them find a job through "links" to employers, paying for their children's school books, and fundraising to establish larger welfare programs. In terms of enforcing the law, he emphasized that his priority was on violent crime and illegal guns, but also on property crimes, as dealing with such matters was the dons' strong suit: "Property crime has the impact of leading to violent crimes, because if somebody believe that if their property is taken they won't get justice, they might just resort to . . . The area leader exacts punishment."

I asked Harry in what situations police work would require having contact with dons. "From time to time you have to work with these leaders," he began to explain. "Not that you're compromising or anything," he hastened to add. "But . . . they have access to the community. They can determine what the community does or does not do. So your connections with communities in many instances are through them. You want to have a meeting, you know, you have to go through them. But," he continued, "what we try to do in instances is to actually use them." He proceeded to describe the nature of police engagement in a way that resembled a form of indirect rule:

> We task them, so they actually end up doing some of our work. For example, if you go into a community and you realize that you're having certain type of crimes—you might have people being shot—and you suspect that they are being shot because, according to them, disrespect or so on. You just say it to someone [the don] that "Listen, you are in charge of this community, so the next time we hear that someone get shot, we coming for you." So rather than we policing to prevent that, they're actually policing themselves. Because they know that if you're in charge, you can prevent things from happening. So we task them to reduce certain acts that you cannot on your own reduce, because you'd have to have eyes and ears in every corner. So you actually task them.

Over time, he explained, the police would develop relationships, where they would ask dons to do certain things. In turn, dons would expect a certain type of reciprocity, a blind eye toward certain acts: "They will expect that certain crimes, if it's not *major*, that . . . Even gun crime, they will expect that . . . For example, you find a gun: you can take it but don't arrest anybody. Things like that." "And if you did arrest someone," I asked, "they would feel that you have violated the terms of the agreement?" "Yes," he answered, "and tacitly they'll kind of withdraw their support."

I was struck by Harry's frankness, which resonated directly with many residents' sense that the police often maintained close connections with dons and other "badmen." His account suggested a clear recognition of the limits of the police in neighborhoods like Brick Town, but also the desire to frame collusion with dons not as the only available option, but rather as a mutually beneficial, even efficient form of "tasking" local leaders with surveillance. We might read such arrangements as indicating a pluralist system characterized by separate "jurisdictions," with some crimes or territories falling under the police and courts and others under the dons' jurisdiction.

Beyond this power-sharing, however, police and justice strategies after the 2010 Tivoli Incursion also suggest that the Jamaican state has appropriated and adopted some of the dons' more popular practices. In such strategies, we can recognize elements of the violent retribution associated with the dons, but also nonviolent initiatives focused on mediation and youth guidance. In addition, in some low-income districts, senior police officers have mimicked dons' social provisioning role—as Harry's financial support of residents also suggests—and their use of popular culture, as part of new attempts to claim authority.

In some cases, JCF officers' frequent use of violence—both as a punitive strategy directed at specific individuals and in a more arbitrary form aimed primarily at demonstrating their capacity to harm at will—suggests deliberate attempts to emulate and displace a don-based model of violent authority.[16] The appeal of this strategy is evident in the popularity of "badman police" discussed in chapter 1, with officers from Keith "Trinity" Gardner to Reneto Adams widely celebrated for their violent approach to crime-fighting.[17] The JCF, while tasked with upholding the law, frequently operates outside of the legal regulatory framework in which it is embedded. Many Jamaicans may support the use of violence by either dons or the police, as long as this violence is directed at people they see as "criminals." As discussed above, the dons' legitimacy is partially rooted in their willingness to wield violence in a way that neighborhood residents consider proper. Such sympathetic assessments of dons' use of violence suggest that social norms not only emphasize fairness. There is also widespread support for more punitive, authoritarian forms of order-making, and the JCF is sensitive to such social norms.[18]

Other JCF practices appear to mimic the dons' "softer" forms of maintaining public order. For instance, in the years following the Tivoli Incursion, the Kingston Western police division introduced a youth curfew, apparently copying the dons' popular curfews, discussed approvingly by the teenagers in my homework club. The JCF's Community Safety and Security Team announced a 9:00 p.m. curfew for children aged seventeen and under, which would rely on local residents trained as "curfew monitors" to implement the policy. In a flyer outlining the initiative, the police division—which includes Tivoli Gardens and Denham Town, areas formerly under Dudus's influence—stated that "the idea of a curfew in the home or even the community is not new, but the uniqueness of this strategy is obvious in the involvement of the police."[19] Implicitly, this statement recognized the longer tradition of a youth curfew, almost seeming to credit Dudus for developing this public order measure.

In this same Division, the officer in charge, Senior Superintendent (SSP) Steve McGregor, also engaged in other forms of apparent appropriation, developing don-like initiatives as part of his community policing approach. As discussed throughout this book, dons' claims to authority are bolstered by their social provisioning, by their "hedonopolitical" ability to create an atmosphere of enjoyment by sponsoring street dances, and by street art inscribing them into a community's history.[20] Drawing on a longer tradition of police welfare, SSP McGregor and the Kingston Western Division organized a Christmas treat with entertainment and holiday gifts for children, and established the "Shut-In Project" to deliver bags of groceries to homebound elderly residents. In addition, McGregor organized a street dance at the Denham Town Police Station with advertisements announcing proudly that "SSp McGregor in asso. with Kingston Western Police presents a night called 'Police Citizen Link Up.'" These events and other investments in the community were promoted on Instagram, spearheading a social media campaign adopted by the JCF more broadly in the years that followed.[21]

The visualization of the new, benevolent police presence did not remain restricted to the digital realm, but was also manifested on community walls. In 2013, under the leadership of the same SSP McGregor, the JCF organized an "anti-mural campaign." Police officers began painting over the memorial murals of men they held to be criminals, seeking to assert their own presence and authority by coating the same walls with their signature "constabulary blue" paint (see figure 4.3). Jokingly but clearly referencing the longer tradition of visualizing authority through mural art, McGregor suggested to West Kingston residents that they could include his likeness on a community wall if he succeeded in bringing order to the area.[22] Indeed, within these various new policing strategies in West Kingston, McGregor emerged as the personification of the police, as the embodiment of the post-Dudus legal order. This model of personified authority, seemingly cultivated through similar aesthetic and sensorial means as that of the dons, was successful to the extent that when McGregor was transferred to another parish, residents protested against his departure. In a small but energetic rally, protestors blocked the road and brandished cardboard signs reading "Crime has gone down, party party's gone up!!!!" Others said "West Kingston is deemed as the mother of all garrisons so we need Mr. McGregor to stay, so the peace in this community can remain," and even "No McGregors No Tivoli." Again, this expression of loyalty for one man, though now a police officer, echoed the tradition of public demonstrations of support for dons.[23]

But perhaps the most explicit form of appropriation of the don's legal order has been the establishment of Restorative Justice Centres (RJCs) in the decade following

4.3 Image of area leader Early Bird painted over by the JCF, Matthews Lane. Photo by Tracian Meikle.

the Tivoli Incursion. Following broader justice reform recommendations, the MOJ established a policy that involved opening several of these centers in low-income urban areas across Jamaica. The opening of the Tivoli Gardens RJC was especially symbolic. Speaking at the event, Prime Minister Andrew Holness framed it explicitly as an alternative to the justice provided by the community's criminal leadership. "I encourage the people of West Kingston, of Tivoli Gardens," he intoned, "to *use* this restorative justice system, which will erode and diminish the power and authority being wielded by criminals over you. When you go to them for justice, you give them power"—"*Power!*" an audience member shouted—". . . over you," Holness continued undeterred. "And that is part of the reason why crime and violence is almost perennial in some community. And we have to break it."[24]

Police, church officials, and community members may refer local disputes to these neighborhood-based centers rather than to the court system or other formal legal institutions. This referral of victims and offenders seems to have a clear analogy in the community justice system, where both police and residents refer incidents to the don. A comprehensive national report on justice reform had already noted that lack of confidence in the state justice system "is manifested by the frequency with which citizens resort to instituting and administering their own form of restorative and retributive 'community justice.'"[25] Echoing this, the National Restorative Justice Policy similarly acknowledged that "dons set the tone for community values and are said to have a hand in all dispute resolutions of significance."[26] Accordingly, the new centers were envisaged as neighborhood-level sites for alternative dispute resolution that could "address a profound disconnect between the formal and informal systems of conflict resolution which is perhaps the most challenging phenomenon for advancing crime reduction strategies."[27] In seeking to overcome this disconnect between formal and informal systems, the RJCs are explicitly envisioned as a restorative, formally sanctioned *alternative* to the dons' punitive, retributive modes of dispute resolution. Notwithstanding, their emphasis on core features of the don's system of justice—proximity, accessibility, and an orientation toward community relations—suggests the hybridization of the state justice system.[28]

These various JCF and MOJ initiatives, from youth curfews to neighborhood-level dispute resolution, are intended to replace the rule of dons but, at the same time, they reproduce some of their most popular measures. This overlap with the dons' methods of norm enforcement both reflects and reproduces the entanglement of dons with the state. This fluidity suggests the need to approach don-based formations of law and order not as outlawry, nor even as a form of legal pluralism, but rather as a form of legal hybridity.

SENSING LAW AND ORDER

The legal order that is centered on dons, and that state agencies may emulate even as they seek to displace it, is also an aesthetic order: it has a material, sensorial dimension that takes shape within the specific built environment of Jamaica's low-income urban areas. In the introduction to this book, I discussed the work that affective atmospheres—the immersive, material-affective relations between bodies and their surroundings—do in normalizing authority. In concluding this chapter, I draw inspiration from recent work in legal studies and criminology in thinking through atmospheres of criminal justice, of law and order. Extending a traditional focus on legal *texts* or even orally transmitted norms, such scholarship draws our attention to how law, or any normative order, is experienced as an embodied, material, and spatial phenomenon.[29] Affective atmospheres, emerging in spaces from the courthouse to the protesting crowd to "the street," help encourage adherence to norms: it *feels* right to engage in certain behaviors and to refrain from others in those spaces. Physical immersion in such atmospheres means that those norms no longer need to be articulated explicitly.

Dons' formations of law and order involve aesthetic interventions into the built environment, shaping the neighborhood and how residents and visitors use it. Whether intentionally or accidentally, these interventions contribute to the production of atmospheres that encourage compliance to local norms. Most obviously, explicit references to public norms are components of such atmospheres: sound systems playing songs condemning informers or public inscriptions warning passersby "No stealing in our community, all thief will be killed."

Other aesthetic features, such as those discussed at the start of this chapter, establish atmospheres of law and order more subtly, through residents' material-affective encounters with visual markers such as graffiti, murals, and urban debris, but also other, less bounded sensorial stimuli, such as sounds or tactile encounters. Security atmospheres take shape within the space of the neighborhood as dons "deploy visual and other sensory signals to fashion aesthetic norms about how security looks, sounds, and feels."[30] The drain covers that are removed, the strategically placed debris, and unfilled potholes can be understood as deliberate forms of design that slow down the movement of vehicles. The burly men hanging out on the corner, some blocking the streets with their cars, are actively engaged in surveilling all passersby and repelling unwelcome intruders. Meanwhile, memorial murals not only serve to visualize a genealogy of local leadership, but also gesture toward the system of surveillance associated with this leadership. The men who populate these portraits gaze directly at passersby, some smiling, some stern—all everyday reminders to residents of who is watching them (figure 4.4). While they

4.4 Commemorative murals.

might appear disorderly or banal to outsiders, these various interventions (or noninterventions) in the built environment materialize the normative order of donmanship.

The spatialized feelings of normative order generated by informal borders, warning signs, and guards are, of course, atmospheres of surveillance and control. Affective atmospheres of surveillance work at the edges of consciousness, with the surveillance system itself remaining almost but not quite unnoticed, the feelings it produces not directly qualified or registered through linguistic representation.[31] Such atmospheres involve a tacit knowledge that, in these surroundings, some interactions are out of bounds: speaking to a police officer is risky, as is taking photographs of the don or his associates, or indeed voicing criticism of them in public. Children, too, can come to internalize the neighborhood rules, staying inside as night falls. These spatial sensibilities reflect and reproduce an autocratic form of rule connected to the personal authority of the don. Even as the don might rarely be seen in public himself, implicit and explicit reminders of who is in charge of the neighborhood can elicit an affective response of wariness, tension, or anxiety.

But as much as—or more than—fear, these atmospheres of surveillance and control involve an enveloping affective spatiality of safety, or even of justice. Residents of neighborhoods like Brick Town do not necessarily move about anxiously, in permanent fear of crime, of the don, or of the police. Feelings of being watched and being watched *over*—of surveillance and protection—blur into each other easily. An enveloping sensation of intimacy and comfort, of being protected, may form when surrounded by graffiti, murals, and bordering technologies connected to the don's order. Such security atmospheres are analogous to those that elite Jamaicans may sense when surrounded by uniformed guards, gates, armed response signs, and CCTV systems in Uptown areas.

The legal hybridity discussed above also makes its way into aesthetic forms and affective atmospheres of law and order. I noticed this during a street dance in Brick Town in April 2010, not long before the Tivoli Incursion. Like many other neighborhoods led by dons, the community had a tradition of hosting an annual event dedicated to the local leadership, the West Side Posse Dance. Stone Love, a well-known sound system, was playing hit after hit, and hundreds of people were packed into the streets, with the crowd including residents from Brick Town as well as from other Downtown neighborhoods. In between songs, Jamaican sound systems engage in a call-and-response dynamic with the public. In this case, Stone Love's DJs made numerous "shout-outs" to the community's former don, shouting "Big up Father General!" into their microphones. These shout-outs were met with loud cheers of approval from the crowd, and a man standing in front me called out "Big up the Donfather!" in response. Following numerous shout-outs to the General, the sound system also paid respect to Dudus, who was said to be at the dance as well. Although the relationship between the two dons had not always been easy, the crowd also responded approvingly to Stone Love's "Big up Dudus!" Not long after, one of the Stone Love DJs called out, "Big up all of the police in the place!" I later realized that the JCF had just entered the neighborhood, and the sound system was explicitly recognizing their presence, seeking to prevent the atmosphere from becoming hostile. Perhaps surprisingly, this shout-out also received a mildly appreciative response although the crowd's reaction was noticeably less enthusiastic than when the sound system celebrated the two dons.

By cheering both for the General and for Dudus, the revelers recognized the authority of both leaders. Institutionalized events such as the West Side Posse Dance, organized in honor of dons or criminal organizations, are sites where claims to authority are made and received. Like the political rallies discussed in chapter 3—dismissed as craziness by Uptown Kingstonians such as Celeste—these street dances are highly political forms of festivity. They can generate intense atmospheres of joyousness, excitement, and energy that encourage a feeling of shared belonging while making the don's authority manifest in a visceral way. However, as the "big up" to the police demonstrates, commitment to dons does not preclude the recognition of other forms of authority. Rather, the shout-outs that characterize these dances render the distinct forms of authority compatible, making it *feel* possible that a normative order could exist in which dons and police need not be pitted against each other.

CONCLUSION

Complementing the reggae and dancehall songs that warn listeners not to become "informers" who share information with the police, there is also a musical tradition of lauding dons as community protectors. Damian Marley's *R.O.A.R.* (2017) is an example of such songs, "bigging up" the lions who "roar for a cause," those who use violence for the greater good. The lyrics outline the system of external defense and internal law enforcement sketched by Second, earlier in this chapter:

> *Big up the lion dem weh roar fi a cause / Defend your community at all cost*
> *Never yet run, stand your ground to the last / Real outlaw, people love we, because:*
> *No old woman purse can get grab off / No juvenile 'pon the road after dark*
> *No visitors can get rob inna the park / Else bwoy will finish before dem start*
> *No shotta can give no juvenile gun / No stinginess when the site money run*
> *No likkle shop can get bruk inna the slum / All who perpetrator haffi pack up and run*

These lyrics emphasize the main elements of the law enforcement that make "people love the real outlaw": old women's purses can't get grabbed, visitors won't get robbed, and no one will break into local shops—perpetrators will have to pack up and run. In addition, the "lions" will ensure that young people can't be out in the street after dark and that these "juveniles" are not given access to weapons. The protectiveness extends to financial support: as discussed more extensively in chapter 5, "the site money" extorted from contractors must be distributed without stinginess. While such depictions of community justice as a fair and functional system do not necessarily reflect how the system works out in practice, this type of musical celebration and the overall positive appraisals I encountered during my own research suggest that the "law and order" provided by dons plays a central role in legitimizing their power. As individual autocrats who can come to personify "the law," the recognition of their authority simultaneously derives from and further strengthens their association with this normative order.

The idea that dons, commonly associated with crime and violence, could play a key role in providing public security and resolving conflicts might strike outsiders as ludicrous. But they have assumed this role in a context where the JCF and the formal justice system have given low-income, black Jamaicans little basis for confidence. This context has allowed various dons to strategically mobilize their reputation for violence in a way that meets the approval of local residents, by balancing their "outlaw" status with an apparent commitment to public order. While community justice is certainly an imperfect system, when residents speak of dons as "splitting justice" in a fair and effective fashion, this should be understand as an assessment made in comparison with the state system of law enforcement and justice.

Such assessments do not always take the shape of conscious decision-making. Justice and security also have felt, affective dimensions. Even to elite Jamaicans such as Celeste, who can move through the city with a sense of untouchability—what she called her "don't mess with me air"—the tactility of police encounters can be unsettling. For residents of Kingston's garrison neighborhoods, when police officers rush through the neighborhood in an aggressive fashion, pushing people aside while barking disrespectful terms, the affective atmosphere this produces is certainly not one of fairness and protection. In contrast, dons have developed the capacity to generate emplaced feelings of lawfulness and safety. They engage in public performances of "splitting justice" that feel just to onlookers. They make their form of security felt through their inventions in the urban landscape, marking their territory, fortifying its borders, and establishing systems of surveillance. While rooted in this territory, dons' role as protectors is also embedded in their person, an image that is upheld through popular culture, from the murals that adorn neighborhood walls to the reggae and dancehall songs played across the island and beyond.

5
Taxation

I sat down on a corner in Brick Town to speak with "Ludlow," an elderly man who had spent most of his life in the neighborhood. He had been telling me about how the area had changed since he moved there as a child, in the 1950s. "Dem time [in those days], it was peace and love," he told me. "When the wickedness start, now, that's way down inna the sixties." He had lived through the worst decades of political violence, when it was "'pon di heights"—at its highest. "You know say mi 'round here already, and mi haffi [have to] go under my cellar when the politics 'pon di heights. Every day you hear gun, you see where we sit down here now, gunshot fire night and day." "Was that around election times?" I asked him. "Yeah, or coming up to election, inna di eighties . . . The 1980 one wicked, man, night and day, and inna di seventies too."

Although Ludlow identified as "a PNP," the political violence had never affected him directly, he explained. "Mi just do mi normal living, you know. 'Cause mi's a easy-going person, you see. No, nobody nuh really trouble me, and mi nuh get involved inna nothing, but mi have friend who get involved and them all dead." He had never had any issues with the General, either. "Him nuh really trouble me you know, him nuh really trouble me. Mi and him get on. Mi nuh really talk to him still, 'cause mi nuh have nothing really fi talk to him [about]."

In the wake of the Tivoli Incursion, Ludlow had become more critical of dons, arguing that "badmanship and donmanship fi cut out"—these formations of crime and leadership, distinct but interrelated, needed to come to an end. Nonetheless, he made a clear distinction between good and bad dons. This distinction, one I had heard many other Downtown residents make as well, seemed to underline the institutionalization of donmanship. The system of donmanship seemed entrenched, but individual dons could be good or bad, a blessing or a curse. "Some of them good too, you know. Yeah, some of them good. The good one them dead." He chuckled. "Yeah, 'cause [it's] a don, you know . . ." Death came with the territory. He began to tell me about dons he considered good: "You know the two first don who mi know? Tony Brown and George Flash, come from over East [Kingston]. Tony Brown dead, and him dead from natural cause. Yeah man, and mi remember when them did want him, want the two of them. And if you never know: them end up a Cuba, and them a PNP, you know. The government did send them away in the seventies."[1] I wanted to know more about why Ludlow considered the dons he mentioned to have been *good* dons. His explanation of why Tony Brown and George Flash had been good ones emphasized a form of rule that did not rely on violence: "'Cause them nuh really go round, go terrorize people, and kill people and tell people to do that."[2] More broadly, he told me, "Them take care a things, make the community run right and things."

Initially, Ludlow had been somewhat cautious in his discussion of Brick Town's affairs, in part because we were in earshot of "Trevor," one of the current corner dons, who often posted at the corner where we were sitting. As Trevor moved off, Ludlow spoke more freely about Brick Town's past leadership, arguing that the General had actually been a bad don, evil even. And that was why he was now in prison, suffering. "A just through evil make him there where him is. You see if him was a good don that get a shot and dead . . ." "Would it be better to be shot dead than to be in prison?" I asked. "Right, and you just go out, go die," he affirmed. "Get a big funeral and everybody come. . . . But from you a evil man, you go prison and suffer, so that's what happen to him. Him wasn't a good don."

Evil, however, was not the only factor leading to the General's imprisonment. Ludlow also read the don's fate as a direct result of his greed: "Him just want everything, you know. Greedy." A more cautious, less greedy don could have escaped imprisonment. "The General too greedy, man. Him nuh use him head. If he did use him head, him would've been here now." I asked him to tell me more about what the General's avarice had entailed. Was it that the General had "taxed" too many people, or taxed them too harshly? Ludlow began to expand. "You haffi really pay. And you know, if you nuh pay, how it go. But you see, the extortion thing, I'm not into it. No sir. You work hard all of your life fi build up your business and every week you haffi give a man money, and him nuh contribute much to it. People fi [should] work for them living. Yeah, it's bad-minded people who extort, you know." I asked him to explain who in Brick Town would be affected by extortion. For instance, would the Rastafari owner of the cook-shop near us have to pay extortion fees? This was not the case, Ludlow explained: "Well, the Rasta now, the Ras not going to be extorted, 'cause a man [associated with the don] will come and him will give them a food and thing, you know." Giving the leaders of the community food for free did not count as extortion, he felt. What about the lady selling juice down the road, I asked. "No man! Me and them people there grow [up together], you know. Them cyaan [cannot] extort them people. [Are] you mad?!"

Extortion was what took place at the wholesale shops on the main streets, he told me: "Like the Chinese people them and the Syrian them. Them extort who can pay." "What about the market people, like vendors?" I probed further. "You call that extortion?" he replied. "I don't know," I asked, "what do you call it?" "Them just pay for a space," Ludlow explained. "Because, alright: government nuh collect no market fee. 'Cause government supposed to go round and collect market fee, 'cause when me grow up people collect market fee. That nuh happen again. So maybe you haffi say them extort them . . ." he concluded reluctantly. "But you just call it a fee?" I proposed. "Yeah, them collect a fee," he answered, sounding relieved. I asked Ludlow what the vendors got in return for the fee. He explained that they would not have to worry about security. "Nobody can come do them nothing." The don would ensure that market operations ran smoothly and safely, no mean feat given that this was one of Kingston's busier markets.

Both "good dons" and "bad dons" assume responsibility for some level of neighborhood-level service provision—at the minimum, they are involved in organizing security and conflict resolution, as chapter 4 described. The various services that they provide come, in many ways, at a cost. Most literally, this may involve a direct financial contribution. From the smallest market vendor to the midlevel private bus route operator to the largest Jamaican corporation, those conducting business in a don's territory will likely have to pay up in one way or another.

Ludlow assured me that the rates the vendors paid in exchange for permission to sell in the market were quite reasonable: "Them pay them a little, a bills a day [about one US dollar]. Nobody not going to really worry you, but you have to pay. So me wouldn't really call the market thing extortion. It's a market fee. The extortion now, that's what happens at the wholesale and business place." Similar to conventional types of permits and licenses, Ludlow saw the fees paid by vendors as an accepted cost of business, a tax that entitled them to conduct their affairs within a certain area. However, this fee only applied to vendors from outside of Brick Town: "You know, there's people down there who nuh pay no market fee. 'Cause me have a little friend who used to work who have her stall down there, she nuh pay no market fee. She born and grow here. You cyaan born round here, and grow round here, and pay man money, you know." Taxable subjects, according to Ludlow, were outsiders: both larger business establishments and smaller vendors from outside the neighborhood. The juice vendor, the friend with a market stall: if these local microentrepreneurs were "born and grow" in the neighborhood, they should benefit from the don's provision of security without having to contribute financially. While locals were not exempted from taxation, I did encounter a general sense amongst residents that they should be left alone.[3]

The "fees" that dons are able to exact from a broad variety of Jamaicans could easily be understood as extortion: the practice of obtaining money or goods through the threat of violence.[4] Indeed, Jamaican newspapers frequently publish articles about the suffering caused by extortionists. Yet I rarely heard the term "extortion" used in Brick Town, or in other Downtown neighborhoods, to describe the money or goods exacted by dons. Over the years, I encountered many instances of transactions that had the outward appearance of extortion but were emphatically not described as such. Rather, I heard a range of alternative terms, euphemisms perhaps, mobilized to refer to dons' ability to claim financial and in-kind contributions from those who conduct business in their territories.

The most common term I encountered was "taxes," used in a non-ironic fashion to describe the financial levy dons can impose. But, as my discussion with Ludlow suggests, these payments might also be called "market fees." In other conversations, my interlocutors framed such exchanges as "parking tickets," or "charitable donations," or forms of "labor regulation." They often described them not so much as direct exchanges, but as forms of *material redistribution*—as broadly justifiable contributions toward a form of public good. I heard the term extortion used mainly in contexts where my interlocutors either considered the rate of taxation to be excessively high, as when dons became "greedy," or where they felt the demands were illegitimate, for instance when freelance extortionists claimed to be associated with the don.

What does this apparent insistence on describing these exchanges as other-than-extortion mean? Might we understand this performance of consent as an authorizing of extortion—and as an enactment of the don's authority more broadly? In this chapter, I focus on the payments that dons exact from small and large urban entrepreneurs, often in exchange for their provision of protection, closely related to their security role described in chapter 4. While the police and media are quick to describe such transactions as "extortion," I take seriously their framing in terms of taxation so as to understand how such payments feature in the claims to authority that dons make and how such claims are received by residents and businesspeople. I am interested in the lengths that the parties involved—both the entrepreneurs and the dons themselves—go to narrate and perform these economic exchanges as *other-than-extortion*. This "theater of consent," which involves material-sensorial practices that legitimize exchanges that do in fact strongly resemble extortion, is an important mode through which dons' claims to authority are made and recognized.[5]

Below, I start with a reflection on how we might understand taxation as a payment extracted and redistributed by political institutions in and beyond the state.

Such payments are informed by a specific moral economy, by a broadly shared "view of social norms and obligations, of the proper economic functions of several parties within the community."[6] I go on to discuss these social norms and obligations as they relate to taxation. Moving across the perspectives put forward by Brick Town residents, dons themselves, and entrepreneurs, the first part of the chapter discusses shared understandings of who has the authority to tax whom, and what public goods they are expected to provide in return. As I show, while such understandings of "fiscal" obligations may legitimize dons' power to extract payments, dons' transgressions of the attendant norms can engender strong affective responses and directly undermine their authority. In the second half of the chapter, which focuses on how those who are the main source of dons' fiscal revenue feel about such payments, I emphasize the importance of specific material objects, specifically documents such as letters and contracts, in assuaging the *feeling* that what is happening is actually extortion.

TAXATION IN AND BEYOND THE STATE

Classic social and political theory has understood taxes as central to a reciprocal relationship between citizens and the state, in which governments extract wealth from individuals and businesses, and redistribute this wealth toward the public good, for instance by providing national security, constructing transport infrastructure, or regulating healthcare systems.[7] Tax compliance, in this view, indicates citizens' submission to the political and regulatory authority of the state while the state's authority to tax is connected to its efficacy in providing public goods and services.[8]

Tax compliance, tax evasion, and protests following tax hikes all emphasize that fiscal relations involve the negotiation of norms related to the public good: who should contribute to collective goods and how far does the state's authority to collect and redistribute resources toward such goods extend? As anthropologist Soumhya Venkatesan notes, "Attitudes toward tax are indicative of ideas about what 'society' is, what constitutes 'the public good,' and where and to whom one's responsibility lies." She highlights how debates about tax articulate not only political views but also ethical positions: "Even if people agree that some taxation is unavoidable, there exist different views on whether the current tax regime is good or 'fair,' on the gulf between 'is' and 'ought,' and on the ideal balance between affordability and responsibility."[9]

Like authority more generally, the authority to tax relies on a large measure of consent—while fiscal relations are not purely voluntary, they cannot be maintained through coercion alone. But fiscal subjects' consent to be taxed is not monolithic. Whether or not they understand a levy to be legitimate is differentiated across the various types of taxes that exist, from income taxes and property taxes, to general sales taxes and the "sin" tax levied on alcohol, tobacco, or sugar in many contexts.[10] And like other forms of authority, fiscal authority reflects and shapes specific political geographies: it is connected not only to a taxable population, but to a fiscal territory within which taxable activities take place. Although taxation is most frequently associated with the nation-state, it also informs international and subnational political relations.[11]

While discussions of the political, ethical, and spatial implications of taxation have been largely state-centric, fiscal anthropologists, sociologists, and geographers are increasingly beginning to recognize that the collective organization and redistribution of contributions toward the public good are not limited to states.[12] We can identify a variety of quasi-political communities in which membership involves some form of "fiscal" obligation. Churches extract tithes, trade unions require union dues, transport associations charge unofficial fees for access to bus routes, and militarized commercial networks charge tolls and import duties as they regulate cross-border trade.[13]

What makes such transactions "fiscal," rather than either extortion or payments for a service, is that they are broadly recognized as social obligations to a centralized authority that engages in some form of redistribution.[14] While these obligations are often balanced by entitlements (for instance, the right to claim protection or to engage in economic activities within a given territory), what distinguishes them from dyadic relations of direct reciprocity is that the payment of tax reflects and reinforces a broader sociopolitical relationship. It is co-constitutive of the regulatory authority and those fiscal subjects who submit to it.

In many contexts, multiple state and nonstate tax authorities operate simultaneously, governing distinct but oftentimes overlapping fiscal spaces. Taxpayers, in turn, must navigate the multiple fiscal obligations that result from this. None of these tax regimes are uncontested. They involve constant negotiations, as different tax authorities compete and collaborate, and fiscal subjects protest, evade, or comply with their demands. It is in these negotiations that authority is claimed, recognized, and contested: Who has the authority to tax within a specific territory? What rates are acceptable? Who should contribute, which activities should be taxed, and toward what ends should these contributions be directed? Such questions are asked of the contributions that dons demand and, most often, receive. While a broad consensus may exist on some types of fiscal obligations, the constant debate around "taxes" highlights their central role in the negotiation of political authority.

THE AUTHORITY TO TAX

As Ludlow's discussion of market fees indicated, dons had taken over the role of the formal state agency in operating Kingston's Downtown markets.[15] Even as dons had become the de facto tax authority, *who* was collecting fees from market vendors or "higglers" (street vendors) made a big difference to whether such payments were viewed as taxation or as extortion. I spoke to my friend Mikey, a small business owner in Brick Town, about how the community had developed since the imprisonment of the General, and his description of recent developments reflected a clear concern with and condemnation of "free range" extortionists. Mikey had moved to Brick Town from the countryside over a decade earlier, when the General was still in charge. At that time, he told me, things still ran smoothly: "When mi just come, the community did more stronger because you'd have a more stronger leader. But the leadership break down now, so mi would say it get weaker."

Mikey explained that the main difference with now was that things had been more organized before the don went to jail. "'Cause you have a good leadership. You have somebody who you can talk to and will reason out things. We nah fi [don't have to] get violent. Or we wouldn't even haffi go to the police station fi try . . . you get what mi a deal with?" He trailed off, checking if I knew what he was referring to. "So, if there was a problem you could take it to the leader and he would sort it out?" I tried to summarize. "Yeah, and we resolve it the best way we can," he responded, emphasizing that the don's form of conflict resolution was a collective one, supported by the "we" of the community.

The don's departure had been accompanied by an increase in violence, he told me, and also by an economic downturn, as vendors and entrepreneurs from outside the neighborhood had become more hesitant to "try their thing" in the neighborhood's commercial district. "From the leadership not there, communication break down. That a go result inna poor business, don't? You a go [are going to] have less people coming in the community, so less money a go turn round." "Is this because they feel less safe?" I asked. "Yeah," he responded. "Them fear fi all type of things: you try your thing, and people rob you and all type of . . . extortion and all kind of things." Where, previously, the nearby commercial district had attracted vendors from across the island, outsiders had begun to reassess the risks of doing business there, he explained.

I asked Mikey to tell me more about the extortion—had this increased since the General was imprisoned? "Yeah, yeah man. You have more people from all about, everywhere them come from now. Them nuh come from Brick Town. Them nuh come into the community itself, them go like on the outskirts. And [target] who a hustle, like the little higgler them, and tell them 'we come from here so'—and them come from over there and them don't even live in the surroundings!" Checking whether I had understood him correctly, I asked: "You mean they don't live here, but they come to prey on the higglers?" He confirmed that this was the case: "Yeah, yeah. You get what mi a deal with. Yeah, and then them give the community a bad name." I could see how this would be the case: "Because then it seems to those market ladies that basically they are getting preyed on, but it's really total strangers doing it?" "Total strangers," he confirmed. "When the General was here now, them things cyaan gwaan [couldn't happen], 'cause them 'fraid fi even steal." Indeed, two years after we first met, Mikey fled the community after he became embroiled in a violent conflict with his housemates. With the General gone and no strong leader to resolve such a dispute, he went back to the rural parish where his mother still lived, and never returned to Brick Town again.

Clearly, then, there was a strong distinction between the General's collection of fees and the practices of free-range extortionists. Under the General, collection was centralized and the payment of market fees allowed vendors from outside to trade safely within the area—both residents and vendors generally considered this to be a legitimate practice associated with his governance role. Outsiders preying on market vendors, in contrast, were extortionists. From this view, removing a strong don does not end extortion. Rather, the lack of a strong central authority encourages the proliferation of extortionists. This logic was also clear in the wake of Dudus's arrest and extradition, as SSP Steve McGregor from the JCF confirmed in 2014: "When it was under the reign of 'Dudus' . . . all of it used to go through him. [Now] everybody wants to collect by themselves."[16]

This general acceptance of a don's right to tax—indeed, his *authority* to tax—did not mean there was no resentment of the way dons such as the General imposed their taxes. Specifically, residents are quick to assess the fairness of the rates that dons charge different economic actors. Overly high rates suggest that the don is not looking out for little people, and that he is motivated by greed. My friend Keith, a long-time West Kingston resident in his late fifties, saw the General's income tax—which he claimed had been 25–50 percent—as excessive, especially given the don's other sources of income. To him, taxing little people rather than focusing on the "big boys"—official contractors—was unfair:

> The General, Dudus, the whole of them, when the [government] contract is issued out, it's always the dons. You know don will get the contract and him get a lump sum of money. But you have the man who works . . . when you get your little pay you still have to give the don money outta your pay, and mi nuh like that neither, 'cause them done get money already from the contract. So them shouldn't even take money from the man who works 'pon it. . . . I think them

shouldn't take nothing from the man who them give the work to work. Just keep on taxing them big boys who do the big work 'cause them can afford it, 'cause eventually them will make back all of them money there.

Keith's disapproval of how the General had implemented his fiscal system did not imply a fundamental denunciation of the don's authority to tax. Rather, his criticism sounds very similar to a demand for progressive taxation, in which it is acceptable to "keep on taxing them big boys."

His critique did point to how a reputation of greed can undermine a don's authority, echoing Ludlow's condemnation of the General. Their accusations of greed also resonated with sentiments expressed by John, whom I first met while he was living in a small room in a Brick Town yard, but who continued to return to the neighborhood frequently for social visits even after he was able to take over a house from his father in another Downtown neighborhood. John described how his opinion of the General had changed over time, telling me: "Well, he is a man who, one time, mi did look up to him. But after a while, mi realize him nuh know weh him a do. Him make greed motivate him instead of people, so him nuh fi mi leader." The don didn't know what he was doing—with greed as his motivation rather than people, John stopped recognizing him as his leader. On occasion, other Brick Town residents quietly shared similar concerns with me, underlining the extent to which a don's taxation regime is always bounded by a clear moral economy. Such discussions of greed underline broadly shared norms of when taxation rates are acceptable and when they become illegitimate.

Still, in many conversations with inner-city residents, I found an acceptance of dons' taxes as a standard governance practice. Like formal state taxes, there is an upper limit to the obligations that taxpayers will accept, and rates considered to be unreasonably high can delegitimize the broader sociopolitical relationship between ruler and ruled. Excessive demands and a reputation of greed will eventually directly undermine a leader's authority, but, by and large, I encountered few residents who actively contested a don's authority to tax as such. Most of those who discussed these payments with me did not speak of them as unjust. Rather, they referred to them in a matter-of-fact way, accepting them as part of life. Still, such discussions of dons' tax regimes entailed staking out political and ethical positions that delineated where fiscal authority began and ended, and why. In indicating where the border between "extortion" and "taxation" lay, residents such as Mikey, Keith, and John reflected on when a commitment to the public good was superseded by greed. They proposed normative differentiations in fiscal obligations by which outsiders and wealthier entrepreneurs should be taxed more; a don "pressuring" low-income residents who were "born and grow" in the community risked being seen as an extortionist. And most clearly, only the don, or those acting directly on his orders, had the authority to tax: all others were rogue tax collectors—extortionists. Even if the money that a don collects may also end up being his personal income, many residents conveyed a sense that these taxes were somehow reinvested in "public goods"—specifically protection but also welfare—within the space of the don's territory.

GIVING BACK TO THE COMMUNITY

Unsurprisingly, dons themselves are also committed to such extortion-as-taxation interpretations. Second, formerly part of the Brick Town leadership, explained to me how the system worked from the perspective of those in charge. He described how men from the area, having soured on "politricks," had turned to what he described as hustling. "When you say hustling, is that what other people would call extortion?" I pressed him to explain. "Yeah, yeah, typically that," he allowed. "Or some people call it taxes?" I suggested. "Yeah, taxes. Yeah, yeah, typically that." Rather than relying on politicians for their income, then, men had turned to hustling. "Some will probably find other ways, but you would call it extortion still. Any way to make money. They might extortion the bus people them, the market, or the business place. So a man says he's responsible for this . . . You understand me? That's where they get their little . . . that nobody breaks into it, and nobody come thief their things." "So when businesspeople pay . . ." I prompted him. "Yes, they are safe too," he replied. "Because is so it set"—that's how the system works. "When you a leader, you know the businesspeople look up to you, any problem they have they come to you."

Here, Second conceded that the system could be recognized as extortion although businesspeople could count on the don's protection in exchange for paying up. Later on in our conversation, though, he described the in-kind contributions that businesses would make, and here he was adamant that this was not a transaction, but a desire to do good. He had been telling me about the expectations of material support that low-income residents would have: "Typically, garrison people have them little daughter, and they have their little thing, and probably sometimes they can come to you with them needs. And you can help them buy some khaki [school uniforms], send them pickney [children] to school."

This type of material support would often be distributed during organized events known as "treats." Back-to-school treats are common annual events, when children receive school bags and notebooks, but holidays are also key occasions for the leadership to distribute food and gifts, for instance the traditional sweet bread "bun" and cheese at Easter treats. Second emphasized the importance of the back-to-school treats: "Book, bags and everything. They [dons and their men] provide the things the government doesn't do, they provide those things through the businesspeople in the area. They go to the businesspeople and, like, they sell book and bag, they will give like three boxes of bags, three boxes of books. Every store gives . . . Then you pile them up, then keep a treat and hand them out." According to Second, the businesspeople made these contributions voluntarily. He was very clear that this was different from extortion: "That is a part of the businesspeople giving back something to the community."

In addition to the regular organization of treats, dons' welfare regimes generally also include free or subsidized access to electricity, water, and housing for residents. They will mobilize, violently if need be, against utility companies seeking to lock off irregular connections to the electricity or water networks. Faced with seemingly intractable rates of electricity theft, the public-private utility company, Jamaica Public Service Company Limited (JPS), has sought to recoup its losses by charging its bill-paying customers—in practice, mostly middle-class Jamaicans—a "loss recovery" fee. We might understand another form of progressive taxation at work here, where wealthier Uptown Kingstonians inadvertently subsidize free utilities for their poorer counterparts. But access to this "freeness" sometimes involves sacrificing political freedom. Second acknowledged this, explaining that residents who were dissatisfied with a don's rule would be hesitant to complain as they could not afford to live in a neighborhood where they would have to pay for housing and utilities: "Most people don't have anywhere else to live . . . they have free light, free water, free everything." In contrast, in the quieter suburb where he had moved, a neighborhood he described as a "residential area" rather than a "garrison," people were more independent: "Over here now, people go to work, people independent. They don't have to rely on nobody, they do their own thing. You pay your bills, you can't beat them [avoid paying]. Over here you have to pay everything. Nothing free. That change me, yeah. Because things you're used to, the free mentality over there . . ." Echoing middle-class criticism of a "freeness mentality" amongst poor Jamaicans, Second told me that moving away from dependency into a self-sufficient, bill-paying life meant achieving a more mature type of masculinity and morality: "It kind of teach me more manhood, reality, face up to life, you have to stand up for your own. If you don't do it nobody will do it. If you want to live good, with respect and principle, you have to keep up to your manhood. You have to do what you have to do." He sounded more sorry for those stuck in a state of dependency than he appeared to condemn them for it, but it was clear that he had come to appreciate having the capacity to pay bills as an important component in "living good."

Although he had moved away from Downtown Kingston, Second continued to help organize treats. Now, he cooperated with the area's Citizens Association and its Councillor. He had no desire to be part of the Citizens Association leadership, but he was happy to help them get donations. "I never want to be in them kind of things. I've been to it still, but I won't be a part of it. I will get sponsors for them. Mi know people. Like treats now, it's me keep treat for the kids them. Mi know people, when mi go around they will give me stuff from same way Downtown. Mi know the same store people them, who respect me and will still give me things." So was this the same stores, from when he still lived in Brick Town, that sent things out for a treat in the suburbs, I asked him, surprised that he could still solicit donations after having left the area so long ago. "Yeah, because they know me. As mi tell you, them look up to me. Me and them is from way back, man. And them principled, them respect me, so I will go to them and say 'Yo! Ray ray . . .' [blah blah blah] and they will assist. Typically you have people, more time, who want to give back to the community, you know. Them want to give back. But if they don't have confidence in somebody who they know will distribute what they're giving—they won't do it." For Second, there was a clear distinction between two types of relationships between dons and businesspeople. Extortion involved an extractive or possibly transactional relationship, in which payments ensured protection. "Giving back to the community," in contrast, involved contributions to the common good made on the basis of confidence that they would be distributed to the needy—a morally informed type of fiscal obligation that functioned only in a context of trustworthy leadership.

PUTTING IN YOUR HAND

Another don I spoke to also framed such contributions as a combination of reciprocity and redistribution, drawing an analogy with the Jamaican system known as *pardna*, a rotating savings and credit association that functions as what economic anthropologist Bill Maurer calls "poor people's finance."[17] Through his direct reference to this socially embedded form of banking, this don, "Toppa," positioned himself as someone who helped resources circulate toward the public good in a horizontal, trust-based fashion. Toppa was the leader of "Hill Courts," a Kingston neighborhood where I spent a summer conducting a pilot study two years before I started working in Brick Town (during the early phases of my research on donmanship). A research assistant who lived in the neighborhood, "Ronnie," helped me find residents willing to be interviewed. Unlike Brick Town, Hill Courts did not have a very powerful leader, perhaps because it was a relatively small housing scheme and its location within Kingston held less economic and political significance. Toppa, the neighborhood don, was often in North America, and many of the residents I spoke to did not seem to recognize him as a major authority figure.

Toward the start of the summer, Ronnie arranged for me to interview Toppa and his two seconds-in-command, "Tony" and "Kevin." I wasn't sure how Ronnie had described me to them, presumably as a foreign researcher who wanted to know more about dons, but it was clear that the three men saw the interview as something of an event and had prepared for the occasion. As Ronnie and I entered the apartment where we were to meet them, the men sat waiting in a dark room filled with ganja smoke, masking their faces with matching bandanas and sunglasses. At this point, I had spoken to a few other dons and seconds-in-command, none of whom had sought to disguise their appearance. Following these previous experiences, this encounter in Hill Courts felt a bit performative, as if the three men were playing the role of "gangsters" for a foreign visitor, perhaps inspired by crime documentaries in which gang members speak to the camera with their face concealed.

The bandanas also made it hard for the men to speak, and initially resulted in somewhat muffled exchanges. Later on, they let their bandanas slip, to speak more easily and to smoke as they explained their role in the neighborhood. Like Second, they emphasized that this role involved organizing treats for the community and especially children's treats. Indeed, Toppa told me, they were organizing an event that same week to raise funds in support of a local church group: "We have to hold all kind of treats and fundraisers. If you come here 'bout 6 o'clock, they have the church right here [in the open air], no tent, no nothing. Just people sitting outside right there, and service and those things. And whatever you can do is just put back, just like that. 'Cause the people for the people, always." I asked him whether his system functioned like a government with different ministries, including a Ministry of Security but also a Ministry of Welfare, where people could apply when they were in need of financial support. He responded enthusiastically to this idea. "Yeah, we have a private ministry said way [in the way that you describe], man. Yeah man, we have a private ministry, man. And that's why we say, like, it always goes back to: as much as you put in, is as much as you always gonna get back when it's your time."

Explaining what he meant by this, Toppa shifted away from the ministerial metaphor to reference another, more horizontal model of economic distribution, that of pardna, Jamaica's long-standing form of rotating savings and credit association (ROSCA). A ROSCA is a type of savings club, commonly defined as "an association formed upon a core of participants who agree to make regular contributions to a fund which is given, in whole or in part, to each contributor in rotation."[18] Members of a pardna group "throw in their hand" at set times, making regular financial deposits into a shared fund. These contributions give them the right to make a relatively large withdrawal or "draw" in the future. In Toppa's words: as much as you put in is what you get back when it's your time. For Toppa, investing in the community ensured that he would be able to "draw" his share in due course.

"Would you say your system connects to the formal system of government, or is it completely separate?" I asked. "It doesn't connect unless they're putting in their share," Toppa explained, extending the analogy further, "and hiring our people when it's time for hiring." The government's contribution to the collective fund, in this view, was mostly through providing jobs for residents. Only after they had put in their "share" in this fashion could they expect to get something back from the community. "Until that time, it's completely different. It's just the people by the people, you haffi understand that part. From they're not putting in their hand and their contributions . . ." he trailed off, seeming to suggest that the political leaders would not be able to claim their share of the pot—the votes—if they did not put in their hand.

I checked that I understood him properly: "Like in pardna, your turn may come around, but if you've been skipping out on your contributions, you can't draw?" "Exactly!" he responded. "And the big MP supposed to know that too, we're due for our pardna draw." "Straight, straight!" Tony and Kevin agreed emphatically. They had put the prime minister in power, Toppa explained, "in the hopes of getting our pardna draw." The JLP, the party they were aligned with, had recently won the elections, and accordingly, as JLP supporters, it was high time for them to get their draw.

By narrating their fundraising activities through the lens of pardna rather than taxes per se, and by extending this metaphor to include political leaders, Toppa and his men reframed what many might read as extortion and clientelism as a long-standing system of mutual support developed to ensure a fair circulation of resources. Anthropologist Trevor Purcell describes pardna as based on "a dual rationality of material gain and cultural solidarity," emphasizing that it is "rooted in pre-established communal/reciprocal relationships," but that the process of participation then also works to reinforce and enhance these social networks.[19] Interpreting his financial and political activities through the logic of pardna allowed a don like Toppa to justify any personal material gain, while positioning himself in a preestablished, horizontal relationship of solidarity and reciprocity with his fellow residents: "the people for the people."

FEELING EXTORTED

As a foreign researcher, I was not an obvious candidate for membership in such pardna-like relations, but this did not mean that my own business was entirely outside of the scope of fiscal demands. As we concluded the interview and I began to pack up my things to leave, the three men asked me whether I could make a donation to the community fundraiser that they were organizing later that week.

It wasn't fully clear to me whether the funds would actually go to that event, but the payment felt logical. It seemed no more than fair for them to ask me for a contribution, whether understood as a tax they could exact as community leaders, a "draw" based on my interest in engaging with the community further, or just direct reciprocity in return for their agreeing to be interviewed. I found some bills and told them I'd be glad to contribute.

Perhaps at the time all of us thought this would be the only exchange. As I returned to the neighborhood over the next weeks to interview other residents, I would run into Tony, who was not hard to recognize despite his disguise during our initial encounter. He began to pressure me for money, both directly and by asking Ronnie to convey the message to me. These requests came without any reference to charitable events, and also came directly from Tony, with no mention of Toppa. The amount of money he was demanding was not dissimilar from requests for support I frequently received and honored from residents. Yet giving Tony money did not feel like voluntary support, given the hint of menace in the tone of the requests. Nor did they feel like a quasi-obligation toward the community leadership, as when Toppa asked me to donate to the children's treat. Although my sensitization toward the exact norms of economic obligation was certainly imperfect, these exchanges *felt* like extortion, where others did not.

While my own small-scale experiences should not be taken as representative, they helped me understand the narratives of consent that were mobilized by both dons and businesspeople as more than self-serving or cynical frameworks—these narratives are part of meaningful performances that have affective impact. The difference between extortion and taxes (or "charitable contributions") is not clear-cut to start with, and depends on multiple factors, ranging from who is asking whom for how much, with what stated purposes, and with what level of implicit or explicit threat. But this difference is also an affective distinction—where one payment feels fair, another may feel illicit.

COMMUNITY DEVELOPMENT AND CONTRACTUAL RELATIONS

How, then, do other outsiders and wealthier entrepreneurs who are the core target of dons' fiscal regime feel about such payments? Perhaps the most common form of "taxation" is the classic "protection racket," where commercial properties, the Chinese- and Syrian-owned stores that Ludlow spoke of, pay a weekly rate to dons for security. Here, in many cases, pragmatic considerations may be at work, in that the cost of paying dons may be less than hiring private security. Ludlow himself suggested that the rates were not unreasonable given the risks such businesses faced: "Them place broke [into] every minute and thing, and burn down and all them things." For them, the payment of US$50 or 100 would be quite affordable; they would reason "A little five thousand [Jamaican dollars], or a little ten thousand a week, a nuh nothing fi [that's nothing to] have my business," Ludlow told me.

I interviewed Andrew, an entrepreneur of Syrian descent in charge of one of Downtown's larger stores, hoping to get an insider view on this type of security arrangement. Sitting with me in his air-conditioned office inside the store, Andrew spent the entire interview denying that he had ever paid any extortion fee, stating that "I would call the police immediately and report it." I asked him whether he knew of any colleagues who had entered such arrangements and he denied this as well: "To be honest with you, I don't. You can have your suspicions, but I don't think they would ever admit it. It's something you don't admit. It's something I would assume." He had internal security, he told me, and an extensive electronic security system with cameras. As I turned off the voice recorder after 45 minutes, feeling slightly frustrated at my inability to get him to open up, he leaned back and chuckled. "Do you ever go to Red Bones?" he asked me, referring to a popular Uptown restaurant and bar. "If you ran into me there . . . ah, the stories I could tell you over rum!"

Despite the difficulty of getting wealthier businessmen to discuss extortion openly—I never did run into Andrew at Red Bones—other accounts suggest that people running shops in the Downtown area often frame their payments to local strongmen as satisfying a security need they would have anyway. Hiring private security guards to protect their properties, some of them argue, would cost more. And if it is known that your business is protected by the don's men, you can be certain that no one will try to mess with you. Such an arrangement, in these accounts, is more effective and cheaper than relying on commercial private security. The question is, of course, what would happen if you tried to get out of this arrangement—opting out definitely comes with the threat of burglaries, robberies, and serious harm to the business or its owner.[20] Yet discussions of these arrangements suggested that many of those paying were less concerned with violence meted out by the "protectors" themselves, and genuinely felt they were getting protection from actually existing security threats separate from the dons and their men.

CORPORATE SOCIAL RESPONSIBILITY

In addition to retail businesses, dons also tax construction companies and contractors. In an interview with a former CEO of a major construction company, I learned more about these arrangements. In addition to pressure for cash payments, another way in which contractors are extorted is through pressure to provide jobs for laborers put forward by the don. In line with the moral economy outlined by residents and dons, "Norman," the retired CEO, described both types of contributions as entailing a form of corporate social responsibility—an obligation that was no more than appropriate for a major company working in impoverished areas.

Describing the labor arrangements his company had developed with dons, Norman told me that these had come to replace a long-standing agreement that major construction companies had had in earlier decades with the politically affiliated trade unions. If the JLP was in power, their trade union BITU would get 60 percent of the jobs on a given contract, and the opposition party's trade union, the PNP-affiliated NWU, would get 40 percent, ensuring a type of balance. Norman described this system as functioning to all parties' satisfaction from the late 1950s, well before he came to lead the company, until into the 1970s. Working with the unions, he explained, also helped contractors resist pressure from politicians to find jobs for their supporters: "It was very well known that if a JLP or a PNP person wanted to get somebody employed, go and talk to the union. And they would put him on the company payroll, because whenever we needed work, we produced a monthly list—transparency is always something that works—and handed it to both unions and said: 'This is what is BITU representation and this is what is NWU representation.'" Whenever workers left, Norman told me, they would be replaced by others affiliated with the same union and the same political party. The first time he ran into "real trouble," he continued, was in the mid-1970s. At that time, his company was building an urban development in St. Catherine, in an area run by a don I call "Bigga" and populated by JLP supporters who had resettled there after having been forcibly removed from a PNP garrison in Kingston. Norman recalled his first visit to the area, accompanied by the MP, who was a JLP Minister at that time:

> The MP said: "Listen, if you're going into the area then you have to deal with Bigga or else you won't get anywhere." I said, "Minister, with all due respect, we only work with the two unions." We had an argument, we had a discussion, and he said, "Okay, but understand: you take your own risk." And I went into that community. And I met with Bigga, I sent for him and I met with him, and I said, "I understand you're the big man here," and so on and so forth. "I want you to understand that I'm not going to pay protection. What I'm prepared to do, however, is to tell you that I will allocate a certain amount of money to the community and develop the community." And I said to Bigga, "Look, it depends on how profitable my project is and so on, but I'm willing to put—I don't know what the number was, a half a million dollars, based on, you know, $5,000 or $10,000 a week, and this was back in the '80s—into the community. And I am prepared for you to be the person to distribute that money in the community.

You can tell me who needs what in the community and what we will do is jointly look after the destitute in the community, you and I." And we became friends.

Norman accepted the new situation quickly, but sought to frame his relationship with the don in other terms than that of a protection racket. He sought to preempt demands for protection money by proposing a type of corporate social responsibility, though tax-like in that the funds allocated toward community development would be dependent on how profitable the construction project was. In the context of this arrangement, then, Norman's company would contribute to "developing the community" and looking after its most destitute members while the don, as "the big man here," would be the one to ensure that these corporate funds were allocated judiciously. Norman also placed Bigga on his payroll, "at a rate higher than his skill level, but he provided me a community link." He gave an example of how well this system would work: Bigga would indicate which resident suffered from a leaky roof, the company would provide zinc sheets, and the don would get another resident to nail them onto the roof.

"Now, I didn't make him an angel," Norman allowed, describing how Bigga still sought to extort other contractors, "I hear that [the utility company] JPS paid him a thousand dollars a pole to provide the security to put in the light poles.... If JPS had come to me, they wouldn't have paid him a thousand dollars a pole." Curious, I asked Norman whether the rate would have gone down with his mediation, or whether Bigga would have permitted JPS to work in his community without paying any sort of fee. "Gone down," he conceded, "But, but: I would have encouraged them to go the same route." JPS, too, he felt, would have been better off in the long run developing a relationship of community development rather than paying protection money.[21]

Notwithstanding, the security dimension of this relationship was of critical importance to the construction company: "I never lost a bag of cement in that area. Because of the insecurity of the people who lived in there, there was a ring of M-16s that used to protect the community, in case the PNP came in there to raid the community at night. And all they did was spread that ring to the outside of my project, I never paid a dollar for it." Interpreting his relationship with the don and his community as one of corporate citizenship meant that, indeed, Norman did not pay a dollar for security. Rather, as he explained it, he made a voluntary contribution of perhaps half a million Jamaican dollars toward community development, and in return, the local gunmen happily extended their existing guarding activities to his construction project.

"Okay," I tried to summarize, "so in the end, it ended up being a security investment, but you were able to . . ." He interrupted me: "But I never paid extortion, right?" "You were able to frame it differently," I suggested. Norman defended his arrangement: "You can call it extortion if you want. But whichever community I have ever been into, we develop the community, or work with the community, and work with the badmen in the community."

Norman went on to explain how in his next project, a few years later, now under a PNP government, he had emphasized the employment and skills development aspect of his engagement. Specifically, he sought to subcontract work that did not require specialist training, such as the construction of curb walls. This subcontracting would allow him to put dons and their men on the payroll, both to engage them in the actual construction business, and to minimize security risks such as a site getting shut down because of theft or violence. This strategic allocation of contracts and employment was widespread, he explained: "What a number of contractors usually do, is to select a don in the area and pay him to provide them with security by giving him some contract. You would give the curb wall, or the grading, or whatever it might be, to a particular subcontractor who is a don of sorts, who would employ thirty or forty people. And he would get paid by the foot or by the square yard or by the whatever. And the presence of his men would ensure that the project never got shut down." He emphasized that you had to be a skilled negotiator to settle on a good price, but also that some of the dons who had started out as curb wall subcontractors had gone on to run major construction companies of their own, winning large contracts from government agencies and successfully completing major development projects.

To some extent, Norman's discussion of his negotiation with dons over contributions in terms of cash, contracts, and jobs struck me as another performance of consent, of enacting what looked a lot like extortion as community development and subcontracting, as building capacity and fostering entrepreneurship. While recognizing that this did not turn dons into "angels," his narrative highlighted dons' governance and entrepreneurial roles, and justified his own transactions as a contribution to the public good that made business sense as well. Emphasizing the contractual nature of these transactions—transforming the don into a subcontractor, with the contract functioning as a material artifact of legality—worked to frame these transactions as legitimate corporate activities.

On another level, Norman's account underlined how dons had come to play a key role in organizing labor, suggesting that his company's previous agreement with the unions had been replaced by a new type of deal. Unions had been powerful labor negotiators both because they could shut down a site and because of their political connections, which tied directly to the clientelist arrangements through which the two political parties controlled the urban poor. Now, dons had become the ones who acted as the main labor organizers, liaising with both corporate

Jamaica and government agencies to ensure that jobs flowed toward their constituents.[22] Their role as employment brokers, and in various cases independent contractors, certainly bolstered their authority as political and economic leaders.

DOCUMENTING CONTRIBUTIONS TO THE PUBLIC GOOD

In other economic sectors, such as the entertainment industry, similar negotiations can be recognized, where entrepreneurs seek to understand their transactions with dons as contributions to the public good, as charitable acts that may additionally make good business sense. During the hearings held by the West Kingston Commission of Enquiry from 2014–2016 as part of a public enquiry into the Tivoli Incursion, Deputy Commissioner of Police (DCP) Glenmore Hinds described the transactions behind Champions in Action, an annual event organized by Dudus's company, Presidential Click. Held at the end of every summer at JamWorld, an entertainment venue in Portmore that could host up to thirty thousand patrons, Champions in Action was one of Jamaica's most famous "stage shows," live concerts with line-ups featuring dozens of reggae and dancehall artists.[23] Referring to police intelligence, Hinds stated that this charitable event, which he described as "done to provide support to children to go back to school," was funded by pressuring reggae artists and companies to make significant cash and in-kind contributions. In his testimony to the Commission of Enquiry, he stressed that this coercion affected the most powerful artists and companies: "It's a stage show, and [at] that stage show, major reggae artists would have to give their service free of charge. Major corporate companies would have to donate products to support the activity. The title sponsor was one of the major corporate companies in Jamaica, I will not call their name but that was the title sponsor. Our intelligence suggests that these persons were coerced to give their services pro bono."[24] Almost immediately, Hinds' depiction of what occurred was contested. High-profile artists swiftly denied having felt any form of pressure. Yes, they had performed for free, but this was a form of charity. Speaking to a reggae radio station, Mr. Vegas, a bestselling dancehall artist who had performed at Champions in Action on multiple occasions, stated that his participation was a voluntary act that centered around "showing love to the people from the ghetto" and that on those occasions that he had declined to perform, there had been no negative consequences:

> It was always a situation where if I'm not busy, or if I'm not booked for another show, and if I was here in Jamaica, I would have offered my service. 'Cause you know, it's an event where artists came together and basically, you know, just showed love to the people, you know, from the ghetto, that turned out in

numbers. I remember you know the first year that I came out, I had like five, six songs at the same time, you know, in the charts. And then they reached out to me and I was not able to do it, and it was no big deal. You know I did it *when* I had the time and when I was available.... I was not forced to be on that concert at no time in my career.[25]

In his rejection of the suggestion of pressure, Mr. Vegas inserted something of a disclaimer, stating that he was speaking on the basis of his own experiences and did not know whether other artists were forced to be part of something they didn't want to be part of. Meanwhile, others rejected the allegations even more forcefully. Queen Ifrica, who was one of the main female headline acts the last time the show was held, in 2009, issued a vehement retort: "Well, I work on Champions in Action from, couple times I think, and every time I was approached, it was always respectful! There was always a letter of appreciation when you finish working, and also money. I was never coerced into performing, never! It is always ultimate respect and honor mi get whenever mi turn up inna that community [Tivoli Gardens] and I cannot tell a lie."[26] The emphasis she placed on the letter of appreciation, and on the material tokens of respect accompanying it, were echoed in a lengthier refutation made by Julian Jones-Griffith, a leading dancehall artist manager, on his blog. Like Queen Ifrica and Mr. Vegas, he began by asserting that there had been no coercion and that the charitable cause and high turnout were the main motivations for his dancehall acts to participate in Champions in Action and the West Kingston Jamboree (another stage show similarly organized by Presidential Click): "I had the privilege of managing some of Jamaica's hottest acts ... there was never any pressure from Dudus or his cohorts. If we weren't on tour we made ourselves available to be a part of either event as they were for a good cause and always well-attended."[27] He similarly underlined the altruistic nature of back-to-school treats connected to these stage shows, which he argued extended far beyond the political boundaries of Tivoli Gardens: "Thousands of kids from PNP and JLP enclaves were given schoolbags stuffed with supplies and enjoyed the day's activities of bounce-a-bouts, clownies, sweet treats, and the like. So even if artists performed for free or a reduced fee, it was a charitable act—giving back to the community ... who needs coercing to do that?"[28]

Like Mr. Vegas, Jones-Griffith does not outright deny the possibility of dons coercing artists. He describes a case involving a different don, where "a very high-profile artist" did not show up to perform at an event organized by that don. Not long after, the manager alleged, two men on a motorcycle rode up to the artist and slapped him hard across the face in retaliation, an act aimed not so much at inflicting physical harm as public humiliation—and an act we can read as an assertion of authority.[29]

Jones-Griffith's main interest in his blog is to establish that the artists he managed were not subject to any pressure and that Dudus did not engage in coercive practices. In support of his claim, he posted two scanned letters of thanks, on his blog and on Twitter, that Dudus had sent to express his gratitude to participating artists. One of these documents, sent to international dancehall star Bounty Killer following the 2006 staging of Champions in Action (figure 5.1), read: "This show is held to raise funds for a back to school treat for youths in and around the West Kingston inner city communities. With the support from your many fans we wish to say thanks for your participation. We are therefore using this medium to express our sincere gratitude and hope, that you will accept this contribution of cash towards your expense prior to the show, as it is our policy to honor our financial obligations. Thanks for a splendid show, your presence made a great difference." Jones-Griffith stated that he had received many similar letters from Dudus and saved them—in the case of the Bounty Killer letter, for nearly a decade—because it was so rare for event promoters to write such letters of appreciation. Beyond written expressions of gratitude, he described artists receiving gifts from Dudus at Christmas, specifically bottles of Hennessy cognac. Having kept the letters as mementos, Jones-Griffith now proffered them as evidence of voluntary participation, arguing that "The content and tone of these letters both prove that money was paid for performing at Champions in Action and disprove all notion that there was coercion to perform."[30] Like Queen Ifrica, he pointed to the existence of a formal letter and a cash contribution toward covering expenses as a material refutation of any allegations of extortion.

I have no way of knowing whether DCP Hinds' intelligence was correct or incorrect, whether artists were subject to any form of coercion or only received "ultimate respect and honor," as Queen Ifrica phrased it. Indeed, the country's most powerful don may not have needed to mobilize any threats of violence, overt or otherwise, to make his requests for charitable donations feel compelling. What interests me in the responses to the allegations of coercion outlined above is, first, that none of those involved seek to distance themselves from Dudus, even years after his conviction and imprisonment. Rather, their main concern is to deny that they were pressured: they seek to publicly narrate their relationship with the don and the transactions involved as voluntary acts, aimed at benefitting children in need and showing love to "the people from the ghetto." The fact that their in-kind contributions—the gift of their labor and the harnessing of their reputation to Dudus's entertainment enterprises—would also have directly bolstered the don's own leadership position is left unstated. Indeed, their responses emphasize the legitimacy of his actions in support of the public good. While none of those involved used the word "taxes," a similar logic and moral economy are at work when their

Presidential Click Productions
1 Seaga Blvd.
Kingston 14.

August 23, 2006

From : Mr. Michael Coke
Re : Performance at Champions in Action 2006

Dear......... Bounty Killa....

This show is held to raise funds for a back to school treat for youths in and around the West Kingston inner city communities. With the support from your many fans we wish to say thanks for your participation. We are therefore using this medium to express our sincere gratitude and hope, that you will accept this contribution of cash towards your expense prior to the show, as it is our policy to honor our financial obligations.

Thanks for a splendid show, your presence made a great difference.

Yours respectfully,

....
Michael Coke (President)

5.1 Letter of gratitude from Dudus to Bounty Killer. Source: https://julianjonesgriffith.files.wordpress.com/2015/05/champions.jpeg.

donations to or through the don's organization are narrated as "contributions to the community" and "for a good cause."

As with other interlocutors' consistent narration of transactions initiated by dons as other-than-extortion, I read the insistence by high-profile players within Jamaica's music industry that their engagements with Dudus were consensual as a key component in enacting the don's authority. What also strikes me about their responses is how such performances of consent mobilize material artifacts: the gift of liquor or a cash gesture toward covering expenses, but more significantly the letter of appreciation. Anthropologists studying documents have emphasized the material politics of bureaucratic paperwork, approaching documents not primarily as texts or representations, but as artifacts, as material mediators.[31] In addition to studying the aesthetic forms of specific genres of documents, they have pointed to the affective, sensorial impacts that documents can have, as material objects, on those who produce them, treasure them, and proffer them as evidence. Yael Navaro, for instance, highlights how documents are frequently "charged with affect," eliciting responses from fear to confidence to cynicism. She urges us to explore "the multiple and contingent affects that documents engender in their holders and transactors."[32]

Dudus himself maintained a general system of documentation. During the Tivoli Incursion, the security forces raided his offices in the neighborhood and seized a large number of documents, enumerated in an eighteen-page Appendix of the Commission of Enquiry's report.[33] Amongst the files, they found various budgets, invoices, receipts, and contracts, many related to Champions in Action. In addition, they came across various lists of names and addresses: of residents of Tivoli Gardens, of unemployed persons in nearby neighborhoods, and of the entire electoral constituency Kingston Western. Such recordkeeping suggests the existence of a bureaucracy aimed at managing a territory and its population, a form of archiving identified in contexts beyond Jamaica amongst criminal organizations and other nonstate governmental actors.[34]

Scholarship on documents highlights their work in processes of state formation, in helping to produce the effect of a boundary between state and society. Similarly, in the examples of dons' use of documentation, paperwork can produce an authoritative boundary between leadership and community, and between extortion and taxation. Just as the contract between the construction company and the don creates a business relationship between them, the letter of appreciation helps enact the relationship between don and artist as one of like-minded benefactors, with a shared commitment to the public good, specifically within the space of "the ghetto."

In the case of Dudus's letters of appreciation, Jones-Griffith stresses the "content and tone" as proof of a lack of coercion. However, their material form also plays a role in making a transaction feel legal and legitimate. The letter to Bounty Killer is a printed form letter with a dotted line to insert an artist's name, printed on Presidential Click Productions letterhead and signed, on another dotted line, by "Michael Coke (President)," using both part of Dudus's government name and his honorific alias. Part of a quasi-bureaucratic genre of papers known as "letters of appreciation," these documents lend an air of formality to artists' in-kind contributions to a don's organization. The recipients of these papers, like Jones-Griffith, may treasure them and present them as evidence that their transactions with the don were voluntary and respectful. In short, these letters are not ephemera—they are part of the material infrastructure of authorization.

PARKING FEES

Beyond such longer-term relationships between businesspeople and dons, other outsiders to Downtown Kingston who find themselves subject to dons' tax regimes may mobilize analogous forms of legitimization. Where I found few businesspeople eager to share their experiences with taxation beyond the state, a more widespread and freely discussed source of dons' income is found in relation to parking. In Downtown Kingston's crowded central commercial districts, parking space is extremely scarce. While some office workers may have access to their employer's private parking lot, other Uptown visitors spend considerable time driving around looking for a spot to leave their often costly vehicles that is both safe and no more than a brief walk from their destination. There are various guarded car parks, some run by private operators, others by the Urban Development Corporation (UDC), a state agency. For both types of parking lots, uniformed guards issue tickets and charge hourly rates.

Another option, when such lots are full, is to park on the street or in empty lots. These "free" parking spaces, however, are not necessarily free. Especially near major markets, drivers seeking to park in an empty spot will soon be assisted. One or more, usually young, men provide guidance on where to "back up, back up, wheel it up" to slot in as many cars as possible. This assistance is generally followed up by a request for money to "watch" the car. In other cases, these men will mark their curbside spots with large stones, making it impossible to utilize the parking space without their assistance. More generally, they will wait until the driver is ready to leave, posting themselves in front of the car until they are remunerated for their guarding services. These requests for money involve a mild threat that the car or its owner might not be safe from the informal guards themselves. Notwithstanding, Uptown parkers with whom I discussed the practice often emphasized that the guards' presence does offer welcome protection from actually existing security threats, from car thieves to homeless persons looking for food, and noted that their rates were not unreasonable. They also argued that accepting this system was ultimately more convenient than wasting time looking for an "official" parking space in the crowded business district.

Newspaper reports and police officers tend to describe this guarding practice as extortion, suggesting that this is the work of individual "hustlers."[35] Indeed, the young men who engage in this type of income generation may be working as freelancers—this form of hustling does not elicit the same opprobrium as the freelance extortionists who pressure market vendors to pay up. Yet in other cases, the regulation of parking may be a much more institutionalized, collective arrangement: rather than "extortion," the payment for protection becomes a don-based "parking fee" that vehicle owners accept as a normal state of affairs. Such arrangements have developed not only in the Downtown business district, but also around the US embassy, where parking space is similarly at a premium. Across from the embassy, parkers from the nearby Uptown ghetto Standpipe describe their "business" as monitored by a "supervisor." In this case, an officer from the nearby police station had only compliments for the orderly fashion in which the "helpers" went about their business, telling a journalist from the *Gleaner* newspaper: "You know, the way these people park the vehicles, they park it so neatly that it appears as if it is the occupants of the premises that park the vehicle."[36]

My friend Keith described to me the level of organization behind the unofficial administration of public parking space. Parking attendants would issue time-stamped parking tickets to drivers, and on their return collect parking fees at an hourly rate that was similar to that of the state-run and commercial parking lots. They would be expected to show their ticket books to the don at the end of their shift, who would then calculate the sum of money he expected to receive based on this administration. The ticket, and the associated calculation of the total parking fee based on an hourly rate, imbue the formally illegal collection of parking fees with a bureaucratic feel, providing drivers with a tangible sense of parking normalcy. In addition to helping dons monitor the amount of money collected by their parking guards, the ticket book also serves as an important material prop in the authorization of extortion while the fact that the hourly parking fee mirrors official rates gives the transaction a sense of fairness. Indeed, one Uptown friend of mine spoke of his confusion regarding such parking paperwork. It had looked just like a UDC ticket, yet he was sure he hadn't parked on a formal lot. Either way, his vehicle was safe and sound when he returned for it. In its ambiguity, the paper ticket also helps Uptown parkers avoid the sensation of being extorted—it *looks* official.

Similar to vehicle owners featured in news items on the topic, those Uptown visitors I spoke to did not seem to view these payments as an egregious form of extortion. However, they did not appear to see them as a form of taxes either—they conveyed no sense that paying for parking was a type of moral obligation toward local communities or their leaders. Rather, these "parking fees" were discussed rather matter-of-factly as a practical payment for protection. Notwithstanding, for many vehicle owners, the institutionalization of the parking system, the standard rates, and the paperwork seem to generate an affective atmosphere of normalcy, authorizing the extraction of fees.

AUTHORIZING EXTORTION

As outlined in this chapter, the money, goods, and favors that dons extract are narrated by those involved in different ways, all of which tend to emphasize that such exchanges are *not* extortion. It stands to reason that dons and their affiliates prefer to present themselves as benefactors rather than extortionists, and that residents who may benefit from their largesse speak of taxes rather than of extortion. Perhaps more surprisingly, the distinction between extortion and "contributions to the community" is also made by those who are expected to pay. Ultimately, across the contexts described here, it is often quite difficult to determine where a voluntary contribution or a moral obligation ends and extortion starts. The threat of violence may be largely implicit and those who pay up may genuinely feel that they are doing good by contributing to a larger cause, whether by providing employment or by supplying low-income children with school supplies. Alternatively, they may understand their contributions as straightforward transactions, as payments for security that are relatively cheap and efficient. At the same time, few people want to see themselves as extortable, and renarrating their payments to dons as other-than-extortion allows those compelled to contribute to maintain their dignity as they continue to operate in dons' territory.

Faced with the difficulty of distinguishing extortion from other types of exchange, I find it more fruitful to ask what the widespread denial of extortion can tell us about political authority. Without ignoring the violence that is involved in the dons' form of rule, it is possible to take seriously the idea that their ability to extract cash and in-kind contributions from a broad range of actors is evidence of an emergent (or indeed, consolidated) fiscal regime. Here, it is important to recognize that state-based systems of taxation are also enforced through the threat of violence, and that paying state taxes can elicit a range of feelings amongst fiscal subjects, from pride in claiming the identity of a taxpayer to frustration over what are felt to be excessively high rates or untenable state expenditures.

The overdetermining narrative of extortion may prevent us from seeing other things that are at play, specifically the authorization of donmanship. I suggest that the frequent framing of payments to dons in terms of fiscal relations—as exchanges that involve some level of redistribution geared toward the common good—plays a key role in enacting dons' authority. Reinterpreting potentially or actually violent exchanges as legitimate political, economic, and moral acts is a way of enacting voluntary, mutually advantageous, and roughly "fair" relationships that extend beyond one-off exchanges.[37] Dons' claims to authority commonly feature references to the delivery of public goods and services. For residents and outsiders, the recognition that dons have the authority to tax is recursive: this recognition of the legitimacy of fiscal demands is informed by a preexisting sense of the don's right to rule, but recognizing such demands as legitimate directly confirms the don's overall political authority.

It is not necessarily the case that residents and businesspeople automatically recognize these claims to fiscal authority. Rather, in their discussions of dons' fiscal regimes, they are constantly negotiating under which conditions payments become extortion. Such discussions are also where the social norms and obligations—the moral economy—within which taxation makes sense are articulated. I found that such discussions centered on who can tax whom and how much. Clearly, it is only the don who has the authority to tax; others demanding protection fees are identified as extortionists or hustlers. Residents, and to some extent businesspeople, largely agreed that those earning income from activities within a don's territory—whether a market vendor, a wholesale owner, or a major corporation—had some level of obligation to contribute financially to the well-being of the community. Whether residents themselves should also pay was less clear, as suggested by Ludlow's indignant response—"You mad!?"—to the idea of a market fee for vendors "born and grow" in Brick Town. I encountered less consensus on when exactly rates were excessively high, but it was evident that a "greedy" don's authority would be diminished—and that whispering accusations that a don was greedy could be a way to undermine his authority.

As the different examples in the second half of this chapter show, dons, residents, and businesspeople navigate the boundary between taxation and extortion through more than narratives. The formation of fiscal relations involves embodied and emplaced performances: specific material-sensorial practices make exchanges *feel* like something other than extortion. Documents in particular do important work here: contracts, letters of appreciation, and parking slips provide a tangible sense of legitimacy. Such "props" in the "theater of consent" help engender positive affects, such as pride in a charitable act, or confidence that one's car is in safe hands.

Conclusion

POLITICAL AUTHORITY IN AND BEYOND THE STATE

Even as marginalized Kingstonians tend to view politicians, the police, and other state institutions with much skepticism, many of them recognize the rule of dons as legitimate. By and large, many residents of the city's most impoverished urban neighborhoods follow the laws that dons set. They support the taxes that dons levy. They vote for the political candidates with whom dons are aligned. They appreciate the painting of murals that commemorate them. And they dance at parties held in their honor. Do dons use violence and terror to coerce residents into obeying them? Do garrison residents support these local autocrats because they hold fundamentally antidemocratic values, belying Jamaica's post-independence history of peaceful democratic transitions? How might other analytical frameworks than those emphasizing coercion and deviance help us to understand how dons have been able to achieve and consolidate power over the past half century?

The figure of the don is commonly understood through the lens of crime and violence. While this emphasis is reasonable enough given Jamaica's persistently high homicide rates and the role of don-led criminal organizations in perpetuating this violence, it sometimes forecloses the possibility of understanding such leaders as *political* figures. I understand dons as political not so much because of their roots in Jamaica's system of garrison politics, and the associated shadow space they occupy within the formal political system—although this is a certainly significant factor. Rather, I approach dons as political figures because they have managed to get others to obey them not simply by coercing them into doing so, but by gaining legitimacy—by achieving a relatively broad measure of consent and consensus amongst those over whom they rule. The reason that donmanship as a system has proved so enduring, I suggest, is that they have managed to transform coercive power into political *authority*.

What does the case of Jamaica's dons tell us about political authority? As I have sought to elaborate throughout this book, we should approach authority as a relational, provisional accomplishment. Such an approach involves asking how dons actively engage in performances that constitute claims to authority, but also under which conditions these claims are recognized. Power cannot become authority if rulers' claims are not recognized: others need to acknowledge their right to rule, whether discursively or practically. Residents recognize this right to rule when they speak of "good" and "bad" dons, when they sing songs celebrating their heroic feats, when they commission commemorative murals or party at street dances held in their honor. But this claiming and acknowledging of authority takes shape both "vertically" and "horizontally." For a ruler to achieve and maintain a position of political authority, they need to gain recognition both from those over whom they rule, and from other rulers. In the case of Jamaica, this means that dons must maintain relationships of recognition not only with the residents of the territories over which they rule, but also with politicians, bureaucrats, and police officers, with business leaders and with other dons. The recognition of their right to rule also involves politicians describing dons as legitimate political representatives and paying respect at their funerals, police officers collaborating with them to secure certain areas, businesspeople paying their "taxes" voluntarily, and other dons respecting the borders of their political and fiscal territory.

And while dons certainly represent a form of personalist, autocratic rule, their enduring entanglement with state actors and institutions suggest that we should not understand them as fully outside, or opposed to, democratic values. Dons operate precisely at this intersection of autocracy and democracy. Scrutinizing their role in electoral politics, justice, security, and taxation, we can recognize how their leadership involves balancing patronage and representation, outlawry and normative order, endangerment and protection, greed and economic redistribution. This strategic straddling of the boundary between "state" and "nonstate" is a key element in dons' claims to authority.

AFFECT, AESTHETICS, ATMOSPHERE

The recognition of these claims is generally not only or primarily the outcome of careful argumentation and deliberation. Power becomes authority through sensorial, affective processes; it works on and through embodied subjects. Aesthetic forms—music, dance, and visual art—enact forms of sensorial persuasion on and through political subjects' listening, seeing, and moving bodies. Consent and consensus are intimately linked to the experience of feeling together, of sharing a sense world: political authority is not only rooted in historically informed, shared narratives of heroic leadership, but also in a common *sense* of who can rule.

In emphasizing this embodied dimension of power, I have followed a broader engagement within anthropology with political affect. Exploring "the sensual life of the state,"[1] this scholarship emphasizes how states rule over citizens through sensorial, affective politics. The legitimization of state power works through generating security affects such as panic and fear while critique can be stifled through the cultivation of doubt.[2] At the same time, state formation also takes a more seductive form, working through the generation of political feelings such as sympathy, hope, love, and joy.[3]

Analyzing how dons generate political feelings draws our attention to the work of political affect in legitimizing forms of power that exceed the nation-state, reminding us that a range of other governing actors can engage in feelingful political projects.[4] Given their strong connection to the space of the marginalized urban neighborhood, an analysis of donmanship and political affect also encourages us to attend more directly to the *spatial* dimension of these processes. Here, drawing on work in critical geography, I have sought to understand where, and through which spatial relations, political affect works to normalize power.

The aesthetic practices that generate a common sense world are *emplaced*. They are especially effective in crafting political community when they involve sights, sounds, and movements experienced in shared places such as the neighborhood. When murals, graffiti, and songs celebrating dons or propagating their rules envelop residents in hardly noticeable ways as they go about their everyday lives—or when they create a shared mood of joy and excitement during festive moments such as street dances held to honor dons—they contribute to the affective atmospheres of authority that normalize donmanship.

The emphasis that many residents place on leaders' spatial proximity shows how shared place-based sense experiences also enhance dons' authority in perhaps less intentional ways. Residents *feel* that dons can represent their concerns better than Uptown politicians and bureaucrats because they inhabit the same urban sense world. Dons, such accounts suggest, can represent them better because they have shared the physical experience of deprivation: living in marginalized areas, sweating in the heat of unairconditioned dwellings, learning to identify security threats by becoming attuned to those neighborhood sounds and movements that indicate danger. Through such associations of representativeness with copresence, the shared sensory experience of hardship—of deeply felt indignities and aspirations shaped by Kingston's geographies of inequality—becomes a political sensation.

The performance and recognition of dons' authority often involve references to such spatial capital, to their reputation of being "born and raise" in the same Downtown territory as residents. But the most powerful dons combine this claim to proximity with an aura of distance and transcendence, of an almost mystical separation from the masses. Here too, memorial murals, street dances, and dancehall songs play an important role in establishing these leaders' authority, representing them as both humble and heroic, as "sons of the soil" who managed to transcend their allotted place in life.

RETHINKING GEOGRAPHIES OF POLITICAL THEORY

What does the case of the dons tell us about political authority *beyond* Jamaica? Might this case provide insights more broadly into political processes and relations at the specific historical conjuncture of the early twenty-first century? The formations of authority associated with donmanship can shed new light on how other extralegal types of rulers, such as the Italian mafia or the Japanese yakuza, maintain positions of power. In addition, I suggest, the political repertoires through which dons are able to claim authority and have those claims received favorably also resonate with the strategies utilized by democratically elected leaders across the world.

Popular and academic understandings of donmanship frequently mobilize terms of failure or weakness to explain the dons' legitimacy—explanations of their success nearly always draw on the language of failed states, weak states, failed postcolonial projects, weak democratic institutions. As others have argued, such normative terms represent an imperialism of categories: they draw on models of European and North American political relations and use these as universal models *for* the rest of the world.[5] Implicitly or explicitly, they not only inaccurately presume a singularly successful model of Euro-American political formation. They also impose Eurocentric indices of success on states and citizenries that have followed very different trajectories than those of the European states or former settler colonies that lie at the basis of much political theory, whether Weberian or Foucauldian. The political formations that characterize postcolonial states, such critiques often suggest, should not be evaluated, or indeed analyzed, through the lens of concepts developed on the basis of historically specific European or North American cases.[6]

The postcolonial critique of Eurocentric political theory resonates with ongoing debates in urban studies on the geographies of theory. Urban scholars have similarly begun to interrogate the supposedly universal concepts developed on the basis of research in European and North American cities. Analyzing Asian, African, Latin American, and Caribbean cities through the lens of such Eurocentric concepts, they argue, often results in the evaluation of these cities as underdeveloped, failed, or otherwise "less-than." The identification of urban forms of nonstate authority in these regions has given rise to terms such as "failed cities," "fragile cities," or even the dehumanizing "feral cities."[7]

Such critiques have played a key role in shifting the parameters of political and urban theory. Yet they should not result in a move toward analytical segregation between the global North and South, between former colonial metropoles and postcolonial states. These divisions may not only obscure patterns that do not conform to these divides; they also risk reviving reductive binaries of the West and the rest. As urban scholar Ananya Roy argues, disrupting theoretical hegemonies does not mean that Euro-American concepts are never applicable to other sites, or vice versa. Rather, we need to theorize from a much broader set of sites, to develop new geographies of theory: "It is not worthwhile to police the borders across which ideas, policies, and practices flow and mutate . . . theories have to be produced in place (and it matters where they are produced), but [t]hey can then be appropriated, borrowed, and remapped."[8]

As I was finishing this book manuscript, the US supreme court had just ruled on former president Donald Trump's claim that he had immunity from prosecution for crimes committed while he was in office. Specifically, Trump sought to avoid prosecution for attempts to obstruct the transition of power to President Joe Biden in the period preceding his supporters' attack on the Capitol in Washington, DC, on January 6, 2021. In Brazil, former president Jair Bolsonaro also faced severe sanctions in the aftermath of his followers' attempts, in January 2023, to block the inauguration of newly elected President Luiz Inácio Lula da Silva by storming government buildings in Brasília. During their period in office and after they were voted out, Trump and Bolsonaro positioned themselves both within and outside of established state institutions: as heads of state and as disruptive outsiders who would "drain the swamp," as electoral favorites and as strongmen threatening their enemies with violence, as blatantly consolidating their private interests while professing a commitment to protecting their supporters' economic welfare. Their popularity and indeed their political authority, I propose, can be understood as directly connected to their strategic engagement with the state and with democratic legitimacy: their frequent referencing of elections, law, and taxes, even as they engaged in all manner of lawbreaking and tax evasion and frequently issued threats or encouraged the actual use of violence.[9] In addition, like dons, these leaders have proved capable of crafting powerful affective atmospheres of shared excitement, resentment, and anger, especially during popular mass rallies attended by supporters dressed in matching colors, wearing red MAGA caps or yellow and green clothing, who shout disparaging slogans in unison.

Certainly, Jamaica's specific, historically shaped political system of garrison politics provided a context in which donmanship was able to flourish. More broadly, donmanship is clearly informed by the legacies of colonialism and plantation slavery and their authoritarian, illiberal formations of power, in ways that resonate with other postcolonies such as Brazil and indeed the United States. Yet I suggest, with caution, that the implications of the analysis proposed in this book may extend beyond postcolonial contexts to shed light on the popularity of elected national leaders such as Vladimir Putin, Viktor Orbán, Giorgia Meloni, and Boris Johnson. Attending to dons' balancing of violence and material gain with their professed commitment to institutionalized norms and redistribution, and to their crafting of affective atmospheres, can extend the political philosophical repertoire through which we apprehend apparently confounding combinations of democracy and autocracy, of liberalism and illiberalism.

DISMANTLING THE GARRISON?

By asserting the broader analytical relevance of donmanship, I do not mean to assert that we are moving toward a world of dons. Indeed, even for Jamaica, this specific formation of authority, while entrenched, may be destabilized. My emphasis throughout this book has perhaps skewed toward those instances where dons' claims to authority are received favorably, both by residents and by influential figures positioned within state institutions. But of course, as with any political system, there are alternatives to donmanship.

The Tivoli Incursion was initially heralded as the event that would finally lead to the "dismantling of the garrison." Given the developments in the years that followed, I am not convinced that Jamaica's system of donmanship will be dismantled in any meaningful way any time soon: the limited interventions aimed at challenging the inequalities cemented into the urban landscape seem to have been replaced by punitive forms of policing, while new and often more violent men have risen to claim power following the death or imprisonment of previous dons. Notwithstanding, it is possible to identify certain changes.

Some of these shifts are actively worrying. One clear trend is the ongoing militarization of policing. Most disturbingly, perhaps, this involves the near continuous deployment of the Jamaica Defense Force to police low-income areas, and the increased use of States of Emergency as a legal strategy to suspend the law in the name of crime-fighting.[10] Another trend is the emergence of new types of violent crime. In the early 2010s, Jamaica's leaders justified the use of these emergency powers by referring to dons. More recently, this legitimization has also shifted to encompass a different set of violent extralegal actors. Specifically, police and media attention shifted beyond dons in Kingston and Spanish Town to focus on the tourist area of Montego Bay where groups of "lottery scammers" were held responsible for a rise in killings. Originally seen as a nonviolent form of crime, the practice of "scamming"—large-scale defrauding of mainly elderly Americans by phone and newer forms of communication technology—came to be associated with violent conflict between rivalling criminal organizations.[11] Unlike dons, scammers and their organizations appear to be less place-based and less invested in assuming a governance role or maintaining connections to established state institutions such as electoral politics. Whether these differences with dons make it more difficult for scammers to consolidate their power, and to persuade others that their activities are legitimate, remains to be seen.

At the same time, back in Kingston, other signs of change—or cracks in the Rancièrean political consensus surrounding donmanship—can also be identified. There have been important critiques and moments of sensory-political dissensus, mentioned more or less in passing at various points throughout the previous chapters. Yet it is important to draw these strands of potentiality together here, not least to highlight the agency of residents in disrupting as well as upholding the status quo of donmanship.

Observers within and beyond Jamaica have often understood the residents of Kingston's garrisons as more or less passive victims, unable to escape the grip of either dons or politicians. This perspective can be nuanced, not only by appreciating that the residents can actively and agentively grant their recognition of dons' authority, but also by attending to the small but potentially incremental ways in which they *withhold* recognition. The acts of dissensus can take a narrative form, for instance by circulating rumors (often related to a don's sexual behavior) that undermine their heroic status, but also through small linguistic choices, such as referring to a payment as "extortion" rather than "taxes." But this withholding of approval can also assume other aesthetic forms: vandalizing the painted visage of a "badman," staying at home during a street dance, or singing songs that celebrate other bodies of authority. While seemingly minor, such aesthetic acts may contribute more to the dismantling of donmanship than any police operation ever will.

Notes

INTRODUCTION

A portion of this introduction is extracted from Jaffe, "Writing around Violence."

1. Most definitions of the term "don" include a reference to their involvement in crime. Charles Price, for instance, defines a don as "a politically connected local leader who wields power, status, and prestige derived from multiple activities, legal and illegal" and "typically provides social welfare and informal justice services." Price, "What the Zeeks Uprising Reveals," 79.
2. See, for example, Arias, *Criminal Enterprises and Governance*; Kivland, *Street Sovereigns*; Michelutti et al., *Mafia Raj*.
3. David Scott refers to this as "the quasi-anthropology of social pathology ... the 'culture of violence' discourse that has such wide purchase among opinion-makers in the Jamaican public sphere." Scott, "Permanence of Pluralism," 297.
4. For example, Curtin, *Two Jamaicas*; Chevannes, "Those Two Jamaicas"; Hall, *Familiar Stranger*.
5. Furnivall, *Colonial Policy and Practice*; Smith, *The Plural Society in the British West Indies*.
6. Meeks, *Envisioning Caribbean Futures*, 77.
7. Meeks, *Narratives of Resistance*, 4. For a similar analysis of these protests as an uprising, see Price, "What the Zeeks Uprising Reveals." Price found these events to be a form of "direct popular action" that is "couched in rhetoric about injustice that focused on people's physical and social welfare" (97). He identifies "a counter-narrative of social relationships and obligations that co-exist alongside the state's juridical, political, and economic obligations and definitions of justice and rights" (98). Christopher Charles also reads the mobilization on behalf of Zeeks as a form of political antagonism, or resistance, that reflects a deep cultural divide, interpreting the protests more expansively as evidence of "counter societies." Writing on Kingston's gangs in the 1970s, Faye Harrison argues that their activities could be seen as a form of "social outlawry," as attempts to evade escape and resist partisan political cooptation. Price, "What the Zeeks Uprising Reveals"; Charles, "Garrison Communities as Counter Societies"; Harrison, "The Politics of Social Outlawry."
8. Meeks, *Critical Interventions*, 178, 179.
9. Meeks, "Reprising the Past," 192.
10. Scott, "The Permanence of Pluralism," 298.
11. Scott, "The Permanence of Pluralism," 298.
12. See, for example, Barrow-Giles, "Democracy at Work"; Leeds, "Cocaine and Parallel Polities"; Benmergui and Soares Gonçalves, "*Urbanismo Miliciano* in Rio de Janeiro."
13. Arias and Goldstein, *Violent Democracies in Latin America*.

14. For example, National Committee on Political Tribalism, *Report of the National Committee*, 6; Rapley, "Jamaica," 28; Meeks, *Critical Interventions*, 185.
15. Jaffe, "The Hybrid State."
16. According to the United States, Presidential Click was the name of Dudus's criminal enterprise, synonymous with the Shower Posse. United States Attorney, Southern District of New York, "Jamaican Drug Lord Christopher Michael Coke Sentenced."
17. Gupta, "Blurred Boundaries"; Ferguson and Gupta, "Spatializing States"; cf. Mitchell, "Society, Economy, and the State Effect."
18. In his conceptualization of sufferation, Jovan Lewis describes it as "an all-encompassing phenomenological condition where the experience of poverty is mobilized as a means for poor Jamaicans to organize and understand their world," experienced as "the lived spatialization of endemic poverty in Jamaica, and the inequalities and adversities that cause it." Lewis, *Scammer's Yard*, 27, 49.
19. Rodgers, "The State as a Gang"; Davis, "Irregular Armed Forces"; Kivland, *Street Sovereigns*.
20. Hansen and Stepputat, "Sovereignty Revisited," 301. This work in turn draws on the strong early twentieth-century interest in Giorgio Agamben's approach to sovereignty; see Agamben, *Homo Sacer*.
21. Hansen and Stepputat, "Sovereignty Revisited," 296. To my mind, the authors cause unnecessary confusion by defining "sovereignty as a tentative and always emergent form of *authority*, grounded in violence that is performed and designed to generate loyalty, fear, and legitimacy" (297, emphasis added).
22. Arendt, "What Was Authority?," 82.
23. Arendt, "What Was Authority?," 82.
24. Weber, *Economy and Society*.
25. For an elaboration of this approach to feeling together, see Rancière, *The Politics of Aesthetics*.
26. See Henriques, *Sonic Bodies*.
27. See Kivland, "Becoming a Force in the Zone."
28. See also Brigstocke et al., "Geographies of Authority."
29. Jaffe, "Security Aesthetics."
30. Closs Stephens, "The Affective Atmospheres of Nationalism," 192. For a distinct but significant related approach to the spatiality of political feelings, see Navaro-Yashin, *The Make-Believe Space*.
31. Such ideas about the difficulties and dangers of a white-identified woman's access were, in my experience, part of a complex dynamic maintained not only by non-black, foreign researchers or audiences but also by Jamaican academics and policymakers. The questions I received resonate with what Victor Rios calls the "jungle book trope," which surfaces in many urban ethnographies: a racialized trope of white researchers immersing themselves in dangerous black spaces and surviving to tell the tale. Rios, *Punished*, 14.
32. Kivland, *Street Sovereigns*, 28.
33. Gunst, *Born fi' Dead*.
34. Zeiderman, *Endangered City*, 29.
35. On representations of Jamaicans as violent, see also Thomas, *Exceptional Violence*.

1. HISTORIES

1. See Cooper, *Sound Clash*, ch. 6.
2. See Lewis, "Walter Rodney."
3. For more on Coral Gardens and its commemoration, see Thomas, *Exceptional Violence*, ch. 5.
4. See, for example, Sheller, *Citizenship from Below*; Thomas, *Political Life in the Wake of the Plantation*.
5. For a longer discussion of the concept, see Jaffe, "Cities and the Political Imagination."
6. It is important to note here that, while many studies of the creative expressions of marginalized groups tend to approach the political imagination as progressive or emancipatory, there are many types of imagination that connect to violent or exclusionary types of political practice and actors, and we should also attend to "the more dystopian potentials of imaginative engagement" (Sneath, Holbraad, and Pedersen, "Technologies of the Imagination," 10). Indeed, as Stuart Hall underscores, popular culture is neither a straightforward form of resistance, nor a simple tool of oppression and control, but rather the site where such struggles play out, see Hall, "Notes on Deconstructing 'the Popular.'"
7. Certainly, a longer genealogy of political authority could be traced to the logic of the colonial slave plantation of earlier centuries. Deborah Thomas, for instance, argues that "contemporary manifestations of garrison politics are grounded in a system of political authority on sugar estates oriented toward loyalty to a powerful figure and reliance on that figure for work, benefits, and protection" (*Political Life*, 13).
8. Thomas, *Political Life*, 7.
9. See Charles, "Garrison Communities as Counter Societies"; Price, "What the Zeeks Uprising Reveals."
10. Palmer, *Freedom's Children*, 47.
11. Singham, *The Hero and the Crowd*. While based on the case study of Grenada, Singham's analysis of the late colonial and early post-independence period closely mirrors the historical development of Jamaica's political parties and their leadership. Specifically, his depiction of the middle-class leader maps easily onto the PNP's forefather Norman Washington Manley while JLP founder Bustamante (if himself also a brown Jamaican, and Manley's cousin) fit the model of the working-class champion.
12. Singham, *The Hero and the Crowd*, 329.
13. Although Singham's analysis reflects a reliance on now-dated theories of political culture and societal "personality types," his characterization of the "hero-crowd" relation has remained an influential model for scholars of Caribbean politics. Deborah Thomas, for instance, similarly connects the development of Jamaica's model of leadership to the type of organized labor that emerged within the plantation economy and, like Singham, describes the power of first union leaders and then political parties as "personalized, ultimately grounded within the charisma and patronage of one or another leader." Thomas, "Time and the Otherwise," 181–82.
14. Sewell, "Music in the Jamaican Labour Movement," 43–44.
15. Sewell, "Music in the Jamaican Labour Movement," 45.
16. Hintzen, "Reproducing Domination Identity and Legitimacy Constructs in the West Indies."
17. Thomas, *Modern Blackness*, 53. Thomas also suggests that, while the brown men who led the unions depicted the black laboring classes as in need of political education, unionization arguably channeled the workers' struggles into a form of organized protest that was politically legible to the colonial government.

18. Gray, *Demeaned but Empowered*, 25–26.
19. For detailed historical analyses of electoral violence in Jamaica, see Sives, *Elections, Violence and the Democratic Process in Jamaica*; Gray, *Demeaned but Empowered*.
20. Kivland, "Becoming a Force in the Zone."
21. Sistren, *Lionheart Gal*, 161. See also Lileth Sewell, whose version of the song includes the lines *Chakka-chakka government, a weh mi do yuh / mi ask yuh fih wuk an' yuh gimme ol' clothes*—Poor quality, sloppy government, what have I done to you, I ask you for work and you give me old clothes. This version demonstrates an even clearer insistence on dignity and autonomy, with voters seeking employment, and spurning a shambolic government's offer of second-hand goods. Sewell, "Music in the Jamaican Labour Movement," 46.
22. For more on garrison politics, see Figueroa and Sives, "Homogeneous Voting"; Lewis, "Party Politics in Jamaica"; Altink, "The Politics of Infrastructure."
23. Figueroa and Sives, "Homogeneous Voting," 85.
24. Scott, "Political Rationalities of the Jamaican Modern."
25. See, for example, Gray, *Demeaned but Empowered*, 134–42.
26. There is no evidence of dons' direct provision of welfare and organized conflict resolution, or their enabling free access to electricity and water, until the 1980s. The first reports of their assuming this larger role within the space of the garrison surfaced at that time and increased in the following decades. See Harrison, "The Politics of Social Outlawry"; Sives, "Changing Patrons"; Sives, *Elections, Violence and the Democratic Process in Jamaica*; Harriott, *Organized Crime and Politics in Jamaica*.
27. Figueroa, Harriott, and Satchell, "The Political Economy of Jamaica's Inner-City Violence."
28. Harriott, *Organized Crime and Politics in Jamaica*, 9.
29. This song followed Twin of Twins' "Which Dudus?," released in 2009 after the United States' initial extradition request, a track in which the duo parody a CIA officer in search of the don, asking why "Babylon," the global capitalist order, is frowning when Dudus was the one providing order: "Mi seh di man set di order Downtown / So how all of a sudden Babylon a come frown?" Presaging the Tivoli Incursion, they also warned those seeking to arrest Dudus to take men from Tivoli Gardens seriously, as these men would not run from the security forces' helicopters: "Like dem tek Garden Man fi some clown / Dem man deh nah go run when helicopter come down."
30. Specifically, Montego Bay's scammers—whose income derives from defrauding (mostly elderly) Americans—do not assume the governance role that dons have, nor do they share the dons' party-political role. Also, until recently, scamming was broadly understood to be a nonviolent form of crime—a rapid increase in murders in Montego Bay associated with scammers was part of the impetus behind the designation of ZOSOs in the tourist zone. For a detailed discussion of the emergence and logic of scamming, see Lewis, *Scammer's Yard*.
31. For more on the normalization of emergency powers in national security, see Campbell, *Citizenship on the Margins*; Campbell and Harriott, "The Resort to State of Emergency Policing."
32. Méndez Beck and Jaffe, "Community Policing goes South," 834–35; research in Mexico similarly suggests that the strategy of "leadership neutralization" increases violence, by catalyzing violent succession struggles and renewed turf wars between criminal organizations, or by weakening the centralized control that previously kept predation of local residents in check; Calderón et al., "The Beheading of Criminal Organizations and the Dynamics of Violence in Mexico."
33. Dacres, "Monument and Meaning," 138.

2. GEOGRAPHIES

1. Brigstocke et al., "Geographies of Authority," 2.
2. Jaffe, *Concrete Jungles*; Ulysse, *Downtown Ladies*; cf. McCallum, "Racialized Bodies, Naturalized Classes."
3. Clarke, *Decolonizing the Colonial City*.
4. Carnegie, "The Loss of the Verandah," 74; see also Carnegie, "How Did There Come to Be a 'New Kingston'?"
5. See Jaffe, "Speculative Policing."
6. See Grossmann and Trubina, "Dignity in Urban Geography."
7. Wacquant, *Urban Outcasts*, 67.
8. See Clarke, *Decolonizing the Colonial City*.
9. See Jaffe et al., "What Does Poverty Feel Like?," on the importance of heat in marking class difference.
10. Helps, "I'm No Soft, Uptown Boy."
11. Thame, "Woman Out of Place."
12. See Ulysse, *Downtown Ladies*, for a detailed analysis of how gender intersects with Kingston's classed and raced hierarchies, and for a description of what she calls a habitus of "tuffness" amongst women from Kingston's low-income areas.
13. For a more detailed discussion of this and other murals, see Meikle and Jaffe, "Scripts Héroïques"; Meikle, "Iconization of Donmanship"; Meikle, "The Multivalency of Memorial Murals."
14. Santino, "Performative Commemoratives."
15. For other instances in which neighborhood soccer teams and politics intersect, see Horowitz, "Football Clubs and Neighbourhoods in Buenos Aires"; Eder and Öz, "Spatialities of Contentious Politics."
16. Helps, "George Phang, 'Dudus,' and That Peace Trip of 20 Years Ago."
17. Helps, "Phang."
18. Henry, "The 'Passa Passa' Phenomenon."
19. For more on street dances and place-based identity, see Stanley-Niaah, "Kingston's Dancehall"; Charles, "Violence, Musical Identity, and the Celebrity of the Spanglers Crew."
20. See, for example, Karandinos et al., "The Moral Economy of Violence in the US Inner City."
21. Eyre, "Political Violence and Urban Geography," 24.
22. Osbourne, "On a Walking Tour to No Man's Land."
23. See Thomas, "Time and the Otherwise," 183, for a discussion of state violence and temporality, where she demonstrates how "recurring moments of exceptional violence . . . lead to an experience of time neither as linear nor cyclical, but as simultaneous, where the future, past, and present are mutually constitutive and have the potential to be coincidentally influential."
24. The role of familial as well as territorial ties in such conflicts was also evident in Tivoli Gardens, after the Incursion. With a leadership vacuum following Dudus's imprisonment, different factions sought to assume control of the area. These contestations frequently pitted members of the extended Coke family, sometimes referred to as "New Generation," with other groups, including at one point family members of Claude Massop, the Tivoli don who was killed by police in 1979 and succeeded by Dudus's father Lester "Jim Brown" Coke. See Helps, "'Dudus' vs Massop War Heats Up."

25. See, for example, Hall, "Science Serving Justice"; *Jamaica Gleaner*, "Desperate 'Dudus' Looks to PNP for Help."
26. Interestingly, the West Kingston Peace Committee that emerged from this treaty met with the United States Ambassador and Embassy officers in February 1978; a diplomatic cable to the US Secretary of State Cyrus Vance (serving under President Jimmy Carter) notes that "the WKPC is composed of the leaders of the gangs affiliated with both of Jamaica's major political parties. . . . The WKPC is a loosely organized entity which claims, probably accurately, to be the only viable representative body in the Western Kingston area." While it is unclear whether the United States actually provided them with support (and perhaps unlikely), the cable concludes: "We were impressed with the vigor, determination, commitment and unity of this group. . . . We are convinced that the interest of the WKPC offers us an excellent opportunity to be helpful in a seriously distressed urban area and to demonstrate our concern for the 'poorest of the poor' in Jamaica and that we must, therefore, respond both promptly and meaningfully." Anonymous, "Political Observations by Western Kingston Peace Committee."
27. Duncan-Waite and Woolcock, *Arrested Development*, 24–25.
28. For a longer version of the following description, see Jaffe, "Crime Watch."
29. Thomas, "Caribbean Studies, Archive Building, and the Problem of Violence," 28.

3. ELECTORAL POLITICS

1. See Sives, "Changing Patrons"; Gray, *Demeaned but Empowered*, 286–90.
2. For a related argument that approaches community leaders as intermediary brokers seeking to gain legitimacy vertically (from residents "below" and state institutions "above" them), see Bénit-Gbaffou and Katsaura, "Community Leadership and the Construction of Political Legitimacy."
3. See Schoburgh, "Local Government Reform in Trinidad and Jamaica."
4. Urbinati and Warren, "The Concept of Representation in Contemporary Democratic Theory," 388; see also Björkman, "'You Can't Buy a Vote'"; Reiter, *The Crisis of Liberal Democracy and the Path Ahead*.
5. While such references to dons as quasi-democratic representatives seem most directly connected to the project of decentralization, there are earlier instances of narratives that mobilize the language of democracy to authorize their actions. In the context of the Cold War, when dons fought proxy battles for the JLP and PNP, politicians from both political parties justified their violent actions in the name of democracy. Those aligned with the JLP were fighting in the name of "the free world," saving liberal democracy and capitalism, while those tied to the PNP were defending Michael Manley's project of "democratic socialism" against a US-based imperialist project. As historian Laurie Gunst described it, "the PNP shootists started seeing themselves as Cuban-style revolutionaries, and the JLP's gunmen thought they were fighting to save Jamaica from Communism." Gunst, *Born fi' Dead*, 93.
6. Gray, *Demeaned but Empowered*, 190; Walker, "Burry Boy and Feathermop."
7. Fitz-Henley, "Burke Defends Move to Invite Phang to NEC." It is important to note that Phang strongly rejects the label of don, see Helps, "Phang."
8. Gray, *Demeaned but Empowered*, 186–87; Paul, "'No Grave Cannot Hold My Body Down'"; Levi, *Michael Manley*, 165. Burry Boy's death was also memorialized in Junior Byles' 1975 reggae

song Bur-o-boy, which includes the following lyrics: "One more life has gone so uselessly / People in the ghetto still fighting to be free / Tell me one more thing / Aren't we all God's children? / What is your meaning of equality when you giving guns to my brothers now? / When will this violence ever cease? / Bur-o-Boy gone check Zackie [i.e., Rudolph "Zackie the High Priest" Lewis, deceased JLP enforcer] down a shut-eye country [i.e., in the land of the dead]." See Byles, "Bur-o-boy"; Chatty Mouth, "Jr. Byles ~ Burr o boy."
9. Gunst, *Born fi' Dead*, 237–39.
10. Sinclair, "Emotional Farewell for 'Haggart.'"
11. *Jamaica Gleaner*, "MPs Turn Out for Funeral." Similar forms of recognition are performed through politicians' presence at birthday parties; for instance, "renowned People's National Party supporter" George Phang's bipartisan political connections were evident when both PNP MPs and a JLP cabinet minister attended his "birthday bash." See Helps, "'Babsy,' Comrades Unite at George Phang's Birthday Bash."
12. Paul, "'No Grave Cannot Hold My Body Down,'" 143.
13. The visual analysis in this section is taken from a longer discussion of the role of art in reproducing or contesting urban orders in Oosterbaan and Jaffe, "Popular Art, Crime and Urban Order beyond the State."
14. Mirzoeff, *The Right to Look*, 5.
15. Rhiney and Cruse, "Trench Town Rock," 6–7.
16. Meikle, "Iconization of Donmanship," 46.
17. See Durkheim, *The Elementary Forms of the Religious Life*.
18. See, for example, Banerjee, "Money and Meaning in Elections"; Michelutti, *Vernacularisation of Democracy*. On how political candidates themselves "feel" democracy and experience elections as emotionally charged moments, see Jakimow, "Feeling/Making Democracy."
19. This and the following sections elaborate on ethnography previously published in Jaffe, "Between Ballots and Bullets."
20. In response, PNP supporters frequently shout "Power." This is likely a reference to the party's engagement with the Black Power movement in earlier decades, but also, and perhaps more importantly, a forceful rhyming rejoinder to chants of "Shower."
21. Kivland, "Becoming a Force in the Zone."
22. For a lengthier discussion of street dances, (political) memory, and place-based identity, see Stanley-Niaah, "Kingston's Dancehall"; Charles, "Violence, Musical Identity, and the Celebrity of the Spanglers Crew."
23. Stanley-Niaah, "Readings of 'Ritual' and Community in Dancehall Performance," 79, 80.

4. LAW AND ORDER

Parts of this chapter appeared in an earlier form in Jaffe, "From Maroons to Dons"; Jaffe, "Criminal Dons"; Jaffe, "Security Aesthetics"; Meikle and Jaffe, "'Police as the New Don'?"
1. On Kingston's colonial urban planning, see Clarke, *Kingston, Jamaica*.
2. Stressing that "a rule's quality as law is not intrinsic to the rule itself, but something attributed to it in social and political interaction," Christian Lund defines law as "the rules and regulations whose creation, protection or enforcement is attributed to the most powerful and credible political institutions in society." Lund, "The Air of Legality," 2. See also von Benda-Beckman, von Benda-Beckman, and Eckert, *Rules of Law and Laws of Ruling*.

3. Notwithstanding this focus on colonialism and its afterlives, legal pluralism can be recognized in nearly any context, for instance, when state laws coexist with international law, religious laws, or the self-regulatory codes of professional or trade organizations.
4. Benton, *Law and Colonial Cultures*.
5. Besson, "Folk Law and Legal Pluralism in Jamaica."
6. For recent exceptions, see Provost, *Rebel Courts*; Cohen, "The 'Debate.'"
7. Benjamin, *Reflections*; see also Rodgers, "The State as a Gang"; Hansen, "Performers of Sovereignty."
8. Amnesty International, *Waiting in Vain*.
9. Ministry of Justice, *Jamaican Justice System Reform Task Force*.
10. As with former prime minister Portia Simpson-Miller—known as Sister P or Mama P—the use of honorific kinship titles enact relations of intimacy and obligation between politicians and their constituents.
11. Spaulding, "Web of Conspiracy."
12. In a survey of four hundred residents in eight low-income communities in Kingston that I coorganized, which sought responses to statements using a Likert scale ranging from "strongly agree" (= 1) to "strongly disagree" (= 5), the statement "In Jamaica, the law treats everyone the same" was met with near-unanimous disagreement, with a mean response of 4.35 (n = 393). See Harbers, Jaffe, and Cummings, "A Battle for Hearts and Minds?"
13. This is a reference to a famous statement made in 1998 by former PNP prime minister (and lawyer) P. J. Patterson, asserting that "the law is not a shackle to enslave; it is a tool of social engineering." See, for instance, Nicholson, "Responsibility."
14. Duncan-Waite and Woolcock, *Arrested Development*, 27–29; Charles and Beckford, "The Informal Justice System in Garrison Constituencies."
15. A study of multiple low-income neighborhoods, for instance, found that "police request the Don to intervene to prevent small gang feuds, petty theft, and shop breaking. Police will also refer criminals . . . so that immediate action can be taken and the community tensions arising from the incident can be calmed to prevent further trouble." Duncan-Waite and Woolcock, *Arrested Development*, 29.
16. Harriott and Jaffe, "Security Encounters."
17. See also Maoz, "Black Police Power."
18. See Harriott et al., *The Political Culture of Democracy*.
19. For an extensive analysis of this and other forms of appropriation by the police described here, see Meikle and Jaffe, "'Police as the New Don'?"
20. On hedonopolitics, see Kivland, "Becoming a Force in the Zone."
21. See, for instance, the campaign #AForce4Good and the JCF's efforts across Instagram, Twitter, Facebook, and TikTok.
22. McFadden, "Jamaica Police Erasing Gang Murals in Slums."
23. *Jamaica Gleaner*, "Video."
24. Thomas, "Holness Insists Tivoli Residents Will Be Compensated"; for audio recording of speech, see NationWide Radio 90FM, "Andrew Holness Must Break Criminal Justice."
25. Ministry of Justice, *Jamaican Justice System Reform Task Force*.
26. Ministry of Justice, *The National Restorative Justice Policy*, 12.
27. Ministry of Justice, *The National Restorative Justice Policy*, 23.

28. Unlike the earlier Jamaican Justice System Reform Task Force's report, in the official policy, the Ministry of Justice frames dons' system of justice as only retributive, as reinforcing values of "revenge, intimidation and force" rather than also encompassing values associated with restorative justice principles (notably "equal respect, dignity, care and concern for others"), Ministry of Justice, *The National Restorative Justice Policy*, 22–23. Pointing to the strong influence of Canadian aid in Jamaica's embrace of restorative justice, political scientist Leanne Levers analyzes restorative justice as a form of opportunistic and inappropriate policy transfer. She argues that the success of the restorative justice policy has been limited precisely because the Jamaican government failed to consider existing informal justice systems, to engage with nonstate stakeholders including dons, and to adapt a model taken from the Canadian province of Nova Scotia to Jamaica's cultural and political context, Levers, "RJ Policy Transfer." This analysis diverges somewhat from legal scholar Inga Laurent's discussion of the origin and development of restorative justice initiatives, which details extensive community consultation in the elaboration of the policy. Laurent, "From Retribution to Restoration," 1137–38.
29. See, for example, Philippopoulos-Mihalopoulos, *Spatial Justice*; Young, "Japanese Atmospheres of Criminal Justice"; Fraser and Matthews, "Towards a Criminology of Atmospheres." Starting from a transnational rather than an urban perspective, Kamari Maxine Clarke makes a related intervention into discussions of justice, approaching international law as sets of social practices, where "affects are legally materialized, discursively and performatively" and, accordingly, "justice making is enmeshed in bodily affects that give rise to emotional expressions and various racialized iconic figures." Clarke, *Affective Justice*, 6.
30. Ghertner, McFann, and Goldstein, "Introduction," 5.
31. Ellis, Tucker, and Harper, "The Affective Atmospheres of Surveillance."

5. TAXATION

Parts of this chapter appeared in an earlier form in Jaffe, "The Hybrid State."
1. Ludlow emphasized their exile to mark the difference between the PNP and the JLP. His party, the PNP, had "sent away" Tony Brown and George Flash of the East Kingston Hotsteppers posse after the two men were charged with the murder of a politician—charges that were later dropped. The JLP, in contrast, had failed to do the same when the United States sought Dudus's extradition, resulting in the Tivoli Incursion and the many deaths. Journalist Sybil Hibbert notes that Tony Brown and George Flash returned to Jamaica in 1993 following their acquittal; all charges were dropped "because the case file was discovered to be missing and there was no trace of the statements on the file." Hibbert, "Permanent Secretary Gunned Down in Broad Daylight"; see also Gray, *Demeaned but Empowered*, 274.
2. This depiction contrasts with academic research on Tony Brown's role in the East Kingston community of Rockfort, which found that "the don was removed by a rebellion on the ground, old age and finally death" following an overly brutal form of rule, with community youth arguing that "Tony Brown use to order a lot of beatings where men hand and foot were broken, some man teeth get lick out because they were accused of not taking the don order.... Tony Brown usually send a squad a man fi yu, him jungle justice system was not working.... Bullyism was the order of the day when Tony Brown ruled." Levy, *Youth Violence and Organized Crime in Jamaica*, 56–57.

3. This also came out clearly in an interview with "Andrew," a resident from another Kingston community, who described how his mother had migrated after an extortion attempt. Andrew's mother had owned a bar and men sent her a letter saying that they wanted a certain amount on a monthly basis. "Through she born and grow inna di place, she say she nuh really deh pan that"—because she had been born and grew up in the area, Andrew told me, she had told them she would not comply. "She must've sent them back a letter with some indecent language," he explained, and then they gave her a warning and one night robbed her while threatening to kill her. It "shook her up violently" that this would happen in what she had felt was *her* place: "She just feel like a nuh fi her place anymore, so she just leave Jamaica"—the fact that this had happened in what she had considered her neighborhood was what caused her to migrate.

4. See, for example, O'Neill, "Terminal Velocity"; Saunders-Hastings, "Du code du barrio à l'idéologie d'une entreprise."

5. Michelutti, "Racket Sociality."

6. Thompson, "The Moral Economy of the English Crowd," 79. For a discussion of the moral economies surrounding illicit trade, see Arias and Grisaffi, "Introduction."

7. Sheild Johansson, "Tax." Geographer Angus Cameron defines taxation as "a specifically instituted and legally sanctioned mode of redistribution." Cameron, "Turning Point?," 236.

8. Elaborating this relational approach, sociologists Isaac Martin, Ajay Mehrotra, and Monica Prasad argue that "Taxation *is* the social contract." As they explain, "Taxes formalize our obligations to each other. They define the inequalities we accept and those that we collectively seek to redress. They signify who is a member of our political community, how wide we draw the circle of 'we.' They set the boundaries of what our governments can do." Martin, Mehrotra, and Prasad, "The Thunder of History," 1.

9. Venkatesan, "Afterword," 143.

10. See Sheild Johansson, "Taxes for Independence."

11. Cirolia, "Contested Fiscal Geographies"; Cameron, "Turning Point?"

12. See, for example, Makovicky and Smith, "Introduction."

13. Kauppinen, "God's Delivery State"; Sheild Johansson, "Taxes for Independence"; Rasmussen, "Inside the System, Outside the Law"; Ference, "'You Will Build Me'"; Fourchard, *Classify, Exclude, Police*; Roitman, *Fiscal Disobedience*.

14. Where centralized authority is less recognized, redistribution may be less a central component of this social obligation. As anthropologist Miranda Sheild Johansson argues, "In the context of societies where populations have historical memories of tribute collection, reciprocity is not necessarily understood as the core logic of a fiscal system." Sheild Johansson, "Taxes for Independence," 20.

15. This responsibility for market operations was previously vested in Metropolitan Parks and Markets (MPM) but shifted to the Kingston and St. Andrew Municipal Corporation. Where Ludlow's account suggested that the government had ceded the fee collection and management of market spaces to dons, rather than continuing to engage actively in competition with them, a former MPM official described the dons' role in collecting market fees in the 1990s more as a constant negotiation, which at that point took the form of literal subcontracting rather than direct replacement. He told me: "I made them collect the fees, but I made sure that we got our fair share out of it. And some of those who evaded the fees were now made to collect fees. And if you didn't pay to them, you'd pay to the market. We took

away a lot of that collection from them because we demanded our fair share of them. But by the same token, instead of using third-party security companies, we used them. So that they earned the security fee that I would have paid to other security companies. And I, you know, I bought them uniforms and put them in uniforms." I sought to clarify whether these "collectors" had been working for MPM. "Yes, as subcontractors," he answered, "But I mean, I gave them money to buy, to provide uniforms for their people, as well as a basic wage. And I didn't collect 100 percent of the money that they collected. I mean, I was aware of that. But instead of collecting 5 percent, I was collecting, you know, maybe 80 percent."

16. Robinson, "Extortion." Swart describes an intermediate situation where men working under the orders of a central don begin to exact a personal "top-up" from entrepreneurs, in addition to the amount that the don expects. Swart, "Producing State-Effect," 18.
17. See Maurer, "The Disunity of Finance," 416–19.
18. Ardener, "The Comparative Study of Rotating Credit Associations," 201. For more on pardna, see Purcell, "Local Institutions in Grassroots Development."
19. Purcell, "Local Institutions in Grassroots Development," 148.
20. See Charles, "Business Ethics in Jamaica," 104; Swart, "Producing State-Effect."
21. Indeed, in the 2010s, JPS developed a new community strategy in low-income areas, aimed in part at electricity theft-reduction, that sought to reconfigure previously antagonistic relations with residents into more collaborative relations of community development. See Jaffe and Pilo', "Security Technology, Urban Prototyping, and the Politics of Failure."
22. However, as Norman emphasized, the unions had worked together to uphold the 60/40 labor deal to ensure that there was a balance between JLP and PNP supporters in a system he called "winner-takes-most." In contrast, the current arrangement, he told me, was different: "Dons are winners-take-all."
23. A *Jamaica Gleaner* review of the last time the event was held, in August 2009, noted that "Champions in Action is known as a well-organised, orderly event and the 2009 staging at Jamworld [sic], Portmore, St Catherine, last Saturday night was no different," and observed that "there were big-ups to the 'President' [Dudus], show organiser, all night." Cooke, "Too Many Champions for Consistent Action."
24. Frances-Pitt, "Did Dudus Force Entertainers to Perform?" The corporate sponsors included well-known national car dealerships, record companies, and television stations.
25. Frances-Pitt, "Did Dudus Force Entertainers to Perform?"
26. Frances-Pitt, "Did Dudus Force Entertainers to Perform?"
27. Jones-Griffith, "No Coercion in Action."
28. Jones-Griffith, "No Coercion in Action."
29. Jones-Griffith, "No Coercion in Action."
30. Jones-Griffith, "No Coercion in Action."
31. For example, Hull, "Documents and Bureaucracy"; Riles, *Documents*.
32. Navaro-Yashin, *The Make-Believe Space*, 33, 125.
33. Ministry of Justice, *Report Western Kingston Commission of Enquiry 2016*.
34. See, for example, Lessing and Willis, "Legitimacy in Criminal Governance"; Nugent, "Governing States."
35. For example, Davis, "Extortionists or Helpers?"; Spaulding, "They're Back!"; Spaulding, "Extortion Menace." The police lament the public's reluctance to report parking hustlers, admitting that they have not prosecuted anyone for extorting people for parking, despite the

existence of legislation that would result in fines or imprisonment for those found guilty of this practice. See Skyers, "Coping with the Hustlers of Downtown Kingston."
36. Bryan, "Visa Vehicle Hustle."
37. See Jensen and Hapal, "Police Violence and Corruption in the Philippines" for comparable attempts to reinterpret violent exchanges between citizens and violent police officers as longer-term state-citizen relationships.

CONCLUSION

1. Linke, "Contact Zones."
2. Masco, *The Theater of Operations*; Thomas, "Public Secrets."
3. Rutherford, *Living in the Stone Age*; Thomas, *Political Life*.
4. For similar work, see Kivland, *Street Sovereigns*.
5. Rudolph, "The Imperialism of Categories," 8.
6. See, for instance, Partha Chatterjee's influential work contrasting a Eurocentric notion of civil society with the concept of political society, but also conceptualizations of politics in the postcolony formulated by Achille Mbembe or Jean Comaroff and John Comaroff. Chatterjee, *The Politics of the Governed*; Mbembe, *On the Postcolony*; Comaroff and Comaroff, *Law and Disorder in the Postcolony*.
7. See, for example, Muggah, "Deconstructing the Fragile City."
8. Roy, "The 21st-Century Metropolis," 820. See Robinson and Roy, "Debate on Global Urbanisms and the Nature of Urban Theory."
9. For related analyses of hybrid forms of legality and authoritarianism, see, for example, McCann and Kahraman, "On the Interdependence of Liberal and Illiberal/Authoritarian Legal Forms"; Corrales, "The Authoritarian Resurgence." On Trump, autocracy, and criminal practices, see Kendzior, *Hiding in Plain Sight*.
10. See Jaffe, "Speculative Policing"; Thomas, "Public Secrets"; Campbell and Harriott, "The Resort to Emergency Policing."
11. Lewis, *Scammer's Yard*; Thorburn, *Scamming, Gangs, and Violence*.

Bibliography

Agamben, Giorgio. *Homo Sacer: Sovereign Power and Bare Life*. Stanford, CA: Stanford University Press, 1998.

Altink, Henrike. "The Politics of Infrastructure in Inner-City Communities in Kingston, Jamaica, from 1962 to 2020." *Journal of Urban History* 50, no. 1 (2022): 165–84.

Amnesty International. *Waiting in Vain: Jamaica: Unlawful Police Killings and Relatives' Long Struggle for Justice*. London: Amnesty International, 2016.

Anonymous. "Political Observations by Western Kingston Peace Committee." Telegram to the US Secretary of State, February 21, 1978. https://search.wikileaks.org/plusd/cables/1978KINGST02040_d.html.

Ardener, Shirley. "The Comparative Study of Rotating Credit Associations." *Journal of the Royal Anthropological Institute of Great Britain and Ireland* 94, no. 2 (1964): 201–29.

Arendt, Hannah. "What Was Authority?" *NOMOS: American Society for Political and Legal Philosophy* 1 (1958): 81–112.

Arias, Enrique Desmond. *Criminal Enterprises and Governance in Latin America and the Caribbean*. Cambridge: Cambridge University Press, 2017.

Arias, Enrique Desmond, and Daniel Goldstein, eds. *Violent Democracies in Latin America*. Durham, NC: Duke University Press, 2010.

Arias, Enrique Desmond, and Thomas Grisaffi. "Introduction: The Moral Economy of the Cocaine Trade." In *Cocaine: From Coca Fields to the Streets*, edited by Enrique Desmond Arias and Thomas Grisaffi, 1–40. Durham, NC: Duke University Press, 2021.

Banerjee, Mukulika. "Money and Meaning in Elections: Towards a Theory of the Vote." *Modern Asian Studies* 54, no. 1 (2020): 286–313.

Barrow-Giles, Cynthia. "Democracy at Work: A Comparative Study of the Caribbean State." *Round Table* 100, no. 414 (2011): 285–302.

Bénit-Gbaffou, Claire, and Obvious Katsaura. "Community Leadership and the Construction of Political Legitimacy: Unpacking Bourdieu's 'Political Capital' in Post-Apartheid Johannesburg." *International Journal of Urban and Regional Research* 38, no. 5 (2014): 1807–32.

Benjamin, Walter. *Reflections: Essays, Aphorisms and Autobiographical Writings*. New York: Schocken Books, 1978.

Benmergui, Leandro, and Rafael Soares Gonçalves. "*Urbanismo Miliciano* in Rio de Janeiro." *NACLA Report on the Americas* 51, no. 4 (2019): 379–85.

Benton, Lauren. *Law and Colonial Cultures: Legal Regimes in World History, 1400-1900*. Cambridge: Cambridge University Press, 2001.

Besson, Jean. "Folk Law and Legal Pluralism in Jamaica: A View from the Plantation-Peasant Interface." *Journal of Legal Pluralism and Unofficial Law* 31, no. 43 (1999): 31-56.

Björkman, Liza. "'You Can't Buy a Vote': Meanings of Money in a Mumbai Election." *American Ethnologist* 41, no. 4 (2014): 617-34.

Brigstocke, Julian, Patrick Bresnihan, Leila Dawney, and Naomi Millner. "Geographies of Authority." *Progress in Human Geography* 45, no. 6 (2021): 1356-78.

Bryan, Chad. "Visa Vehicle Hustle: Parking Business Booms outside US Embassy." *Jamaica Gleaner*, January 26, 2014. https://jamaica-gleaner.com/gleaner/20140126/auto/auto1.html.

Byles, Junior. "Bur-o-boy." YouTube, September 30, 2011. Video, 6:52. https://www.youtube.com/watch?v=rGSXefnZjYg.

Calderón, Gabriela, Gustavo Robles, Alberto Díaz-Cayeros, and Beatriz Magaloni. "The Beheading of Criminal Organizations and the Dynamics of Violence in Mexico." *Journal of Conflict Resolution* 59, no. 8 (2015): 1455-85.

Cameron, Angus. "Turning Point? The Volatile Geographies of Taxation." *Antipode* 38, no. 2 (2006): 236-58.

Campbell, Yonique. *Citizenship on the Margins: State Power, Security and Precariousness in 21st-Century Jamaica*. London: Palgrave Macmillan, 2020.

Campbell, Yonique, and Anthony Harriott. "The Resort to Emergency Policing to Control Gang Violence in Jamaica: Making the Exception the Rule." *Journal of Latin American Studies* 56, no. 1 (2024): 115-36.

Carnegie, Charles. "How Did There Come to Be a 'New Kingston'?" *Small Axe* 21, no. 3 (2017): 138-51.

Carnegie, Charles. "The Loss of the Verandah: Kingston's Constricted Postcolonial Geographies." *Social and Economic Studies* 63, no. 2 (2014): 59-85.

Charles, Christopher. "Business Ethics in Jamaica and the Problem of Extortion by Counter Societies." In *Ethical Perspectives for Caribbean Business*, edited by Noel M. Cowell, Archibald Campbell, Gavin Chen and Stanford Moore, 95-117. Kingston: Arawak Publications, 2007.

Charles, Christopher. "Garrison Communities as Counter Societies: The Case of the 1998 Zeeks Riot in Jamaica." *IDEAZ* 1, no. 1 (2002): 29-43.

Charles, Christopher. "Violence, Musical Identity, and the Celebrity of the Spanglers Crew in Jamaica." *Wadabagei* 12, no. 2 (2009): 52-79.

Charles, Christopher, and Orville Beckford. "The Informal Justice System in Garrison Constituencies." *Social and Economic Studies* 61, no. 2 (2012): 51-72.

Chatterjee, Partha. *The Politics of the Governed: Reflections on Popular Politics in Most of the World*. New York: Columbia University Press, 2004.

Chatty Mouth: Reggae, Rants and Reasoning. "Jr. Byles ~ Burr o boy." Posts by Stinking Bishop and blakbeltjonez Cheddar on January 2 and January 3, 2013. https://djgreedyg.proboards.com/thread/21503/jr-byles-burr-boy.

Chevannes, Barry. "Those Two Jamaicas: The Problem of Social Integration." In *Contending with Destiny: The Caribbean in the 21st Century*, edited by Kenneth Hall and Denis Benn, 179-84. Kingston: Ian Randle Publishers, 2001.

Cirolia, Liza Rose. "Contested Fiscal Geographies: Urban Authority, Everyday Practice, and Emerging State-Finance Relations." *Geoforum* 117 (2020): 33-41.

Clarke, Colin G. *Decolonizing the Colonial City: Urbanization and Stratification in Kingston, Jamaica.* Oxford: Oxford University Press, 2006.

Clarke, Colin G. *Kingston, Jamaica: Urban Development and Social Change, 1692-2002.* Kingston: Ian Randle Publishers, 2006.

Clarke, Kamari Maxine. *Affective Justice: The International Criminal Court and the Pan-Africanist Pushback.* Durham, NC: Duke University Press, 2019.

Closs Stephens, Angharad. "The Affective Atmospheres of Nationalism." *cultural geographies* 23, no. 2 (2016): 181-98.

Cohen, Corentin. "The 'Debate' and the Politics of the PCC's Informal Justice in São Paulo." *Contemporary Social Science* 17, no. 3 (2022): 235-47.

Comaroff, Jean, and John L. Comaroff, eds. *Law and Disorder in the Postcolony.* Chicago: University of Chicago Press, 2008.

Cooke, Mel. "Too Many Champions for Consistent Action: Bounty Killer, Mavado Bring Concert to Thunderous Climax." *Jamaica Gleaner*, August 19, 2009. http://old.jamaica-gleaner.com/gleaner/20090819/ent/ent4.html.

Cooper, Carolyn. *Sound Clash: Jamaican Dancehall Culture at Large.* New York: Palgrave Macmillan, 2004.

Corrales, Javier. "The Authoritarian Resurgence: Autocratic Legalism in Venezuela." *Journal of Democracy* 26, no. 2 (2015): 37-51.

Curtin, Philip. *Two Jamaicas: The Role of Ideas in a Tropical Colony, 1830-1865.* Cambridge, MA: Harvard University Press, 1955.

Dacres, Petrina. "Monuments and Meaning." *Small Axe* 8, no. 2 (2004): 137-53.

Davis, Carlene. "Extortionists or Helpers? Motorists Fume over Being Charged to Park on the Streets of Kingston but the Men Who Charge Say They Are Offering a Service." *Jamaica Gleaner*, April 27, 2018. https://jamaica-gleaner.com/article/lead-stories/20180429/extortionists-or-helpers-motorists-fume-over-being-charged-park.

Davis, Diane E. "Irregular Armed Forces, Shifting Patterns of Commitment, and Fragmented Sovereignty in the Developing World." *Theory and Society* 39, nos. 3-4 (2010): 397-413.

Duncan-Waite, Imani, and Michael Woolcock. *Arrested Development: The Political Origins and Socio-Economic Foundations of Common Violence in Jamaica.* Brooks World Poverty Institute Working Paper 46. Manchester: Brooks World Poverty Institute, 2008.

Durkheim, Émile. *The Elementary Forms of the Religious Life.* Translated by Joseph Ward Swain. New York: Free Press, 1965. First published 1912 by George Allen and Unwin (London).

Eder, Mine, and Özlem Öz. "Spatialities of Contentious Politics: The Case of Istanbul's Besiktas Neighborhood, Çarsi Footfall Fandom and Gezi." *Political Geography* 61 (2017): 57-66.

Ellis, Darren, Ian Tucker, and David Harper. "The Affective Atmospheres of Surveillance." *Theory and Psychology* 23, no. 6 (2013): 716-31.

Eyre, L. Alan. "Political Violence and Urban Geography in Kingston, Jamaica." *Geographical Review* 74, no. 1 (1984): 24-37.

Ference, Meghan E. "'You Will Build Me': Fiscal Disobedience, Reciprocity and the Dangerous Negotiations of Redistribution on Nairobi's Matatu." *Africa* 91, no. 1 (2021): 16-34.

Ferguson, James, and Akhil Gupta. "Spatializing States: Toward an Ethnography of Neoliberal Governmentality." *American Ethnologist* 29, no. 4 (2002): 981-1002.

Figueroa, Mark, Anthony Harriott, and Nicola Satchell. "The Political Economy of Jamaica's Inner-City Violence: A Special Case?" In *The Caribbean City*, edited by Rivke Jaffe, 94–122. Kingston: Ian Randle Publishers, 2008.

Figueroa, Mark, and Amanda Sives. "Homogeneous Voting, Electoral Manipulation and the 'Garrison' Process in Post-Independence Jamaica." *Journal of Commonwealth and Comparative Politics* 40, no. 1 (2002): 81–108.

Fitz-Henley, Abka. "Burke Defends Move to Invite Phang to NEC." NationWide Radio FM90, June 27, 2016. https://nationwideradiojm.com/burke-defends-move-to-invite-phang-to-nec/.

Fourchard, Laurent. *Classify, Exclude, Police: Urban Lives in South Africa and Nigeria*. Oxford: Wiley, 2021.

Frances-Pitt, K'Shema. "Did Dudus Force Entertainers to Perform on Champions in Action?" *IrieFM.net*, May 26, 2015. https://www.iriefm.net/did-dudus-forced-entertainers-to-perform-on-champions-in-action/.

Fraser, Alistair, and Daniel Matthews. "Towards a Criminology of Atmospheres: Law, Affect and the Codes of the Street." *Criminology and Criminal Justice* 21, no. 4 (2021): 455–71.

Furnivall, J. S. *Colonial Policy and Practice: A Comparative Study of Burma and Netherlands India*. Cambridge: Cambridge University Press, 1948.

Ghertner, D. Asher, Hudson McFann, and Daniel M. Goldstein. "Introduction: Security Aesthetics of and beyond the Biopolitical." In *Futureproof: Security Aesthetics and the Management of Life*, edited by D. Asher Ghertner, Hudson McFann, and Daniel M. Goldstein, 1–32. Durham, NC: Duke University Press, 2020.

Gray, Obika. *Demeaned but Empowered: The Social Power of the Urban Poor in Jamaica*. Kingston: University of West Indies Press, 2004.

Grossmann, Katrin, and Elena Trubina. "Dignity in Urban Geography: Starting a Conversation." *Dialogues in Human Geography* 12, no. 3 (2022): 406–26.

Gunst, Laurie. *Born fi' Dead: A Journey through the Yardie Underworld*. New York: Henry Holt, 1996.

Gupta, Akhil. "Blurred Boundaries: The Discourse of Corruption, the Culture of Politics, and the Imagined State." *American Ethnologist* 22, no. 2 (1995): 375–402.

Hall, Arthur. "Science Serving Justice: Forensic Lab Steps Up Its Game to Deal with Greater Use of Technology in Crime-Fighting." *Jamaica Observer*, December 2, 2019. https://www.jamaicaobserver.com/news/science-serving-justice-forensic-lab-steps-up-its-game-to-deal-with-greater-use-of-technology-in-crime-fighting_181166?profile=1470.

Hall, Stuart. "Notes on Deconstructing 'the Popular.'" In *People's History and Socialist Theory*, edited by Raphael Samuel, 227–40. London: Routledge, 2016. First published in 1981.

Hall, Stuart, with Bill Schwartz. *Familiar Stranger: A Life between Two Islands*. Durham, NC: Duke University Press, 2017.

Hansen, Thomas Blom. "Performers of Sovereignty: On the Privatization of Security in Urban South Africa." *Critique of Anthropology* 26, no. 3 (2006): 279–95.

Hansen, Thomas Blom, and Finn Stepputat. "Sovereignty Revisited." *Annual Review of Anthropology* 35 (2006): 295–315.

Harbers, Imke, Rivke Jaffe, and Victor Cummings. "A Battle for Hearts and Minds? Citizens' Perceptions of Formal and Irregular Governance Actors in Urban Jamaica." *Política y Gobierno* 23, no. 1 (2016): 97–123.

Harriott, Anthony. *Organized Crime and Politics in Jamaica: Breaking the Nexus*. Kingston: Canoe Press, 2008.

Harriott, Anthony, and Rivke Jaffe. "Security Encounters: Negotiating Authority and Citizenship During the Tivoli 'Incursion.'" *Small Axe* 22, no. 3 (2018): 81–89.

Harriott, Anthony, Balford Lewis, Carole Wilson, and Elizabeth Zechmeister. *The Political Culture of Democracy in Jamaica and in the Americas, 2018/19: Taking the Pulse of Democracy*. Nashville: Vanderbilt University, 2020.

Harrison, Faye V. "The Politics of Social Outlawry in Urban Jamaica." *Urban Anthropology* 17, nos. 2–3 (1988): 259–77.

Helps, H. G. "'Babsy,' Comrades Unite at George Phang's Birthday Bash." *Jamaica Observer*, April 2, 2016. https://www.jamaicaobserver.com/news/-babsy—comrades-unite-at-george-phang-s-birthday-bash_56484.

Helps, H. G. "'Dudus' vs Massop War Heats Up." *Jamaica Observer*, August 25, 2013. https://www.jamaicaobserver.com/news/-dudus—vs-massop-war-heats-up_14941075.

Helps, H. G. "George Phang, 'Dudus,' and That Peace Trip of 20 Years Ago." *Jamaica Observer*, May 7, 2016. http://www.jamaicaobserver.com/news/george-phang—dudus—and-that-peace-trip-of-20-years-ago_59482.

Helps, H. G. "I'm No Soft, Uptown Boy: Mark Golding Says He Can Handle the 'Don' Element." *Jamaica Observer*, June 4, 2016. http://www.jamaicaobserver.com/news/I-m-no-soft—uptown-boy_62957.

Helps, H. G. "Phang: I Never Ordered a Hit on Omar." *Jamaica Observer*, October 21, 2012. https://www.jamaicaobserver.com/news/Phang—I-never-ordered-a-hit-on-Omar-_12804881.

Henriques, Julian. *Sonic Bodies: Reggae Sound Systems, Performance Techniques, and Ways of Knowing*. London: Continuum, 2011.

Henry, Balford. "The 'Passa Passa' Phenomenon." *Jamaica Observer*, November 21, 2003. http://www.jamaicaobserver.com/lifestyle/html/20031120T210000-0500_51896_OBS_THE__PASSA_PASSA__PHENOMENON.asp.

Hibbert, Sybil E. "Permanent Secretary Gunned Down in Broad Daylight." *Jamaica Observer*, January 8, 2013. https://www.jamaicaobserver.com/news/Permanent-Secretary-gunned-down-in-broad-daylight_13318490.

Hintzen, Percy C. "Reproducing Domination Identity and Legitimacy Constructs in the West Indies." *Social Identities* 3, no. 1 (1997): 47–76.

Horowitz, Joel. "Football Clubs and Neighbourhoods in Buenos Aires Before 1943: The Role of Political Linkages and Personal Influence." *Journal of Latin American Studies* 46, no. 3 (2014): 557–85.

Hull, Matthew S. "Documents and Bureaucracy." *Annual Review of Anthropology* 41 (2012): 251–67.

Jaffe, Rivke. "Between Ballots and Bullets: Elections and Citizenship in and beyond the Nation-State." *Citizenship Studies* 19, no. 2 (2015): 128–40.

Jaffe, Rivke. "Cities and the Political Imagination." *Sociological Review* 66, no. 6 (2018): 1097–110.

Jaffe, Rivke. *Concrete Jungles: Urban Pollution and the Politics of Difference in the Caribbean*. New York: Oxford University Press, 2016.

Jaffe, Rivke. "Crime Watch: Mediating Belonging and the Politics of Place in Inner-City Jamaica." In *Stories of Cosmopolitan Belonging: Emotion and Location*, edited by Hannah Jones and Emma Jackson, 159–69. London: Routledge, 2014.

Jaffe, Rivke. "Criminal Dons and Extralegal Security Privatization in Downtown Kingston, Jamaica." *Singapore Journal of Tropical Geography* 33, no. 2 (2012): 184–97.

Jaffe, Rivke. "From Maroons to Dons: Sovereignty, Violence and Law in Jamaica." *Critique of Anthropology* 35, no. 1 (2015): 47–63.

Jaffe, Rivke. "The Hybrid State: Crime and Citizenship in Urban Jamaica." *American Ethnologist* 40, no. 4 (2013): 734–48.

Jaffe, Rivke. "Security Aesthetics and Political Community Formation in Kingston, Jamaica." In *Futureproof: Security Aesthetics and the Management of Life*, edited by D. Asher Ghertner, Daniel M. Goldstein, and Hudson McFann, 134–55. Durham, NC: Duke University Press, 2020.

Jaffe, Rivke. "Speculative Policing." *Public Culture* 31, no. 3 (2019): 447–68.

Jaffe, Rivke. "Writing around Violence: Representing Organized Crime in Kingston, Jamaica." *Ethnography* 20, no. 3 (2019): 379–96.

Jaffe, Rivke, Eveline Dürr, Gareth Jones, Alessandro Angelini, Alana Osbourne, and Barbara Vodopivec. "What Does Poverty Feel Like? Urban Inequality and the Politics of Sensation." *Urban Studies* 57, no. 5 (2020): 1015–31.

Jaffe, Rivke, and Francesca Pilo'. "Security Technology, Urban Prototyping, and the Politics of Failure." *Security Dialogue* 54, no. 1 (2023): 76–93.

Jakimow, Tanya. "Feeling/Making Democracy: Emotions of Candidates Contesting Dehradun Municipal Elections." *Ethnos* 88, no. 1 (2023): 130–48.

Jamaica Gleaner. "Desperate 'Dudus' Looks to PNP for Help." June 6, 2010. https://jamaica-gleaner.com/gleaner/20100606/lead/lead1.html.

Jamaica Gleaner. "MPs Turn Out for Funeral." May 9, 2001. http://old.jamaica-gleaner.com/gleaner/20010509/lead/lead1.html.

Jamaica Gleaner. "Video: West Kingston residents protest transfer of SSP McGregor." March 23, 2015. https://jamaica-gleaner.com/article/news/20150323/video-west-kingston-residents-protest-transfer-ssp-mcgregor.

Jensen, Steffen, and Karl Hapal. "Police Violence and Corruption in the Philippines: Violent Exchange and the War on Drugs." *Journal of Current Southeast Asian Affairs* 37, no. 2 (2018): 39–62.

Jones-Griffith, Julian. "No Coercion in Action." *No Retreat No Surrender* (blog), May 31, 2015. https://julianjonesgriffith.wordpress.com/2015/05/31/no-coercion-in-action/.

Karandinos, George, Laurie Kain Hart, Fernando Montero Castrillo, and Philippe Bourgois. "The Moral Economy of Violence in the US Inner City." *Current Anthropology* 55, no. 1 (2014): 1–22.

Kauppinen, Anna-Riikka. "God's Delivery State: Taxes, Tithes, and a Rightful Return in Urban Ghana." *Social Analysis* 64, no. 2 (2020): 38–58.

Kendzior, Sarah. *Hiding in Plain Sight: The Invention of Donald Trump and the Erosion of America*. New York: Flatiron Books, 2020.

Kivland, Chelsey. "Becoming a Force in the Zone: Hedonopolitics, Masculinity, and the Quest for Respect on Haiti's Streets." *Cultural Anthropology* 29, no. 4 (2014): 672–98.

Kivland, Chelsey. *Street Sovereigns: Young Men and the Makeshift State in Urban Haiti*. Ithaca, NY: Cornell University Press, 2020.

Laurent, Inga N. "From Retribution to Restoration: Implementing Nationwide Restorative Justice Initiatives: Lessons from Jamaica." *Fordham International Law Journal* 42, no. 4 (2017): 1095–166.

Leeds, Elizabeth. "Cocaine and Parallel Polities in the Brazilian Urban Periphery: Constraints on Local-Level Democratization." *Latin American Research Review* 31, no. 3 (1996): 47–83.

Lessing, Benjamin, and Graham Denyer Willis. "Legitimacy in Criminal Governance: Managing a Drug Empire from Behind Bars." *American Political Science Review* 113, no. 2 (2019): 584–606.

Levers, Leanne Alexis. "RJ Policy Transfer: The Case of Jamaica." PhD diss., University of Warwick, 2017.

Levi, Darrell E. *Michael Manley: The Making of a Leader*. Athens: University of Georgia Press, 1990.

Levy, Horace. *Youth Violence and Organized Crime in Jamaica: An Examination of the Linkages and Disconnections*. Kingston: Institute of Criminal Justice and Security, 2012.

Lewis, Jovan Scott. *Scammer's Yard: The Crime of Black Repair in Jamaica*. Minneapolis: University of Minnesota Press, 2020.

Lewis, Rupert. "Party Politics in Jamaica and the Extradition of Christopher 'Dudus' Coke." *The Global South* 6, no. 1 (2012): 38–54.

Lewis, Rupert. "Walter Rodney: 1968 Revisited." *Social and Economic Studies* 43, no. 3 (1994): 7–56.

Linke, Uli. "Contact Zones: Rethinking the Sensual Life of the State." *Anthropological Theory* 6, no. 2 (2006): 205–25.

Lund, Christian. "An Air of Legality: Legalization under Conditions of Rightlessness in Indonesia." *Journal of Peasant Studies* 50, no. 4 (2022): 1295–1316. https://doi.org/10.1080/03066150.2022.2096448.

Makovicky, Nicolette, and Robin Smith. "Introduction: Tax beyond the Social Contract." *Social Analysis* 64, no. 2 (2020): 1–17.

Maoz, Eilat. "Black Police Power: The Political Moment of the Jamaica Constabulary." *Comparative Studies in Society and History* 65, no. 1 (2023): 115–40.

Martin, Isaac William, Ajay K. Mehrotra, and Monica Prasad. "The Thunder of History: The Origins and Development of the New Fiscal Sociology." In *The New Fiscal Sociology: Taxation in Comparative and Historical Perspective*, edited by Isaac William Martin, Ajay K. Mehrotra, and Monica Prasad, 1–27. Cambridge: Cambridge University Press, 2009.

Masco, Joseph. *The Theater of Operations: National Security Affect from the Cold War to the War on Terror*. Durham, NC: Duke University Press, 2014.

Maurer, Bill. "The Disunity of Finance: Alternative Practices to Western Finance." In *The Oxford Handbook of the Sociology of Finance*, edited by Karin Knorr Cetina and Alex Preda, 413–30. Oxford: Oxford University Press, 2011.

Mbembe, Achille. *On the Postcolony*. Berkeley: University of California Press, 2001.

McCallum, Cecilia. "Racialized Bodies, Naturalized Classes: Moving through the City of Salvador Da Bahia." *American Ethnologist* 32, no. 1 (2005): 100–117.

McCann, Michael, and Filiz Kahraman. "On the Interdependence of Liberal and Illiberal/Authoritarian Legal Forms in Racial Capitalist Regimes . . . The Case of the United States." *Annual Review of Law and Social Science* 17 (2021): 483–503.

McFadden, David. "Jamaica Police Erasing Gang Murals in Slums." *AP News*, October 17, 2013. https://apnews.com/article/bc4614bf5b3f45ef9c15854609db8fad.

Meeks, Brian. *Critical Interventions in Caribbean Politics and Theory*. Jackson: University of Mississippi Press, 2014.

Meeks, Brian. *Envisioning Caribbean Futures: Jamaican Perspectives*. Kingston: University of the West Indies Press, 2007.

Meeks, Brian. *Narratives of Resistance: Jamaica, Trinidad, the Caribbean*. Kingston: University of the West Indies Press, 2000.

Meeks, Brian. "Reprising the Past, Imagining the Future." *Small Axe* 20, no. 2 (2016): 187–98.

Meikle, Tracian. "Iconization of Donmanship and Popular Culture as Site of Struggle." In *Most Wanted: The Popular Culture of Illegality*, edited by Rivke Jaffe and Martijn Oosterbaan, 43–47. Amsterdam: Amsterdam University Press, 2019.

Meikle, Tracian. "The Multivalency of Memorial Murals in Kingston, Jamaica: A Photo-Essay." *Interventions* 22, no. 1 (2020): 106–15.

Meikle, Tracian, and Rivke Jaffe. "'Police as the New Don'? An Assessment of Post-Dudus Policing Strategies in Jamaica." *Caribbean Journal of Criminology* 1, no. 2 (2015): 75–100.

Meikle, Tracian, and Rivke Jaffe. "Scripts Héroïques: Le Cas de Christopher 'Dudus' Coke, Don Jamaïcain." *Terrain* 74 (2021): 152–67.

Méndez Beck, Max, and Rivke Jaffe. "Community Policing goes South: Policy Mobilities and New Geographies of Criminological Theory." *British Journal of Criminology* 59, no. 4 (2019): 823–41.

Michelutti, Lucia. "Racket Sociality: Investigating Intimidation in North India." *Journal of the Royal Anthropological Institute of Great Britain and Ireland*, forthcoming.

Michelutti, Lucia. *The Vernacularisation of Democracy: Politics, Caste and Religion in India*. New Delhi: Routledge, 2008.

Michelutti, Lucia, Ashraf Hoque, Nicolas Martin, David Picherit, Paul Rollier, Arild E. Ruud, and Clarinda Still. *Mafia Raj: The Rule of Bosses in South Asia*. Stanford, CA: Stanford University Press, 2018.

Ministry of Justice. *Jamaican Justice System Reform Task Force: Final Report*. Kingston: Ministry of Justice, 2007. https://moj.gov.jm/sites/default/files/2019-10/JJSRTF%20FINAL%20REPORT_6Jun07.pdf.

Ministry of Justice. *The National Restorative Justice Policy*. Kingston: Ministry of Justice, 2012. https://moj.gov.jm/sites/default/files/2020-10/Restorative%20Justice%20Policy_Revised_%20Final_Policy_March_18.pdf.

Ministry of Justice. *Report Western Kingston Commission of Enquiry 2016*. Appendix 26: List of Documents Found at Christopher Coke's Office. Kingston: Ministry of Justice, 2016. https://moj.gov.jm/news/report-western-kingston-commission-enquiry-2016.

Mirzoeff, Nicholas. *The Right to Look: A Counterhistory of Visuality*. Durham, NC: Duke University Press, 2011.

Mitchell, Timothy. "Society, Economy, and the State Effect." In *State/Culture: State Formation after the Cultural Turn*, edited by George Steinmetz, 76–97. Ithaca, NY: Cornell University Press, 1999.

Muggah, Robert. "Deconstructing the Fragile City: Exploring Insecurity, Violence and Resilience." *Environment and Urbanization* 26, no. 2 (2014): 345–58.

National Committee on Political Tribalism. *Report of the National Committee on Political Tribalism (Kerr Report)*. Kingston: Jamaica Information Service, 1997. https://rightstepsandpouitrees.files.wordpress.com/2016/06/kerr-report.pdf.

NationWide Radio 90FM, "Andrew Holness Must Break Criminal Justice." MP3 audio. https://nationwideradiojm.com/wp-content/uploads/2017/07/Andrew-Holness-must-break-criminal-justice-July-13.mp3.

Navaro-Yashin, Yael. *The Make-Believe Space: Affective Geography in a Postwar Polity*. Durham, NC: Duke University Press, 2012.

Nicholson, A. J. "Responsibility: The Conversation." *Jamaica Gleaner*, June 21, 2009. http://old.jamaica-gleaner.com/gleaner/20090621/focus/focus9.html.

Nugent, David. "Governing States." In *A Companion to the Anthropology of Politics*, edited by David Nugent and Joan Vincent, 198–215. Malden, MA: Blackwell, 2004.

O'Neill, Kevin Lewis. "Terminal Velocity: The Speed of Extortion in Guatemala City." *Environment and Planning A: Economy and Space* 53, no. 5 (2021): 977–91.

Oosterbaan, Martijn, and Rivke Jaffe. "Popular Art, Crime and Urban Order beyond the State." *Theory, Culture and Society* 39, nos. 7–8 (2022): 181–200. https://doi.org/10.1177/02632764221076429.

Osbourne, Alana. "On a Walking Tour to No Man's Land: Brokering and Shifting Narratives of Violence in Trench Town, Jamaica." *Space and Culture* 23, no. 1 (2020): 48–60.

Palmer, Colin. *Freedom's Children: The 1938 Labor Rebellion and the Birth of Modern Jamaica*. Chapel Hill: University of North Carolina Press, 2014.

Paul, Annie. "'No Grave Cannot Hold My Body Down': Rituals of Death and Burial in Postcolonial Jamaica." *Small Axe* 11, no. 2 (2007): 142–62.

Philippopoulos-Mihalopoulos, Andreas. *Spatial Justice: Body, Lawscape, Atmosphere*. New York: Routledge, 2014.

Price, Charles. "What the Zeeks Uprising Reveals: Development Issues, Moral Economy, and the Urban Lumpenproletariat in Jamaica." *Urban Anthropology and Studies of Cultural Systems and World Economic Development* 33, no. 1 (2004): 73–113.

Provost, René. *Rebel Courts: The Administration of Justice by Armed Insurgents*. New York: Oxford University Press, 2021.

Purcell, Trevor W. "Local Institutions in Grassroots Development: The Rotating Savings and Credit Association." *Social and Economic Studies* 49, no. 1 (2000): 143–81.

Rancière, Jacques. *The Politics of Aesthetics: The Distribution of the Sensible*. New York: Continuum, 2004.

Rapley, John. "Jamaica: Negotiating Law and Order with the Dons." *NACLA Report on the Americas* 37, no. 2 (2003): 25–29.

Rasmussen, Jacob. "Inside the System, Outside the Law: Operating the Matatu Sector in Nairobi." *Urban Forum* 23, no. 4 (2012): 415–32.

Reiter, Bernd. *The Crisis of Liberal Democracy and the Path Ahead: Alternatives to Political Representation and Capitalism*. London: Rowman and Littlefield International, 2017.

Rhiney, Kevon, and Romain Cruse. "'Trench Town Rock': Reggae Music, Landscape Inscription, and the Making of Place in Kingston, Jamaica." *Urban Studies Research* (2012): 1–12. https://doi.org/10.1155/2012/585160.

Riles, Annelise, ed. *Documents: Artifacts of Modern Knowledge*. Ann Arbor: University of Michigan Press, 2006.

Rios, Victor M. *Punished: Policing the Lives of Black and Latino Boys*. New York: NYU Press, 2011.

Robinson, Corey. "Extortion: Culture of Silence." *Jamaica Gleaner*, April 10, 2014. https://jamaica-gleaner.com/gleaner/20140410/lead/lead1.html.

Robinson, Jennifer, and Ananya Roy. "Debate on Global Urbanisms and the Nature of Urban Theory." *International Journal of Urban and Regional Research* 40, no. 1 (2016): 181–86.

Rodgers, Dennis. "The State as a Gang: Conceptualizing the Governmentality of Violence in Contemporary Nicaragua." *Critique of Anthropology* 26, no. 3 (2006): 315–30.

Roitman, Janet. *Fiscal Disobedience: An Anthropology of Economic Regulation in Central Africa*. Princeton University Press, 2005.

Roy, Ananya. "The 21st-Century Metropolis: New Geographies of Theory." *Regional Studies* 43, no. 6 (2009): 819–30.

Rudolph, Susanne Hoeber. "The Imperialism of Categories: Situating Knowledge in a Globalizing World." *Perspectives on Politics* 3, no. 1 (2005): 5–14.

Rutherford, Danilyn. *Living in the Stone Age: Reflections on the Origins of a Colonial Fantasy*. Chicago: University of Chicago Press, 2018.

Santino, Jack. "Performative Commemoratives, the Personal, and the Public: Spontaneous Shrines, Emergent Ritual, and the Field of Folklore." *Journal of American Folklore* 117, no. 466 (2004): 363–72.

Saunders-Hastings, Katherine. "Du code du barrio à l'idéologie d'une entreprise: L'extorsion et l'économie morale de la violence des gangs au Guatemala." *Cultures et Conflits* 110 (2018): 121–40.

Schoburgh, Eris D. "Local Government Reform in Jamaica and Trinidad: A Policy Dilemma." *Public Administration and Development* 27, no. 2 (2007): 159–74.

Scott, David. "The Permanence of Pluralism." In *Without Guarantees: In Honour of Stuart Hall*, edited by Paul Gilroy, Lawrence Grossberg, and Angela McRobbie, 282–301. New York: Verso, 2000.

Scott, David. "Political Rationalities of the Jamaican Modern." *Small Axe* 7, no. 2 (2003): 1–22.

Sewell, Lileth. "Music in the Jamaican Labour Movement." *Jamaica Journal* 44 (1979): 43–55.

Sheild Johansson, Miranda. "Tax." In *The Cambridge Encyclopedia of Anthropology*, edited by Felix Stein, 1–16. Cambridge: Cambridge University Press, 2020; online ed., 2023. http://doi.org/10.29164/20tax.

Sheild Johansson, Miranda. "Taxes for Independence: Rejecting a Fiscal Model of Reciprocity in Peri-Urban Bolivia." *Social Analysis* 64, no. 2 (2020): 18–37.

Sheller, Mimi. *Citizenship from Below: Erotic Agency and Caribbean Freedom*. Durham, NC: Duke University Press, 2016.

Sinclair, Glenroy. "Emotional Farewell for 'Haggart.'" *Jamaica Gleaner*, May 9, 2001. http://old.jamaica-gleaner.com/gleaner/20010509/news/news1.html.

Singham, A. W. *The Hero and the Crowd in a Colonial Polity*. New Haven, CT: Yale University Press, 1968.

Sistren, with Honor Ford-Smith. *Lionheart Gal: Life Stories of Jamaican Women*. Kingston: University of the West Indies Press, 2005. First published in 1986.

Sives, Amanda. "Changing Patrons, from Politician to Drug Don: Clientelism in Downtown Kingston, Jamaica." *Latin American Perspectives* 29, no. 5 (2002): 66–89.

Sives, Amanda. *Elections, Violence and the Democratic Process in Jamaica*. Kingston: Ian Randle Publishers, 2010.

Skyers, Javene. "Coping with the Hustlers of Downtown Kingston: Police Say Shoppers in Market District Not Reporting Acts of Extortion." *Jamaica Observer*, October 17, 2015. https://www.jamaicaobserver.com/news/Coping-with-the-hustlers-of-downtown-Kingston_19234055.

Smith, M. G. *The Plural Society in the British West Indies*. Berkeley: University of California Press, 1965.

Sneath, David, Martin Holbraad, and Morten Axel Pedersen. "Technologies of the Imagination: An Introduction." *Ethnos* 74, no. 1 (2009): 5–30.

Spaulding, Gary. "Extortion Menace: Crime on the Rise As Downtown Kingston Returns to Pre-Tivoli Incursion State." *Jamaica Gleaner*, September 10, 2013. https://jamaica-gleaner.com/gleaner/20130910/lead/lead1.html.

Spaulding, Gary. "They're Back! Extortionists Extracting a Heavy Toll." *Jamaica Gleaner*, September 19, 2011. https://jamaica-gleaner.com/gleaner/20110919/lead/lead5.html.

Spaulding, Gary. "Web of Conspiracy." *Jamaica Gleaner*, August 22, 2012. https://jamaica-gleaner.com/gleaner/20120822/lead/lead1.html.

Stanley-Niaah, Sonjah. "Kingston's Dancehall: A Story of Space and Celebration." *Space and Culture* 7, no. 1 (2004): 102–18.

Stanley-Niaah, Sonjah. "Readings of 'Ritual' and Community in Dancehall Performance." *Wadabagei* 9, no. 2 (2006): 47–73.

Swart, Floor. "Producing State-Effect in the Inner-Cities of Kingston, Jamaica: How Does the Extraction of Taxes Influences the Ability to Govern and Enhances Feelings of Citizenship?" Master's thesis, Utrecht University, 2014.

Thame, Maziki. "Woman Out of Place: Portia Simpson-Miller and Middle-Class Politics in Jamaica." In *Black Women in Politics: Demanding Citizenship, Challenging Power, and Seeking Justice*, edited by Julia S. Jordan-Zachery and Nikol G. Alexander-Floyd, 143–64. Albany, NY: SUNY Press, 2018.

Thomas, Deborah A. "Caribbean Studies, Archive Building, and the Problem of Violence." *Small Axe* 17, no. 2 (2013): 27–42.

Thomas, Deborah A. *Exceptional Violence: Embodied Citizenship in Transnational Jamaica*. Durham, NC: Duke University Press, 2011.

Thomas, Deborah A. *Modern Blackness: Nationalism, Globalization, and the Politics of Culture in Jamaica*. Durham, NC: Duke University Press, 2004.

Thomas, Deborah A. *Political Life in the Wake of the Plantation: Sovereignty, Witnessing, Repair*. Durham, NC: Duke University Press, 2019.

Thomas, Deborah A. "Public Secrets, Militarization, and the Cultivation of Doubt: Kingston 2010." In *Caribbean Military Encounters*, edited by Shalini Puri and Lara Putnam, 289–309. New York: Palgrave Macmillan, 2017.

Thomas, Deborah A. "Time and the Otherwise: Plantations, Garrisons and Being Human in the Caribbean." *Anthropological Theory* 16, nos. 2–3 (2016): 177–200.

Thomas, Michelle. "Holness Insists Tivoli Residents Will Be Compensated." NationWide Radio FM90, July 14, 2017. https://nationwideradiojm.com/holness-insists-tivoli-residents-will-be-compensated/.

Thompson, Edward P. "The Moral Economy of the English Crowd in the Eighteenth Century." *Past and Present* 50 (1971): 76–136.

Thorburn, Diana, with Joanna Callen, Herbert Gayle, and Laura Koch. *Scamming, Gangs, and Violence in Montego Bay*. Kingston: CAPRI, 2019.

Ulysse, Gina. *Downtown Ladies: Informal Commercial Importers, a Haitian Anthropologist and Self-Making in Jamaica*. Chicago: University of Chicago Press, 2007.

United States Attorney, Southern District of New York. "Jamaican Drug Lord Christopher Michael Coke Sentenced in Manhattan Federal Court to 23 Years in Prison." Press release, June 8, 2012. https://www.justice.gov/archive/usao/nys/pressreleases/June12/cokechristophersentencing.html/.

Urbinati, Nadia, and Mark E. Warren. "The Concept of Representation in Contemporary Democratic Theory." *Annual Review of Political Science* 11 (2008): 387–412.

Venkatesan, Soumhya. "Afterword: Putting Together the Anthropology of Tax and the Anthropology of Ethics." *Social Analysis* 64, no. 2 (2020): 141–54.

Von Benda-Beckman, Franz, Keebet von Benda-Beckman, and Julia Eckert, eds. *Rules of Law and Laws of Ruling: On the Governance of Law*. London: Routledge, 2009.

Wacquant, Loïc. *Urban Outcasts: A Comparative Sociology of Advanced Marginality*. Cambridge: Polity Press, 2007.

Walker, Karyl. "Burry Boy and Feathermop: The Violent Duo That Helped and Shamed the PNP." *Sunday Observer*, January 20, 2008. https://www.jamaicaobserver.com/news/Burry-Boy-and-Feathermop:-The-violent-duo-that-helped-and-shamed-the-PNP.

Weber, Max. *Economy and Society: An Outline of Interpretive Sociology*. Edited by Guenther Roth and Claus Wittich. Berkeley: University of California Press, 1978. First published 1922 by Mohr Siebeck (Tübingen).

Young, Alison. "Japanese Atmospheres of Criminal Justice." *British Journal of Criminology* 59, no. 4 (2019): 765–79.

Zeiderman, Austin. *Endangered City: The Politics of Security and Risk in Bogotá*. Durham, NC: Duke University Press, 2016.

Index

abolition of slavery, 29, 108
aesthetics: and authority, 5, 14-15, 20, 79, 92, 162-64; of documents, 156; and party politics, 84, 94, 103; police use of, 125; security, 104, 105, 128-31
affective atmospheres: of authority, 13-14, 20, 30, 162-63; of festivity, 31, 102; of intimacy, 78; of security, 128-30
Agamben, Giorgio, 170n20
air-conditioning, 50, 57, 59, 62, 85, 158, 163
Alkaline, 22
Allen, Edward Vivian, 31-32
anti-mural campaign, 93, 125-26
Apartheid, 56
archiving: of affect, 26; and authority, 78; by dons, 156
Arendt, Hannah, 12-13
Arnett Gardens, 34, 71; Football Club, 67-68, 88-89; George Phang and, 88-89; Willy Haggart and, 63, 88, 90-91
authenticity, 36-37
autocracy, 129; and antidemocratic values, 161; and democracy, 6, 21, 162, 166; and jurisprudence, 117, 131

ballot boxes, 35, 38
Barth, Dennis "Copper," 36
baz, 6, 16
Beenieman, 67, 89
Benjamin, Walter, 108

Biden, Joe, 165
BITU, 22, 29, 30, 149
blackness, 58; and class and gender, 60-61; and policing, 58, 106, 114, 131; and politicians, 23, 30, 60, 79, 171n17; and sufferation, 11; and urban space, 52-54, 56
Black Power, 23, 175n20
Black radicalism, 23
Black Roses Crew, 63, 88, 90-91
Bogle, Paul, 89
Bolsonaro, Jair, 6, 165
borders, 69-73; transcending of, 74-78
Bounty Killer, 154-57
Brazil, 6, 165
Brown, Jim, 26, 48, 173n24; and community justice, 118; funeral, 88; Memorial Dance, 101-2; and Shower Posse, 101
Brown, Tony, 77, 134, 177nn1-2
bureaucracy: dons' entanglement with, 7, 10, 20, 41-42, 162; dons' own, 156-58. *See also* documents
Burry Boy, 88, 174n8
Bustamante, Alexander, 89, 171n11; and BITU, 22, 29-30; and labor riots, 28; and music, 22-23, 29-30

Canada, 74, 76, 177n28
capitalism, 4, 35, 172n29, 174n5
Carnegie, Charles, 54
cell phones, 81, 120-21, 166
Cham, 37-39

Champions in Action, 152–57, 179n23
Charles, Christopher, 169n7
Christianity. *See* religion
Chronixx, 22–24, 47
Chubby Dread, 76
churches, 10, 127, 138, 145
Citizens Association, 85–86, 133–34
citizenship, 25, 137, 180n37; corporate, 150; and elections, 30, 33, 96, 99; and unions, 30
Cocoa Tea, 27–29
Coke, Christopher. *See* Dudus
Coke, Lester Lloyd. *See* Brown, Jim
Cold War, 4, 24, 35–36, 96, 103, 174n5
Colombia, 19
colonialism, 24, 28, 44, 165, 171n7; and legal pluralism, 107–8; and urban development, 58, 105
community justice, 106, 115–21
construction companies, 39; and extortion, 50, 148–52
consumption, 56–57
contracts. *See* documents
corulers, dons as, 39–44
counterarchives, 78
Cuba, 35, 88, 134. *See also* Cold War

Dacres, Petrina, 49
dancehall. *See* music; musical heroes; music industry; street dances; *and individual artists*
dances. *See* street dances
democracy: and autocracy, 6, 162, 166; participatory, 21, 84
democratic institutions, 21, 164
democratic socialism, 35, 174n5
democratic values and ideals, 11, 27, 96
diaspora, 76–78
documents, 111, 154–59
drug dealers, 69, 77
drug trafficking, 4, 5, 17–18, 19, 38
Dudus, 1–5, 8, 26, 173, 179n23; donmanship after, 44–47; and extortion, 140, 153–57; extradition of, 99, 177; and peace treaties, 27, 68, 75; popular music references to, 42–44, 48, 75; 172n29; and religious references, 28, 30; and security, 117, 118; and street dances, 68–69, 130; and youth curfews, 119, 124

Early Bird, 26, 36, 101, 126
elections: 1944, 29, 30; 1949, 31–33, 40; 1980, 36, 37–38, 133; 1985, 35; 2011, 17, 40, 99–101; and hedonopolitics, 31, 94–96, 102, 109. *See also* ballot boxes; democracy; electoral fraud; violence: electoral
electoral campaigns, 29, 31–33, 94–95, 99–102, 103, 109–10
electoral fraud, 35, 38
electricity theft, 41, 143, 172n26, 179n21
Europe, 10, 164

FBI, 61
fear, 17, 79, 156; affective atmospheres of, 129–30, 163; of dons, 5, 11, 13, 19, 65, 81, 87, 139; of the police, 45; of the urban poor, 6, 57
Feather Mop, 88
femininity, 60–61
firearms, 19, 31–32, 35, 74, 77, 82–83, 84, 131
Flash, George, 134, 177n1
football, 67–69, 81, 88–89, 90, 173n15
Fraser-Price, Shelly-Ann, 67
freedom, 11, 20, 56–58, 79, 96, 143; of movement, 78
funerals, 63, 88–89, 93, 103, 134, 162
Furnivall, J. S., 7

garrison, dismantling of, 44–45, 48, 166–67
garrison politics, 2–4, 21; definition of, 34; governmentality and, 34, 38; history of, 33–39
Garvey, Marcus, 48, 89, 90
Gaza, 86–87
gender, 16–17, 32, 56, 60–62, 173n12
geographies: of dignity, 52; of inequality, 52–59, 79, 163; political, 14, 51, 138; of protection, 16; of theory, 164–66
Golding, Bruce, 1, 43–44, 55, 99

Golding, Mark, 60, 61
graffiti, 128, 130, 163; don-related, 71, 104; party political, 34, 72, 90, 104
Gunst, Laurie, 18

Haggart, Willy: funeral of, 88–89; memorial dance for, 101; murals of, 63–64, 90–91
Haile Selassie, 90
Haiti, 6, 16–17
Half Pint, 3, 8
Hall, Stuart, 171n6
Hamas, 86–87
Hansen, Thomas Blom, 11
Harrison, Faye, 169n7
hedonopolitics, 31, 125
Holness, Andrew, 99, 127
homicides, 17, 73, 80; rates of, 21, 75, 161, 172n30; police, 75, 108–9
hope, 94, 102, 163

illiberalism, 165–66, 180n9
immobility, 51, 65, 57, 78, 79
informers, 17, 77, 121–22, 128, 131
Italy, 6, 164

Jamaica Constabulary Force (JCF). *See* police
Jamaica Defense Force (JDF). *See* military
Jamaica Public Service Company Limited (JPS), 143, 150, 179n21. *See also* electricity theft
Japan, 164
Johnson, Boris, 166
Jones-Griffith, Julian, 153–57
Jungle. *See* Arnett Gardens
jungle justice. *See* community justice

Kartel, Vybz, 22, 122
Kivland, Chelsey, 16–17, 31

labor: organizing by dons, 136, 148–52, 179n22; movement, 30, 33, 171n13, 171n17; unrest, 25, 28, 29–30. *See also* BITU; NWU; TUC

land tenure, 108. *See also* squatter settlements
language. *See* Patois
legal hybridity, 121–27
letters. *See* documents
Lewis, Cleve, 31–32
Lewis, Jovan, 170n18
London, 75
Louie Culture, 27–29
love, 13, 58, 99, 119, 163
Lula da Silva, Luiz Inácio, 165
Lund, Christian, 175n2

mafia, 6, 108, 164
Mafia Raj, 6
Mandela, Nelson, 90
Manley, Michael, 35, 75, 88, 90, 174n5
Manley, Norman Washington, 29, 89, 171n11
marijuana, 145
markets: dons' governance of, 43; and extortion, 70, 75, 135–36, 139–40, 142, 158, 160, 178n15; shopping at, 15, 56
Marley, Bob, 90
Marley, Damian "Junior Gong," 3, 131
Marshall, Bucky, 26, 74–75
masculinity, 61–62, 143
Massop, Claudie, 26, 36, 48, 74–75, 101, 118, 173n24
Maurer, Bill, 144
media: coverage of dons, 3, 5, 68, 76–78, 89, 136, 166; coverage of extortion, 136, 158; coverage of politicians, 60; scandals, 109; social, 125, 176n21
Meeks, Brian, 8–9
Meloni, Giorgia, 166
methodology, 15–20
Mexico, 172n32
migration, 43–44, 47, 56, 178n3
militarization of policing, 15, 44–47, 56, 166–67
military, 1, 10, 16, 45, 56, 166. *See also* militarization of policing; security operations
Miller, Jacob, 75
Mirzoeff, Nicholas, 90

INDEX 195

Miss Lou, 48, 90
mobility, 51, 78–79; social, 54, 65; transnational, 78
monarchy, 12, 86
Montego Bay, 45, 166, 172n30
moral economy, 137, 141, 149, 154, 160, 178n6
Morgan, Natty, 36
Mr. Vegas, 152–53
murals, 13–14; assemblage, 89–91, 103; memorial, 14, 63–66, 71, 77, 125–26, 128–29, 161; of local heroes, 67, 90–93; of politicians, 34, 89–91, 93; tradition of, 14, 84, 89; vandalization of, 90, 92–93, 103, 167. *See also* anti-mural campaign
murders. *See* homicides
music: and bodily sensations, 13–14, 95, 102, 162; and elections, 31–33, 172n21; and political imagination, 24, 25, 29–30, 36, 131. *See also* musical heroes; music industry; street dances
musical heroes, 48, 67, 90–92
music industry, and connections to dons, 10, 39, 69, 152–57

Nanny of the Maroons, 48, 89
National Heroes, 22–24, 28, 29, 47, 48, 89
Navaro, Yael, 156
neoliberalism, 10, 39, 42
Netherlands, 86, 105
New York, 76, 77
No Man's Land, 71
nongovernmental organizations (NGOs), 10, 16, 42, 59
NWU, 29, 149

Obama, Barack, 86, 90
Orbán, Viktor, 6, 166

pardna, 144–47
parking, and extortion, 70, 136, 157–60
Passa Passa, 43, 68–69, 72. *See also* street dances
Patois, 54, 56, 60, 111

Patterson, P. J., 90, 176n13
peace treaties, 27, 68, 74–75, 78, 174n26
Phang, George "Pepper," 68, 88, 89, 174n7, 175n11
Phipps, Donald. *See* Zeeks
Phipps, Glenford. *See* Early Bird
place-making, 67–69
plantations, and colonialism, 28, 108, 165, 171n7, 171n13
pleasure, 14, 31, 95, 125. *See also* hedonopolitics
pluralism, 10; legal, 106–9, 121, 123–24, 127, 176n3; violent, 9
plural society theory, 7–9
police: colonial, 28; entanglement with dons, 7, 10, 123–24, 162, 176n15; elite encounters with, 109–15, 132; killings, 75, 108–9; corruption, 114; brutality, 19, 49, 114–15; legendary officers, 37–38, 124–25. *See also* informers; militarization of policing; security operations; Tivoli Incursion; violence: state
political imagination, 25–26, 47, 49, 171n6
political philosophy, 95, 166
postcolonial nations, 7–9. *See also* states: postcolonial
poverty, sensorial experience of, 54–57, 59–60, 79, 163
Presidential Click, 10, 69, 152, 153, 157, 170n16
Price, Charles, 169n1, 169n7
protests: in support of dons, 1, 8–9, 23, 25, 27–28, 85, 169n7; labor, 25, 28, 171n17; in support of police, 125; against taxes, 137, 138; in support of Walter Rodney, 23. *See also* riots
Protoje, 22–24, 48
Purcell, Trevor, 146
Putin, Vladimir, 6, 166

Queen Ifrica, 48, 153–54

Rae Town, 67, 94–95
Rancière, Jacques, 167

Ranks, Cutty, 75
rape, 115, 119
Rastafari, 22–23, 34, 39, 90
reggae. *See* music; musical heroes; music industry; *and individual artists*
religion: dons and references to, 1, 26, 28, 30, 62–65; and the middle class, 8; and musical traditions, 29–30. *See also* Rastafari
Rema. *See* Wilton Gardens
representation, political, 84–87
restorative justice, 177n28
Rios, Victor, 170n31
riots: labor, 28; Rodney, 23; Zeeks, 8–9, 26–28, 75, 169n7
robberies, 38, 115, 148, 176n15
Rodney, Walter, 23

Sandokhan, 36
Santino, Jack, 65
scamming, 45, 166–67, 172n30
Scott, David, 8–9, 38, 169n3
Seaga, Edward, 3, 33, 68, 75, 88, 90, 102
security: affective atmosphere of, 128–30; private, 16, 39, 147–48. *See also* fear; military; police; security operations
security operations, 1, 9–10, 26, 42, 43–44, 54, 58, 69, 74, 99. *See also* Tivoli Incursion
sensorial politics, 13–15, 90–93, 103, 125, 128–31, 156, 162–64, 167. *See also* affective atmospheres
sexuality, 17, 61, 167
Sharpe, Michael, 2–5, 6, 9, 26
Sharpe, Sam, 48
Shearer, Hugh, 22–23
Sheild Johansson, Miranda, 178n14
shootings, 74, 81, 88; drive-by, 72, 104
Simpson-Miller, Portia, 55, 60–61, 90, 176n10
Singham, A. W., 28, 171n11, 171n13
slavery, 24, 29, 89, 107–8, 165, 171n7
Smith, M. G., 7–8
snitching. *See* informers

soccer. *See* football
South Africa, 56
South Asia, 6
sovereignty, 10, 11, 28, 96, 170nn20–21
Spanish Town, 166
spatial imaginaries, 52
speech acts, 87, 103
spirituality. *See* Rastafari; religion
sports. *See* football
squatter settlements, 3, 108
states: of emergency, 45, 47, 108, 166; parallel, 9, 41, 121; postcolonial, 6, 164–66, 180n6
Stepputat, Finn, 11
street dances, 14, 15, 55, 125, 130–31, 162–63, 167; and place-making, 67–69; police sponsoring of, 125; memorial, 101–2
street vendors, 43, 70, 139–40
sufferation, 11, 170n18
Super Cat, 36–37

Tel Aviv, 45, 77
territorial stigmatization, 52, 57–58, 60, 62, 67
Thame, Mizuki, 60
Thomas, Deborah, 26, 78, 171n7, 171n13, 171n17, 173n23
Tivoli Incursion, 1, 15, 26, 42, 72, 75, 156; impact of, 15, 44, 54, 57–58, 99, 133; popular culture representations, 9–10, 43–44; public enquiry into, 152, 155, 156. *See also* garrison, dismantling of; security operations
Toronto, 76
tourism, 3, 45, 69, 166, 172n30
trade unions. *See* BITU; labor; NWU; TUC
Trench Town, 58, 67, 71–72, 90, 92–93
Trump, Donald, 6, 165
TUC, 29, 30
Twin of Twins, 43–44, 172n29

UDC (Urban Development Corporation), 157–58
United Kingdom, 74

United States: criminal violence in, 69–70; engagement with dons, 174n26; extradition requests to Jamaica, 1, 15, 16, 88, 99, 172n29, 177n1; illiberalism in, 165; transnational networks between Jamaica and, 74–77. *See also* Cold War
uprising. *See* riots
USSR, 4. *See also* Cold War

violence: borders and, 69–74; causes of, 22, 25; collective, 115; criminal, 18, 38, 41, 73–74, 80, 127, 139, 151, 172n32; culture of, 169n3; electoral, 3–4, 8, 31–40, 70–72, 94, 98, 133; extortion and, 136, 160; dons' reputation for/use of, 5, 42, 51, 61–62, 65, 115–21, 131–32, 154, 159, 161, 177n2; football and, 68; glorification of, 8; illiberalism and, 6, 21, 165–66; law and, 108–9; scammers and, 166; sovereignty and, 11, 170n21; state, 4, 9, 15, 23–24, 37, 44, 49, 114, 122–24, 173n23, 180n37; unions and, 31–31; writing around, 18–20. *See also* firearms; homicides; peace treaties; rape
violent pluralism, 9

Wailer, Bunny, 42–43
waste management, 19, 41
Waterhouse, 67
weapons. *See* firearms
Weber, Max, 9, 12–13, 164
whiteness, 16–18, 58, 110, 170n31
Wilton Gardens, 34, 75
World Bank, 42, 85

yakuza, 164

Zeeks, 8–9, 26–27, 169n7; and peace treaty, 75; popular music references to, 27–29, 75; and security, 117. *See also* riots: Zeeks
Zeiderman, Austin, 19
Zones of Special Operations (ZOSOs), 45, 172n30